Oglala Women

Women in Culture and Society
A series edited by Catharine R. Stimpson

Oglala Women
Myth, Ritual, and Reality

Marla N. Powers

The University of Chicago Press
Chicago & London

The University of Chicago Press, Chicago 60637
The University of Chicago Press, Ltd., London
© 1986 by The University of Chicago
All rights reserved. Published 1986
Paperback edition 1988
Printed in the United States of America
97 96 95 94 93 92   6 5

Library of Congress Cataloging in Publication Data
Powers, Marla N.
  Oglala women.

  (Women in culture and society)
  Bibliography: p.
  Includes index.
    1. Oglala Indians—Women. 2. Indians of North
America—South Dakota—Women. 3. Oglala Indians—
Social life and customs. 4. Indians of North America—
South Dakota—Social life and customs. I. Title.
II. Series.
E99.Q3P67 1986   305.8′97   85-24499
ISBN 0-226-67748-6 (cloth)
ISBN 0-226-67749-4 (paper)

To Bill, Jeff, and Greg

Contents

Illustrations

Series Editor's Foreword

In "The Trick Is Consciousness," Paula Allen Gunn, a Native American writer, states: "The key is in remembering, in what is chosen for the dream. / In the silence of recovery we hold / the rituals of the dawn, / now as then."[1] *Oglala Women: Myth, Ritual, and Reality* powerfully remembers. Scrupulously, Marla Powers helps to recover the history of the Native Americans who called themselves the Lakotas. For them, "tradition" is the time before that bloody intrusion, that nightmare, the "coming of the white man."

Despite that invasion, the Oglalas survived. Perhaps twenty thousand now live at Pine Ridge, South Dakota, the second largest reservation in the United States. As aware of the "now" of the present as of the "then" of the past, Powers also tells of the modern Oglalas, after the coming of the white man. In so doing, she offers an original contribution to any analysis of colonization and of the adaptation, struggles, and resistance of the colonized. For example, the colonizers had fixed attitudes about how men and women ought to behave. Ironically, those notions may have enabled Native American women to move more flexibly than Native American men between traditional patterns of action and those the reservation demanded of them.

Powers shows how official voices, such as historians, government officials, psychologists, and travelers, have ignored, blurred, trivialized, sentimentalized, and slandered Native American women. Unhappily, even some feminists, acutely sensitive to women and their work, have distorted Native American realities. To picture them fairly and accurately, Powers calls for an "Indian perspective." She wants the Oglalas to interpret

---

1. In *That's What She Said: Contemporary Poetry and Fiction by Native American Women*, ed. Rayna Green (Bloomington: Indiana University Press, 1984), 18.

themselves. As she mediates between her subject and her readers, she is discreet, sympathetic, and respectful.

Sustaining that perspective, *Oglala Women* looks at women: their roles, duties, and pleasures; the sacred and secular representations of their life cycle from birth, through maturity, to death—in brief, their dawns and dreams. Legitimately, Powers asks not only about women, but about gender. The architecture of the social roles of men and women, gender is as thoroughly woven into various societies as are patterns of food production or burial ceremonies. Indeed, one of the obligations of myth is to explain the origins of gender, rationalize its presence, and justify its future.

Powers argues that Oglala society rebukes the theory that gender is a hierarchy universally demanding female subordination, a theory that women's studies has frequently found plausible. Particularly today, Oglala women may devise a fiction of male superiority. In actuality, relations between female and male tend to be those of "complementarity," with female and male roles having equal strength and power. For the Oglalas and for their traditions, sexual difference breeds mutual respect.

Few—too few—books like *Oglala Women: Myth, Ritual, and Reality* exist. Its care and scholarship will not treacherously trick consciousness but will generously, and authentically, illuminate it.

Catharine R. Stimpson

Preface

This book is about the twenty thousand Oglalas of Pine Ridge, the second largest Indian reservation in the United States, situated in southwestern South Dakota.

For twenty-seven years I have been privileged to know a number of Lakotas, as they call themselves, particularly those families living in what is now Red Cloud Community, a hamlet named after one of the most famous of all "Sioux" chiefs.

It is impossible to list the hundreds of people I have met over such a long period, but some have made a lasting impression on me and deserve to be recognized. My mentioning their names does not mean they necessarily endorse this work, but I do hope they will understand that I have tried to be as faithful as I can to their life and culture. Any errors or omissions are certainly not intentional and are mine alone.

Nor are the people whose names I mention here necessarily those who agreed to be interviewed. I have preserved the anonymity of the people I worked with, except in some rare cases where real names are used either because the respondents wanted it that way or because it was already a matter of public record.

I would particularly like to express my gratitude to the following relatives and friends who have shared their lives and culture with me and my family with kindness, hospitality, and generosity: Zona Fills the Pipe, Sadie and Clarence Janis, Darlene Shortbull, Starlet and Peter Fills the Pipe, Frank Afraid of Horses, Etta and Pugh Young Man and family, Charlotte Ortiz, Bessie and John Cornelius and family, Judy Cornelius, Laura and Charles Red Cloud, Nancy and Bill Horn Cloud, Lottie and Edgar Red Cloud, Alice Red Cloud, Agnes Red Cloud, Julie and George Plenty Wolf, Marie and Melvin Red Cloud, Celeste and Owen Brings, Helena and Oliver Red Cloud, Agnes Lamont, Frances Red Shirt, Millie He Crow, Jessie Means, Barbara Red Cloud Jones, Hildegarde and Everet Catches and family, Francis Shangreaux, Lily Shangreaux, Carol and Richard Whitecalf, Benny Lenard, and all the other Lakota women and men who have made us feel that Pine Ridge was our home. And my thanks go to Vanessa, Shirley, Jennifer, and Iris, the Oglala women leaders of the future.

I would especially like to thank David P. McAllester, for his many years of encouragement and support of my work, and Catharine R. Stimpson, whose probing questions and insightful comments, editorial and otherwise, have contributed immensely to the clarity of this manuscript.

I am indebted to the Department of Anthropology of Rutgers University for two years of support and to the Wenner Gren Foundation for Anthropological Research for a grant-in-aid to support my field research in the summer of 1980.

Thanks also:

To Myron Aronoff, Ximena Bunster B., Robin Fox, and Lionel Tiger for commenting on an earlier version of this work.

To the Theis family for their many years of hospitality to our family.

To Jill Dolezal, who shares my love of horses and with whom I have enjoyed many hours of riding. The beauty and solitude of the hills overlooking Pine Ridge helped me put things into their proper perspective.

To Ron and Don Forgey, whose home was the site of countless late-night discussions.

To Brother C. M. Simon, S.J., for sharing his office, library, photographs, affection, and good humor.

That I grew up in a family where there were no limitations based on gender gave me an objectivity I might not otherwise have had. For that I thank my maternal grandfather and my parents and particularly my aunt, Helen Rose.

And finally I am deeply indebted:

To my sons Jeff and Greg for their patience and constant encouragement throughout my entire academic career. Their willingness to help with numerous chores at home and at Pine Ridge enabled me to get on with my work. They were with us at Pine Ridge from the time they were two years old until they started college. The ease with which they participated in Lakota culture from the very beginning was gratifying to us, and I believe their lives have been enriched by this bicultural experience.

To my husband, William K. Powers, who first introduced me to the Oglalas twenty-eight years ago and with whom I share that special attachment to the Plains and their people that casual visitors never comprehend. His contribution is immeasurable. His constant encouragement, respect, and keen sense of humor have been a stabilizing force both personally and professionally. His insightful research with the Oglalas has provided the foundation of my own; his influence will be evident to those who know his work. I thank him also for his help with the translations.

Janet Bascomb typed the manuscript with great care.

Introduction

I propose to examine the broad relationships between sex roles and social structure by focusing on the effect of gender on the organization of Oglala society—on the role of women and their relations with men. Change in the present condition of Oglala women is inseparable from change in the social position of Oglala men. I address the fact that gender is integral to the *total* social system, which some studies of women overlook. As one anthropologist has written,

> Gender has not been adequately addressed as a social fact. We are beginning to understand that sex, which has generally been viewed in biological terms and relegated to the infrasocial domain, must be viewed from the perspective of economics, politics, religion, philosophy, art. In brief, sex differences take on meaning and function within wider cultural systems and play an important role in the structure and maintenance of those systems. (Shapiro 1982, 720)

Another purpose of my research is to correct a second problem in ethnographic studies. Although temporal dimensions are usually lacking in standard structural and functional approaches to ethnographic studies, I employ a biographical approach that provides a systematic analysis of change. Life histories can provide some indication of the extent to which individuals' values or evaluation of their places in society change over time. To this end I have collected life histories of Oglala women ranging from sixteen to ninety-six years of age to discover their sense of their own lives in their own culture from earliest recollections up through the present. I elicited information about attitudes toward their own childhood, pubescence, courtship, marriage, pregnancy, and childbirth; their philosophy of child rearing; how they evaluate their parents; and how they perceive continuity

1

and change between their own lives and those of their children and grandchildren. I was interested in whether they had professional training of any kind; whether they worked outside the home and whether they wanted to; whether they encountered resistance to this and what strategies were available to them.

One persistent question was the degree to which traditional Lakota culture influences modern Lakota life. In particular, I was concerned with how far contemporary female behavior was modeled after the traditional roles of women. Although the anthropologist may often have difficulty distinguishing between *traditional* and *modern* on analytic grounds, the Oglalas do not. The category "traditional" encompasses all the cultural artifacts and behaviors that are perceived to have existed before the coming of the white man. All modern culture at least partly originates with or has been established by whites, not the least of which is the reservation. Traditional and modern, then, are ideal and idealized categories, but the Oglalas agree on their defining characteristics and try to understand the similarities and differences in human behavior according to these two dissimilar, but not always contrasting, classes. Most active women (Oglala women in leadership roles, whether on the tribal council or in their own business) are adept at distinguishing between the two categories and the behavior each entails. The women are also capable of living part of their lives in each, often moving back and forth from traditional to modern on purely situational grounds. Seeing themselves as both traditional and modern under certain conditions, they are not afraid to switch between the two with the same ease with which most, if not all, can switch from, say, the Lakota langauge to English when circumstances so dictate.

In either case, a high value is placed on women's roles as wife and mother. A number of traditional women move freely along a continuum between what might be regarded as high-status Euramerican positions (judge of the Oglala Sioux tribal court, treasurer of the Oglala Sioux tribal council, director of curriculum for Oglala Lakota College, etc.) and traditional high-status Native American positions (wife and mother) simultaneously and without conflict. Furthermore, women's participation in what are regarded as Euramerican occupations in no way impinges on or detracts from their traditional roles, since in Lakota culture maternal and managerial roles are not regarded as antithetical.

However, these options are not so readily available to Oglala men. Those who occupy high-status positions (in the tribal council, for example) are usually criticized for behaving like white men. They are accused of not being able to speak their native language (whether they can or not), of exploiting kinsmen and friends, of stealing money from the tribal treasury, of selling land illegally, of embezzling government funds, even though their participation in tribal politics may benefit the tribe. Furthermore, in contrast to females, whose traditional roles have continued over time, as a result of European contact males have relatively few full-time traditional occupations available to them. Many traditional male options have, in fact, been usurped by federal welfare programs. As Lurie writes (1972, 33): "Indian women seemed to have held up better under the stresses of reservation life than men and were often in the forefront of work in tribal councils and business committees. A possible explanation is that Indian males had suffered greater identity dislocation. The male roles of hunter, warrior, and shaman had been destroyed but women still had children to be reared and domestic tasks to attend to."

The establishment of the reservation, and the usurpation of political and economic power by the federal government, had a profound effect upon Indian males. Little has been said about its effect on females. During the reservation process, men were stripped of their political and economic responsibilities, whereas women continued to function as wives and mothers, the implication being that their roles did not change, or at least changed very little. What is not widely understood is that all the new positions for Indians created by the Indian Reorganization Act of 1934— which included the tribal administrative council, law-and-order commissions, boards of education, the judicial system, and ultimately all the bureaucracies that have provided hundreds of services to Oglala people from that time to the present—were open to women as much as to men. Of course men occupied most of the positions in the burgeoning bureaucracies (which were essentially controlled by the federal government), but the egalitarian relationship traditionally maintained between men and women continued to manifest itself under the new administration just as it had during the old buffalo-hunting days.

The most important change was in education. Before 1934, Indian males and females were totally segregated in education, mainly in mission schools such as the Holy Rosary Mission at Pine Ridge, established in 1888 by German Jesuits. Boys were taught manual skills—shoemaking, baking, farming, dairying, carpentry, and other forms of manual labor. Indian girls were taught what the dominant white society believed they should learn—the domestic skills such as cooking, sewing, and home-making that would help them grow into the stereotype ideal of Euramerican womanhood. Some also learned typing and other clerical skills, and others were trained as nurse's aides. With the Indian Reorganization Act, which was intended in part to place some decision making about the Indians' future into the hands of the tribes, the education system became more liberal. In the federal schools the same academic classes were opened to both boys and girls, but girls, with their newfound liberal education plus their training in home management, became more qualified for administrative jobs than the men, most of whom never received administrative training at all since the thrust of their training was in manual labor. Men returned from federal vocational schools to find there were few opportunities on the reservation for employment in their areas of training, whereas clerical and domestic jobs were available for women.

In Oglala society, attitudes toward gender, rules for proper sexual conduct, sexual strategies, ideas about maleness and femaleness, marriage rules, and reproductive symbolism all receive significant expression in myth and ritual. Since myth is a reflection, conscious or unconscious, of social structure and of feelings and perceptions about social relations, hierarchies, and proper behavior, I shall discuss relevant myths and rituals that pertain to female sex roles. I join many scholars, feminists and otherwise, who point out that myth and ritual frequently serve as a charter for social behavior as well as a rationale for behaving in sexually distinctive ways. Peggy Sanday writes:

> Creation stories contain within them a conception
> of the natural or initial order of things. By articu-

lating how things are in the beginning, people
supply more than a logic for sexual life styles—
they make a basic statement about their relationship with nature and about their perception of
the source of power in the universe. This relationship, and its projection into the sacred and
secular realms, holds the key for understanding
sexual identities and corresponding roles. (Sanday
1981, 57)

Part of the Indian perspective on what it means to be an Indian
woman is rooted in the cosmology and early history of the
Oglalas and in their change from a semisedentary subsistence
pattern in the Great Lakes region to nomadic buffalo hunting on
the Plains. And while Oglala society may be viewed as male
dominated, primarily as a consequence of missionary and federal
education, in ritual and myth females are its prime movers. For
example, the most important figure in myth is Falling Star
(Woȟpe), who when she appears on earth is transformed into
White Buffalo Calf Woman, a female who in her sexual prime
gives the Lakotas all their sacred ceremonies. In modern times,
even secular rituals such as the War Dance partly stem from the
Drum Religion, which was founded by a woman in the Great
Lakes region (Densmore 1932). To a lesser extent the Native
American Church, for those who participate in it on the Pine
Ridge reservation, was founded by a woman (Petrullo 1932).
However, this is not to say that the Oglalas believe women are
dominant. In myth and ritual, Oglala women clearly do domi-
nate; in history, the males are regarded as superior. But in the
reality of everyday living, females and males complement each
other, with reality establishing a perfect dialectic between the
myth of history and the history of myth.

Any attempt to separate the myth from the reality of Indian
womanhood must begin by understanding women not in a preor-
dained asymmetrical relationship to men, but rather in a complementary way: "Complementarity between man and woman
being based on differences precludes competition. Sexual differentiation implies the mutual dependence of specialization"
(Ardener 1972, 8). If we examine women from an *Indian* perspective, there is overwhelming agreement that the roles of men
and women in traditional Oglala society were complementary,

exemplified in the Lakota concept of *okicicupi* 'sharing,' which was a philosophy that underlay not only relationships between men *or* women, but between men *and* women. For the Oglalas and other Native American societies where the sexes complement each other, women are neither inferior nor superior to men, merely different. Both sexes are valued for the contributions they make to the society. They are cooperative rather than competitive. The French sociologist Marcel Mauss provided an explanation for such complementarity over sixty years ago when he pointed out that exchange creates and maintains a social relationship (Mauss 1924). "Thus the conceptualization of sexual differences as specialization, entailing mutually necessary functions in economic life as well as in reproduction, establishes mutual interdependence" (Ardener 1972, 8).

The empirical status of women is frequently clouded by two claims that do not obtain cross-culturally. One is that reproductive roles cause women to be subordinate; the second is a belief that males are somehow intrinsically and universally dominant.

A number of feminist writers view women's productive and reproductive roles as the basis for female subordination. They see sexual asymmetry as a social fact of life in which women are universally subordinate to men. They contend that a woman's biological and reproductive (private, domestic) role is the basis for her inequality because it precludes her active involvement in the powerful, prestigious (public) spheres open to men (Rosaldo and Lamphere 1974; Ortner 1974).[1] For the Oglalas, it is just the opposite. My research shows that the fulfillment of an Oglala woman's traditional role—that of wife and mother, according to those values perceived to be irrefutably Lakota—has facilitated her movement into economic and political roles modeled after Euramerican concepts of propriety, albeit in part inadvertently. Necessarily, I view the assumptions of universal male dominance and the seemingly marginal status of women as problematic. A wide range of relationships exist between males and females in societies of differing economic and political complexity. Examining a particular aspect of a female's (or male's) life out of context can be misleading. A major difficulty in many of the early feminist writers' analyses of women's lives has been the erroneous assumption of universality. In their haste to correct earlier misperceptions about women's roles (particularly in Euramerican culture) feminist scholars themselves have failed to see particularities in women's lives. Overgeneralization on their part has resulted in still another distorted view of American Indian women's place in their own culture. Rather than uncritically accepting a woman's status as secondary, it is necessary to examine the different social contexts in which males and females coexist (Tiffany 1979, 4). Oglala society provides a good example of what others have called the myth of male dominance (Rogers 1975). I suggest that Oglala women purposely perpetuate this myth by making males and outsiders believe that men are in charge. Cross-cultural studies have shown that male dominance, despite its frequent assertion, simply does not exist as a social fact. According to Eleanor Leacock, "women were not as literal 'equals' of men (a point which has caused much confusion), but as they were—female persons, with their own rights, duties, and responsibilities which were complementary to and in no way secondary to those of men" (Leacock 1978, 252; cf. Briggs 1974; Schlegel 1977). In summary, equating women's productive and reproductive roles with subordination, plus an unfounded belief in the universality of male dominance, precludes the possibility of seeing more complex relationships. Even today it is still common to contrast the roles of women with the roles of men and then to make some generalization, usually with regard to the universality of the lower status of women. But these errors do not apply to women exclusively. Rather, they are a function of viewing any non-Western group, and even certain segments of Western society, ethnocentrically.

Another common misconception has been that *values* placed on certain behaviors in Western society can be equated with values placed on those same behaviors in non-Western society. This approach is suspect, since much of the argument is based on the division of society into political and domestic spheres. This is a false dichotomy among the Oglalas and serves as another example of the imposition of Western categories on non-Western societies. Reinforcing this has been a long history of treating Native American women voguishly. In both scholarly and popular writing, there have been trends and popular themes ranging from the noble *sauvagesse* to the scornful squaw. As is true for most studies of other women, studies of Native American women have been selective, stereotypic, and damaging (Green 1980, 249).

An examination of the stereotype of the Oglala woman is instructive. Generally, Indian women impressed non-Indians as being ugly drudges, while the men were usually described as lazy. Early travelers who visited the Plains were likely to agree with Parkman:

> Except the dogs, the most active and noisy tenants
> of the camp were the old women, ugly as Mac-
> beth's witches with hair streaming loose in the
> wind and nothing but the tattered fragment of an
> old buffalo-robe to hide their shriveled limbs.
> . . . The heaviest labors of the camp devolved
> upon them; they must harness the horses, pitch the
> lodges, dress the buffalo robes and bring in meat
> for the hunters. With the cracked voices of these
> hags, the clamor of the dogs, and laughing of chil-
> dren and girls, and the listless tranquility of the
> warriors, the whole scene had an effect too lively
> and picturesque to be forgotten. (Parkman
> 1950, 70)

Views of camp life seem to highlight the activities of women, since they were more visible than men's. For the most part, men's work was outside the camp—a point rarely mentioned. Parkman, of course, was not only an adventurer but a man of letters. His descriptions of camp life are vivid but exaggerated. The idea of juxtaposing dogs and women in a case in point. To have one's hair streaming loose in the wind might have been considered stylish by the Oglalas, and what he regards as a tattered fragment might very well have been common everyday dress. For Parkman limbs must be shriveled, voices must be cracked, tranquility must be listless. In another passage he continues:

> The moving spirit of the establishment was an old
> hag of eighty. Human imagination never conceived
> hobgoblin or witch more ugly than she. . . . From
> morning till night she bustled about the lodge
> screaming like a screech-owl when anything dis-
> pleased her. (Parkman 1950, 102)

So we encounter another "hag," again compared to a witch and a screech owl. Parkman also described the Oglala camp as "infested by little copper-colored naked boys and snake-eyed girls" (105). Indian women served as "tawny mistresses" to the trappers (173). About an Indian woman's marriage to a trapper, he observed:

> He had taken to himself a wife, for whom he had paid the established price of one horse. This looks cheap at first sight but in truth the purchase of a squaw is a transaction which no man should enter into without mature deliberation since it involves not only the payment of the price, but the burden of feeding and supporting a rapacious horde of the bride's relatives . . . who gather about him like leeches and drain him of all he has. (102)

In the preceding description Parkman reveals his ignorance of Oglala culture, particularly the rules that govern marriage. It was customary then and still is common for the couple and their respective in-laws to exchange gifts, a practice Parkman calls "a purchase." Additionally, every major event was accompanied by great feasting. Neither the relatives of the bride nor those of the groom suffered any particular hardship. Giving gifts and food was considered a sign of generosity, and prestige accrued to the person who gave away the most.

Parkman's observations were followed by a proliferation of accounts by military men and missionaries, particularly after the great Sioux reservation was established with the Fort Laramie treaty in 1868 and some of the Oglalas began to pitch their camps near the military forts. These Indians were looked down upon by the whites living in the fort. One writer observed:

> Still another level of Fort Laramie society were the Indian squaws, who lived with their children and some transient braves in a non-descript community known as "Squaw Town" upstream from the fort. It was part of the long-established community of "tame" Oglala that under Chief Smoke, had settled down to live by the favors and the trade of Fort Laramie and the California emigrants. Some of the women worked as servants for the officers'

wives; others simply existed on the scourings of
the fort, degraded to the roles of hangers-on in the
white man's establishment. To receive special gifts
of food they sometimes organized dances, and
other entertainment after which the officers took
up a collection and purchased flour, meat and rice
from the commissary and gave it to them. Squaw
Town was not so romantic as it was pathetic. In
the Indian tradition, the male inhabitants believed
themselves above menial work, and the women
employed as servants at the fort could not afford
the high prices at the sutler's store. (Nadeau 1967,
152)

While this is a fair description of Indian life around the fort, it
should be emphasized that the Oglalas themselves had nothing
but disdain for those who chose to live near the whites. In fact
these Indians received a special name, wagluȟe*—convention-
ally translated as loafers. It is unfair to say Indian tradition
dictated that males were above menial work. Indian males did
not take part in the white man's economy; they were hunters and
warriors stripped of their normal economic pursuits and political
independence. The women were employed as servants, the beginning of female participation in the white man's society at the
very start of the reservation period. Also depicting hardships
around the fort, the missionary Mrs. Collins wrote (to the Indian
commissioner): "The consequence is that many of them are in
almost a starving condition and they will gather up from the
ground scraps that our dogs have left untouched. There is only
one other way by which they can save themselves from sharp
hunger, and that is too humiliating to a woman and a Christian to
more than allude to" (Nadeau 1967, 152–53).

Clearly Indian men were restless, and even after the establishment of the reservation, bands of hunters frequently left its
boundaries to hunt buffalo. Indian women accompanied them.
During one of the more famous historical events involving the
Oglalas, the annihilation of George Armstrong Custer, it was

---

*The following diacritics will be used in writing Lakota words: š, pronounced
as in shake; ȟ, pronounced as in the German nach; and an apostrophe indicating a
glottal stop.

reported that Indian women stayed with their men during the battle. The appearance of Indian women on the battlefield gave observers still another opportunity to distort female behavior. For example, reporters of the Custer battle observed: "Hordes of squaws and old, gray-haired Indians were roaming over the battlefield howling like mad. The squaws had stone mallets and mashed in the skulls of the dead and wounded. Many were gashed with knives and some had their noses and other members cut off" (Graham 1953, 260). Not only is there continual reference to Indian women as hags, but here an added dimension of extreme brutality and mutilation is attributed to the women. To continue:

> The real mutilation occurred in the case of Reno's
> men, who had fallen near the village. These had
> been visited by the squaws and children and in
> some instances the bodies were frightfully butch-
> ered. Fortunately not many were exposed to such
> a fate. Custer's field was some distance from the
> village and appears not to have been visited by
> these hags, which probably explains the exemption
> from mutilation of those who had fallen there.
> (Graham 1953, 167)

The stereotype was maintained even after the turn of the century, when "the squaws are squatty, yellow, ugly, and greasy looking. Hard work disfigures them, for their lazy brutes of sons, husbands, and brothers will do no work, and the unfortunate women are as so many pack mules" (Finerty 1890, 69). Descriptions become even more graphic, and in addition to being ugly, the women are "greasy" and "yellow," which is unusual since stereotypically Indians have incorrectly been described as "red"—in fact many Europeans still refer to them as "Red Indians." Again a comparison is made with animals, in this case pack mules. One of the foremost historians of the Sioux concurs: "Of course the squaw was always available as a beast of burden, but manifestly a great skin tipi was beyond even her extraordinary power to transport for a day's journey" (Robinson 1904, 29). In one popular book there is no listing for women in the index except under "squaw" or "best of burden" (Tibbles 1905, 274).

Even writers who were not critical spoke of the virtues of Indian women in a condescending way:

> General Sully, who rarely had a good word for Indians, officially stated that "the females of the wild bands of Sioux, called the Teton Sioux, set an example of virtue worthy of being copied by any civilized nation." What wonder that in a society where divorce was easy and celibacy unknown, the Sioux abhorred harlots? When a harlot fell into the hands of those virtuous dames, it went hard for her. When the Sioux women found out that a female Crow captive who was to be adopted into the tribe was a whore, "they seized the unfortunate creature, tore off her clothing, lashed her to a pine tree, and piled brush about her intending to burn her alive." (Vestal 1956, 24)

These were the same women who "were remarkable among those of the prairie nations . . . they are generally tall and straight, without the thick ankles, and ungainly walk, and the stooping shoulders of their less favored sisters. Taking them altogether, the wild prairie Sioux have no superiors among the Indians in appearance and domestic virtues" (Vestal 1956, 23–24). In this passage, of course, Sioux women are being compared with other Indians, not with whites. Still other writers discerned what they understood to be Victorian values in Indian society:

> The Sioux women are, according to the traditional Sioux code of morals, moral. That is, they are given a standard of virtue and live up to it. It may not meet the approval of orthodox whites, and it may be somewhat less rigid than the rule prescribed in Turkey, but it nevertheless serves its own purpose and obliterates among the savages one of the greatest scourges that afflicts our boasted civilization. There is no "social evil" among the Sioux. There are people in this world who cannot appreciate the fact that a savage is capable of those finer sensibilities so much dwelt upon by sentimentalists and writers of fiction among the civilized nations. They are perfectly willing to ascribe instinct and even knowledge to

> their favorite horse or dog . . . but somehow or
> other, these good people are loath to believe that
> the Indian youth or the aged savage has any con-
> ception of sentiment or any of the attributes of
> love. (DeBarthe 1958, 42)

Ironically, contemporary investigators are no more enlight-
ened than their predecessors. For example, some psychological
anthropologists and psychiatrists who spent only brief periods at
Pine Ridge attributed what they perceived as male dominance to
their assumption that "the restrictions placed upon women in the
past society made them objects of man's sexual aggression. . . .
Since there had been tacit approval for sexual aggression in the
old society. . . . it is not surprising to find occasional reports of
rape or murder and extremes of sexual license" (Macgregor
1946, 154–55). "Sexual aggression" refers to an early practice
whereby a husband disfigured the face of an adulterous wife,
usually by cutting off her nose, a practice Oglala society con-
doned.

Just as early investigators were prone to examine "proper"
female (and male) behavior through the critical lens of
Euramerican culture, recent investigators were quick to explain
"improper" behavior. In addition to claims of approval for
sometimes heinous acts of sexual aggression, as indicated above,
the inevitable matter or childbearing and rearing, prostitution,
and sexual preference all came under scrutiny. For example, a
prominent psychiatrist who visited the Oglalas for two weeks
made this observation: "The Dakota women who gave us information on the old methods of child training were at first
reticent. To begin with, they were Indians. Then also, Mekeel,
whom they had known as anthropologist and friend, was now a
government man. And then, it was not quite decent to talk to
men about things concerning the human body. Especially the
subject of the unavoidable beginning, namely pregnancy, always
caused some giggling" (Erikson 1950, 33).

The statement above is both racist and sexist. Women were
hesitant to talk with him because he was an obvious outsider who
according to Oglala custom was asking inappropriate and
meaningless questions. The human body is taken matter of factly
by traditional Oglalas. In Lakota there are no vulgar words; the

category of obscenity simply does not exist. Although Euramerican ideas equating sexual practices with despicable, and thus unmentionable, behavior have been integrated into the language since the turn of the century, these correlations were foreign to traditional Oglalas.

Not talking about sexual things has nothing to do with decency in Oglala tradition; the reticence has to do instead with modesty. Yet though the same psychiatrist recognized the women's reticence about discussing such topics with a male (a white male at that), it did not prevent him from using the data to analyze Oglala female sexuality—of course, from a Euramerican perspective.

While errors made by early investigators could often be attributed to the fact that they were by no means trained social scientists and, as in Parkman's case, were often "men of letters" writing to impress a popular audience, the most grievous errors are made by Royal B. Hassrick, an anthropologist who has been regarded by many Siouanists as perhaps the foremost ethnographer of the Lakota people. Hassrick's degree of projection is extraordinary; virtually all of his comments on sexuality (female and male) mirror Euramerican attitudes and concerns. About child rearing he writes:

> Bearing children was an attribute which pragmatically expressed the Sioux acceptance of life. There was no confusion about the role of women, for being a mother and rearing a family was the ultimate achievement. As a matter of fact, there seems to have been no other acceptable pattern for feminine existence. Women might become dreamers to practice certain curings, and rites associated with child rearing and tipi-building but these in no way appear to have precluded the role of motherhood. The Sioux placed this role among the highest virtues. . . . There was no question of the probability of motherhood; rather a forthright acceptance of an acknowledged predestined fact. (Hassrick 1964, 41)

All of this is correct from an Oglala point of view, but it is misleading in that it ignores other roles played out by Oglala women.

As another example of categories Hassrick judged significant, prostitution was obviously worthy of some attention. The Oglala woman emerged as moral in the view of some investigators because the category of prostitution was irrelevant to traditional Oglala society. Because of the white man's ignorance of Oglala kinship and marriage practices, morality could be discussed only in the most patronizing terms. For example, Hassrick writes:

> It is possibly surprising, in light of the dual standard with respect to sex, that the Sioux failed to consider prostitution. But there is no evidence it entered their lives—probably for several good reasons. In a war directed society, men were at a premium and women were plentiful. In a close-knit society where the reputations of all women were known and ideally all were placed upon a pedestal, there was little opportunity for a man to attempt to satisfy secretly or consistently his sexual aggression without public disapproval. . . . Where goods and horses were the only medium of exchange, there was no money in prostitution and even a mistress could not be maintained. The entire matter was unnecessary for the Sioux could enjoy the complications of polygamy rather than the hollow despair of prostitution or keeping a mistress. Moreover, divorce was a comparatively simple method of disposing of one woman for another. (Hassrick 1964, 112)

There are a number of errors in this statement. The idea of a dual standard is Euramerican, not traditional Oglala. Furthermore, there is simply no evidence that women were "more plentiful." In the ravages of battle, women and children were killed along with their menfolk, and women frequently accompanied their men on the warpath, exposing themselves to the same hazards. True, reputations were important to both females and males, but there were no pedestals in the Oglala camp. And one wonders what Hassrick had in mind when he discussed satisfying "secretly or consistently . . . sexual aggression."

Moreover, that prostitution did not exist because "there was no money in it" makes no sense, for if the idea of prostitution had been relevant then goods and horses would be adequate compensation in a society that practiced subsistence economy. Therefore the idea that even a mistress could not be maintained is a non sequitur.

Hassrick's claim that polygamy makes prostitution or keeping a mistress unnecessary is also irrelevant. Most Oglalas (over 90 percent) were not polygamous. They practiced serial monogamy upon death or desertion of a spouse or divorce by common consent. The idea that divorce was simply "disposing of one woman for another" fails to take into consideration that women often initiated divorce with full societal approval.

As one more example from the same author of how categories assumed to be important to Western culture are imposed upon non-Western peoples (whether or not the categories exist at all), I turn to the subject of lesbianism:

> Lesbianism seems to have played a much less obvious part in the life of the Sioux. Certain dream instructions given to young women—in particular, the Double Woman's appearance—hint at a kind of sanction for female perversion.

Even when there is no evidence for lesbianism among Plains societies, he appears to congratulate women for making the "right choice." He continues:

> Rattling Blanket Woman for example underwent a true choice situation during her dream experience and selected, albeit unwittingly, the role of wife and mother in opposition to a career of professional craftsmanship and suggested spinsterhood. And yet there exists no record of old maids among the Sioux. Furthermore, there seems to be no examples of female inversion, and the role of women within the society appears to obviate the development of any meaningful causes. (Hassrick 1964, 123)[2]

In fact, dreams of the Double Woman appeared to males, who then chose to become berdache or not depending on the outcome of the dream. Berdaches (men who dressed like women and assumed female behaviors) were thought to have auspicious powers related to childbirth and child rearing. There is no evidence that berdaches were necessarily homosexual among the Lakotas (Powers 1983, 461–62). There is no "hint" that there were any kind of sanctions for "female inversion." "Old maid" also is not a significant category in Oglala culture.

Although female historians and anthropologists and missionary wives often wrote prolifically about Plains Indians, even when they attempted to write from the female perspective the early documenters of Indian women neglected to portray them from their own Indian viewpoint. The argument is clouded today not so much because Indian women are not portrayed at all or because they are portrayed from a male perspective. And it is not simply that non-Indian females' descriptions of Indian life are still overwhelmingly influenced by the male point of view. Rather, Indian women remain stereotyped because they are never portrayed from the perspective of *Indians*—male or female.

Few except for Indian writers, both male and female, have been able to understand clearly the freedoms and constraints of Oglala social organization within which males and females maintain social relations. Ella Deloria, herself a Sioux and an anthropologist, identified the problems and prejudices of observers of Indian life:

> Outsiders seeing women keep to themselves have frequently expressed a snap judgement that they were regarded as inferior to the noble male. The simple fact is that woman had her own place and man his; they were not the same and neither inferior nor superior. The sharing of work also was according to sex. Both had to work hard for their life made severe demands. (Deloria 1979, 26)

And more recently Lily Shangreaux, an Oglala woman, notes:

> One must also consider that the Lakota man and woman comprised an economic unit whose basic goal was survival. Each benefitted from the other, and both found it extremely difficult (but not impossible) to live singly. This mutual dependence was probably a factor in their traditional attitudes held toward women.[3]

Even those aspects of female life that are customarily treated as subservience are from the Indian perspective only a necessary part of a person's survival:

> Women and children were the objects of care
> among the Lakotas and as far as their environment
> permitted they lived sheltered lives. Life was soft-
> ened by a great equality. All the tasks of women—
> cooking, caring for children, tanning and sewing—
> were considered dignified and worthwhile. No
> work was looked upon as menial, consequently
> there were no menial workers. Industry filled
> the life of every Lakota woman. (Standing Bear
> 1928, 90)

In this work I shall refute some of the old stereotypes. I begin with a historical prelude that describes, for those unfamiliar with the Oglalas, something of their prereservation social and political organization and their transformation from nomadic warriors into a society almost totally dependent on the United States government.

In part 1, I examine the traditional female role, one rooted firmly in the cosmological past. The Oglalas believe that women have always played an important part in Lakota life, and the respect and honor paid to them is nowhere better enunciated than in the early myths.

I then investigate ideas about Lakota culture from the perspective of the Oglala female growing up in what is perceived to be the dim past of the prereservation era. These beliefs and values are based mainly on what my respondents consider to be representative of Lakota culture during the buffalo-hunting days before the establishment of the Pine Ridge reservation in 1878.

Of course very few living Lakotas witnessed these times, although there are still a few men and women who were born in a tipi and may even have taken part in a buffalo hunt (if they are one hundred years old, for it was roughly in 1880 that the buffalo were nearly exterminated). Certainly those Oglalas now in their seventies heard stories about this period of life firsthand and grew up vicariously reliving through their parents and grandparents the nomadic, equestrian culture that became the stereotype of the Plains Indians.

The information on traditional culture is organized around Lakota concepts of the life cycle. According to the Lakota system, there are four stages of life: childhood, adolescence, adulthood, and old age. These four stages correspond with other sacred mysteries of the Oglalas. The life process itself is considered sacred because, traditionally, it is a reincarnative system. The life cycle, then, continues to repeat itself as certain aspects of what we may analogously call "soul" are reborn.

In part 2 I shall explore just what it means to grow up as an Oglala woman in the twentieth century, always conscious of her unique past that continues to provide an ideological basis for contemporary life quite different from her non-Oglala and non-Indian counterparts.

All my information has been obtained from Oglala women and men except where otherwise noted. In some cases I have had to consult various literary sources to provide a continuous story. Otherwise the ideas are those of countless Oglala women and men I have known over the past years.

Wherever possible I try to let the Oglalas speak for themselves about the varied aspects of their lives. I am particularly interested in how Oglala women perceive themselves to fit into what is often unjustly seen as a world of men.

In each chapter I offer a brief historical statement about the important institutions affecting Oglala women, but my primary concern is with the present and with the status and role of Oglala women in the 1980s in light of their adventurous past.

The Past

1 Historical Prelude

While the white man was calling the Indian woman a
drudge, old He Dog, at ninety-two, told me: "It is well
to be good to women in the strength of our manhood
because we must sit under their hands at both ends of
our lives."[1]

Introduction

It has been generally accepted in anthropology and history, and
echoed continually through popular literature and the mass
media, that the "Sioux," of which the Oglalas are a major
constituent, are the most typical of all American Indians. The
Sioux attained notoriety in the middle to late nineteenth century
because of what have generally been branded as "hostilities"
against the United States government. But from the Indians'
point of view, hostile actions were necessary to thwart the inces-
sant advance of the European and American soldiers, settlers,
and entrepreneurs. A number of grim encounters, in particular
the Indian wars of the West, culminating with the Battle of
the Little Big Horn in 1876 and the Ghost Dance movement
and Wounded Knee massacre of 1890, rendered the "Sioux"
notorious.[2]

Although my major concern is with Oglala women, some
review of early "Sioux" history and culture is in order, because
many of the traditional beliefs of Oglala men and women are
anchored in the prereservation past—perceptibly, if not empirically.

The Oglalas are the largest subdivision of the political division
known as Titunwan (Tetons). The term Sioux, is a misnomer,
being a French corruption of the Algonquian *nadowesiih* 'little
adders,' a derogatory term applied by various tribes and the
French, during the seventeenth century, to a loose affiliation of

Siouan (*sic*) speakers calling themselves Oceti Šakowin 'Seven Fireplaces.'[3]

Table 1 illustrates the linguistic and political breakdown of the Seven Fireplaces as customarily idealized by the native people themselves and by historians and anthropologists. Table 1 also shows that the Oglalas speak a Siouan dialect called Lakota, one mutually intelligible with Dakota and Nakota.[4] *Lakota* means "allied" or "affiliated," perhaps an unusual or at least idealistic reference to a loose confederation of "Sioux" that, when they were not uniting to fight against their traditional enemies the

Table 1   Political Organization of the Seven Fireplaces

Division	Dialect	Gloss
		(Teton)
Teton	Lakota	
Oglala		Prairie dwellers; they scatter their own
Sicangu		Burned thighs (also known by the French term, Brulé)
Hunkpapa		End of the circle
Mnikowoju		Planters beside the stream
Sihasapa		Black foot (not to be confused with the Algonquian tribe of the same name)
Oohenunpa		Two boilings or two kettles
Itazipco		No bows (also known by the French term Sans Arcs)
		(Yankton)
Yankton	Nakota	End dwellers
Yanktonais		Little end dwellers
		(Santee)
Mdewakanton	Dakota	Spirit or mystery lake dwellers
Wahpeton		Leaf dwellers
Sisseton		Fish-scale dwellers
Wahpekute		Leaf shooters

Source: Powers 1977, 13.

Crees and Ojibwas in the Great Lakes region, were fragmenting and fighting among themselves. Even after they moved out onto the prairies (Teton is often glossed "prairie dweller"), they fought virtually every tribe around them with the exception of the Cheyennes and Arapahos in later historical times. And they continued to fight each other after receiving horses from the Missouri River tribes about 1750 up through the near annihilation of the buffalo about 1880.

Early History

By the beginning of the sixteenth century the Sioux were living in semisedentary villages in the forests of Minnesota. They gathered wild rice, hunted, practiced limited horticulture, and engaged in trade with other Indians. Their social organization was characterized by a cognatic descent system coupled with Iroquoian kinship terminology and patrilocal band residence. There is some speculation, based on kinship terminology, that the Dakotas were originally matrilineal.

In the 1700s they were driven out of Minnesota by the Crees and Chippewas, who had been armed by the newly arrived French and British. They were forced westward onto the Central Plains, where the Oglalas, along with other Siouan speakers, occupied what are now South Dakota, North Dakota, parts of Montana, Nebraska, Wyoming, and Colorado. The Oglalas as a politically discrete unit did not exist before about 1700.[5]

By 1750 the Sioux had obtained horses from the Missouri River tribes, and from approximately 1780 to 1868 they roamed the Plains. Within two generations they became exemplary nomadic hunter-gatherers, hunting buffalo on horseback and living in tipis.

During the nineteenth century a highly complex set of institutions such as the Chief Society, warrior societies, and various women's sodalities, the Sun Dance, and other rituals characterized the florescence of the Sioux. The new political organization of the Sioux was highly developed. An individual belonged to the *tiyoŝpaye* 'band,' the *oyate* 'tribe,' and finally the Teton. Each of these units had its own governing body, and the criteria for attaining political power in each were well defined. The rules of conduct for an individual were clearly designated for each class of kin. It was a relatively well ordered society, free from the ambiguities that characterize more complex societies.

The *tiyošpaye*, sometimes numbering several hundred, came into existence as migrating groups of extended families fused with others. The seven original Oglala *tiyošpaye* were Payabya 'pushed aside'; Tapišleca 'spleen'; Kiyaksa 'cut band'; Wajaja 'Osage'; Itešica 'bad face'; Oyuȟpe 'untidy'; and Wagluȟe 'loafers.'[6] Within each *tiyošpaye* there were several camps or *wicoti*, each with upwards of twenty-five people. Each *wicoti* and *tiyošpaye* was under the leadership of one or more men commonly designated as *itancan*, chief or leader. A man was elected leader and maintained his status with the consent of the people who followed him. At no level of organization was there a permanent leader. Each *wicoti* had a leader who lasted as long as he could keep the group together. Thus leadership, status, and tenure were not absolute. A leader had to continually demonstrate his ability to lead, particularly by providing game and protection from enemies.

Leadership among the Oglalas was closely tied to the Oglala worldview and concept of the individual. Personal power accrued to those who propitiated the proper spirits. Leaders acquired status through generosity, fortitude, bravery, and hunting ability. Accumulating material things was not important in itself, but the way such goods were redistributed was extremely important.

A number of sodalities were found among the Oglalas during the development of Lakota culture on the Plains: for example, (1) the *akicita* 'soldier society,' whose primary function was to maintain law and order, especially during the summer buffalo hunts and at large tribal gatherings such as the Sun Dance; (2) civil societies, such as the Chief Society, which served as the true policymaking bodies of the Oglalas; (3) warrior societies, whose primary function, as the name indicates, was to organize forays against enemies; (4) feast and dance associations, whose essential interest was in organizing various leisure pursuits; (5) religious sodalities, often called "dream cults," which were made up of individuals who had received similar visions or who served as ritual curers; and (6) women's sodalities, whose activities ranged from artisan interests—for example, quilling and tanning—to performing rituals centered on the celebration of war, hunting, and religion. It should be emphasized here that, though women formed their own sodalities, most of the men's sodalities invited a number of women to participate, often in ritual capacities such as singer (Wissler 1912).

There were six *akicita* societies, and each year a different one was chosen to police the band, thus guarding against any one society's becoming too powerful. Each *akicita* had its own distinctive organization and ceremonies.

Of the civil societies the most distinguished was the Chief Society. This society, composed of men over forty, served as a governing council that elected seven chiefs for lifetime service. The Chief Society delegated authority to those seven. However, this office was short-lived and disappeared when the Oglalas were confined to the reservation (Grinnell 1967; Powers 1977; Wissler 1912).

The seven chiefs in turn delegated authority to four younger men known as Shirt Wearers. The Shirt Wearers were considered the supreme councilors and actually controlled the camp. Together the Chief Society, the seven life-term chiefs, and the Shirt Wearers appointed four men, *wakicunze*, who were responsible for the organization and control of the band camp and the sun dance camp. The *wakicunze* controlled the general social, political, and economic aspects of Oglala life.

Leaders were able to influence policy but never made it. Obedience and discipline were required during communal hunts and war expeditions, but civil authority was by common consent. Councils were the main policymaking bodies in Oglala culture. Theoretically they consisted of all the members of the group the council represented. They met frequently to discuss proposals, and issues were debated by all members:

> Determination of policy among the Oglalas was
> the result of a highly informal process in which
> through councils and other policy groups a consen-
> sus was arrived at through a continuous weighing
> of views until objections to the proposals under
> consideration had been reduced to a minimum. . .
> . Even after a decision was reached, it was possi-
> ble for dissenters to leave the group thus evading
> the necessity for obeying a decision to which they

were opposed. The binding force of majority rule
as evidence in a formal vote by a representative
assembly has no acceptance in Oglala culture
(Grinnell 1967, 132).

With the coming of the white man and his colonial administration, the situation changed drastically. The buffalo were exterminated, and the Sioux were conquered and confined to reservations. The Indian condition deteriorated as the nation pros-
pered. Not only did Euramerican dominance inhibit Indian
potential, but westward expansion depended on the exploitation
of the subordinate group to the extent that "one could probably
write a history of the U.S. in terms of fraudulent real estate
transactions, often pushed through at gunpoint. These real
estate transactions were called treaties" (Burnette and Koster
1974, 105).

Between 1778 and 1871, 371 treaties were signed and ratified
between the United States government and American Indians,
all of which were broken or abrogated.

Westward settlement gathered momentum after the Civil
War. The discovery of gold in California and the Rocky Moun-
tains, along with plans for the construction of transcontinental
railroads, resulted in demands to reduce Indian landholdings to
make way for westward migration. In 1874, after gold was discovered in the Black Hills, white men began to invade the Sioux
treaty lands. The government offered to buy the Black Hills, but
the Sioux refused to sell. Later, threatening the Sioux with
starvation if they did not relinquish the Hills, the United States
government took them over.

Since 1871 United States policy has been to legislate, not
negotiate, in Indian matters. The federal government has not
consulted Indians no matter what effect the legislation has had
on their civil and property rights. As one leading authority
stated: "When we were weak and the Indians were strong we
were glad to make treaties with them and live up to those
treaties. . . . The misfortune of the Indians is that they hold
great bodies of rich lands which have aroused the cupidity of
powerful corporations and powerful individuals" (McNickle
1973, 76).

After the beginning of the reservation period, in the late

1870s, the authority of the traditional governing bodies diminished considerably. The *akicita* societies were disbanded and disarmed because Indian agents of the Bureau of Indian Affairs recognized the need for a police force loyal to them and not to the traditional Oglala leaders. Valentine McGillycuddy, a particularly strong agent in the 1880s, used the threat of army intervention to convince the Oglalas to permit the creation of an Indian police force answerable to him alone—not to the traditional leaders. (Grinnell 1967; for a discussion of Indian police see Hagan 1966).

The Chief Society remained in operation, but its importance as an advisory group depended on the agent in power. The early Indian agents dealt with the council of the Chief Society. In fact, it was this council that had negotiated with the United States government during the last years of the hostility between the Oglalas and the federal government. (Grinnell 1967; Maynard and Twiss 1970).

Ultimately the Bureau of Indian Affairs, through its local representative the Indian agent, took control of most phases of Oglala life. The Indian agent was in charge of distributing rations, law and order, education of children, disposal and allotment of Indian land, issuing permits for Indians to leave the reservation to hunt, payments to individual Indians under provisions of treaties or land cessions, and even the regulation of Indian religion. Indian agents had dictatorial powers on the reservation that came from their control of rations and the threat of armed intervention from the army should the Oglalas resist federal policies.

From the beginning, the colonists mistakenly assumed that leadership was vested in one man who could make decisions for the whole tribe. This led to a number of misunderstandings; for example, the 1868 Treaty of Fort Laramie was not considered binding by all bands of Sioux because only one leader had been consulted (Maynard and Twiss 1970). The term "chief" was not indigenous to the Oglalas; rather, it was a Euramerican term. Among the Sioux no leader existed who was supreme in all aspects of life. But the colonial administration had to have native leaders for successful takeover, so out of a group of *tiyošpaye* council leaders the United States government chose those they thought would be most cooperative.

The Indian style of leadership changed to deal with the federal government, which insisted on negotiating with a small number of chiefs. Leaders such as Red Cloud came to have tremendous power. Although Red Cloud was never more than a war leader to the Oglalas, owing to white pressure and influence he was selected "treaty chief" to sign the treaty ending the Red Cloud War. Later he was recognized by whites as head chief of the entire Sioux nation and was taken to Washington, D.C., to negotiate with the federal government. Later, when strong chiefs began to interfere with government policies, Indian agents tried to discredit them and weaken their power.

With the establishment of the reservation system, the United States government espoused policies designed to assimilate the Oglalas into non-Indian society. In 1887 the Dawes Act was passed, and in the early 1900s it became operational throughout South Dakota. The allotment act provided for parceling out land to individuals according to a formula and was billed as giving Indians the right to own land individually so that they could become small farmers. It was unimportant that most of the land was not suited for farming and that the Indians had no capital to start farms and were not interested in agriculture. Moreover, the policy was in direct conflict with traditional Indian attitudes toward the land. Land was sacred and could be possessed by no man, since it was the mother of all living creatures. To whites this belief was pagan and had to be eradicated (Burnette and Koster 1974).

This program to "civilize" Indians by giving them a plow and a plot of land was in reality a strategy to open up Indian land for white settlement, since the allotment act specified that surplus lands—that is, lands remaining after individual allotments were made—could be sold to the United States. Subsequently, the most valuable lands, such as the Black Hills, fell into the hands of the federal government and white settlers.

During the time the Dawes Act was in effect, American Indians lost four-fifths of their land. In 1880 Indians owned 241,000,000 acres. Between 1887 and 1934 they lost 190,000,000 acres to whites, and 27,000,000 acres were appropriated by the federal government for national parks, leaving the Indians with only 24,000,000 acres (Powers 1969).

The allotment process whereby Indians lost land has been

described as "the second slaughter of the buffalo as far as Plains Indian economy was concerned" (Burnette and Koster 1974, 113). The Indians slumped from near self-sufficiency back into poverty, while whites and the United States government profited from Indian land. Moreover, the Sioux had been promised that their rations would remain the same. However, immediately after the agreement was concluded, Congress cut the beef ration by one million pounds at Pine Ridge and by two million pounds at nearby Rosebud (Burnette and Koster 1974, 147).

The Bureau of Indian Affairs

The reduction of original tribal domains to reservations situated on lands deemed unfit for white settlement caused severe disruption of tribal economies, which made it even more important for the government to honor its treaty obligations. Under the terms of the treaties, in exchange for their lands the government was obligated to supply the Indians with food, education, and clothing, often in perpetuity. These treaties, along with trusteeship over reserved land, have been the basis for the unique legal relationship between the Indian people and the United States government.

To fulfill treaty obligations and help assimilate Indians into the mainstream of American life, the federal government created the Bureau of Indian Affairs (BIA). The role of the BIA is controlled by Title 25 (Indians) of the Federal Code and is directly under the control of the Department of the Interior. Jobs in the bureau were and continue to be political rewards. As the bureaucracy of the BIA grew it became more self-serving and self-contained and less concerned with assisting Indian people. At every juncture, efforts on behalf of Indians that held any promise of permanent relief were undermined by the very structure and nature of the agency: "The reward system of the BIA discourages leadership on purpose. It not only serves to reward unaggressive behavior and docility but punishes, usually by transfer, those who persist in behaving like leaders. It is therefore not possible to conceive of change and improvement within the present structure" (Cahn 1969, 147).

A major obstacle to innovation is the process that imposes review upon review of every idea proposed. Consequently, each idea is subject to distortion and resistance by officials who see their empires threatened.

On the reservation, Indian contact with the federal government was through the superintendent (earlier called the Indian agent). The superintendent held the real power on the reservation, for he distributed and withheld resources. Rations and purchase orders were cut off from whole families who protested his decisions. The superintendent acted as judge, police chief, gardener, cowboy, banker, real estate agent, and secret head of state all wrapped in one (Burnette and Koster 1974, 187). Moreover, because land in trust status was held in the name of the United States on behalf of the Indian owner, he could do nothing with his land without the permission of the BIA superintendent, who acted for the United States government (Burnette and Koster 1974, 118). In 1915 an independent organization conducting an investigation of Indian administration reported that "the Indian Superintendent is a czar within the territorial jurisdiction prescribed for him. He is ex-officio both guardian and trustee" (Costo 1968, 87).

Under the New Deal administration and commissioner of Indian affairs John Collier (1933–45), the bureau was reorganized and its earlier emphasis on assimilation of Indians changed to one of adapting as much as possible to the local needs of various tribes. Collier's solution to the economic situation of the 1920s concentrated on tribal development and on government planning for reservation development. A program of acquisition and consolidation of tribal lands was started. Collier pushed for the Indian Reorganization Act of 1934, which ended the open sale of land. Collier supported the development of strong tribal units, organized to act politically and economically for the Indians' own benefit.

One provision of the act offered tribes the opportunity to engage in self-government (albeit under the direction and guidance of the bureau). The Indian Reorganization Act authorized the establishment of tribal councils and the drafting of tribal constitutions:

> At the heart of the Act were the sections authorizing tribes to operate under governments of their own choice, either formalized by written docu-

ments or following customary usage and to establish business corporations for the management of
their resources. This made explicit in statutory law
for the first time the principle which the courts had
followed since the 1830's recognizing the residual
rights of Indian tribes to govern themselves
(McNickle 1973, 94).

The act was not compulsory, and tribes had the option of
voting to accept or reject it. To those tribes adopting it, it
prohibited further division of tribal lands into individual allotments and provided for the secretary of the interior to return to
tribal ownership lands that had been withdrawn from home-
steading but not occupied.

Oglala traditionalists fought bitterly against the act, but in the
end they lost owing to a provision that allowed it to be adopted
with the consent of 30 percent of the eligible voters on the
reservation. Thus it allowed a minority to rule. The Oglala Sioux
constitution, based largely on the United States Constitution,
was formulated in 1935 and accepted by a vote of 1,348 to 1,041,
with many traditional Oglalas abstaining (Burnette and Kostner
1974; Maynard and Twiss 1970).

Many problems arose, because the new form of tribal government worked out at Pine Ridge did not reflect the Indian culture
that had existed before the coming of white man. The tradition-
ists felt that to conduct an election campaign for the tribal council
was demeaning, since their status was determined by tradition.
Another objection stemmed from the fact that in organizing
electoral districts *tiyošpaye* divisions were ignored. Thus the
establishment of an elected council under the terms of the 1935
constitution displaced the band structure and made no provision
for traditional leadership.

As we enter this study of twentieth-century Oglala women,
little of substance has changed since the Indian Reorganization
Act. Although the Lakotas technically are not wards of the
federal government, it is still the responsibility of various tribes
to prove that they are capable of governing themselves without
"benefit" of the Bureau of Indian Affairs. This demonstration of
ability becomes increasingly important for the Lakota people,
not only of Pine Ridge, but of all the Lakota and Dakota reservations.

Today the Oglalas are experiencing population expansion coupled with a shrinking land base, waiting for the federal courts to settle the Black Hills claims. The Hills are still sacred to them—as to all the Lakotas—and the Oglalas are the foremost among the reservation Indians in voicing their demand to regain title to their sacred Hills.

In many ways, to be Oglala, to be Lakota, today requires the same fortitude that was required in prereservation days when the threat of cultural extinction was imminent. Much of the hopes of the Oglalas are based on a long tradition of religious beliefs, one that distinguishes them both from other Indians and from non-Indians. An understanding of this wisdom of the ages, passed down from one generation to the next, makes it possible to understand the relationships between Oglala men and women, which in the past have often been neglected or ignored by Western writers.

2 The Buffalo Nation

O You, Grandmother, from whom all earthly things
come, and O You, Mother Earth, who bear and nourish
all fruits, behold us and listen: Upon You there is a
sacred path which we walk, thinking of the sacredness of
all things.[1]

The Cosmological Matrix

If we are to understand the ideological basis for male/female
behavior and the way the Oglalas assess the role of women, we
must begin with what is perceived to be the Lakota beginning:
the creation of the universe and the emergence of humans from
an earlier subterranean existence to the surface of what the
Lakota people call Maka Ina 'Mother Earth.'

Even though from a Western perspective Oglala women are
portrayed as subordinate to men—particularly in matters pertaining to politics, economics, and religion—women have fared
much better in the cosmological sphere, where even non-Indians
agree that the woman reigns supreme.

In the cosmology it is woman whose social transgression leads
to the creation of time and space. It is woman who, bored with
the natural universe, conspires with the culture hero to coax
humans, her own people called the Buffalo Nation, from their
subterranean world to the earth. It is she who in concert with the
trickster teaches the people about culture, and it is she who
suddenly then leaves them to face the vicissitudes of nature
alone. Finally, it is a sacred woman who drops to earth in the
form of a falling star and unites with the most virile of sacred
beings, the South Wind. In the transformation of Falling Star
into the sacred White Buffalo Calf Woman, she brings to a
starving Lakota nation that instrument of prayer the Calf Pipe,
which along with the Seven Sacred Rites will intervene in their
lives whenever they are experiencing hardship and danger.

What follows is a synopsis of some of the most important myths and beliefs. I believe that a better understanding of the Lakota conception of the spiritual condition of women will help us to understand the way the Lakotas see themselves in terms of male/female relationships in real life. It will also be of interest to see to what extent the symbolic representation of sexual ideology reflects and reinforces social relations between men and women (Tiffany 1979, 20). In a society where complementarity between the sexes is highly valued, it is unlikely that either male chauvinism or feminism can adequately explain people's behavior.

Thanks largely to the work of James R. Walker, a physician at Pine Ridge between 1896 and 1914, many of the stories about the creation of the Oglala universe have been preserved (Walker 1917, 1980). Although Walker's point of view on Oglala cosmology has been challenged in part, recent critical evaluations of his work demonstrate that most of his analysis of Oglala myth is consistent with contemporary analysis.[2]

To shed light on the position of Oglala women in the cosmology, I will begin with a review of the characters who figure prominently in literally hundreds of short stories collected by Walker and others and relate these characters to the series of myths that deal with the creation of the universe out of a void, ultimately resulting in the emergence of humans. I should note here that it is the emergence story that is most frequently told by Oglala people today, while the creation of the universe is largely taught in bilingual and bicultural programs sponsored by public, federal, and mission schools on the Pine Ridge reservation.

Creation of the Universe

According to the Walker myths, Inyan 'the rock' existed in a scenario devoid of time and space; only Hanhepi 'the darkness, night' surrounded Inyan. Inyan desired another thing so that he could exercise his power over it, but to do so he had to create it out of himself, using his own power and his own blood, which was blue. What he created would also have power, but the amount of power would depend on the amount of blood he gave up. He then constructed a great disk out of himself, shaping it around him, and he called it Maka 'earth.' The creation of Maka required that he open all his veins, and so much blood flowed from him that he shriveled into something hard and powerless. His blood formed not only Maka, but all the waters on it. But the powers of his blood that now formed the earth and waters could not live in the waters, so the powers separated, shaping part of themselves into a great blue dome called Maȟpiyato 'sky' (literally, 'blue sky'). Thus was created from rock, once powerful and oldest of all, the earth, sky, and waters. Since rock originally contained all the powers of the universe in his blood, those powers were then diffused into the earth, the sky, and the waters. The powers of these areas are often equated with their "spirits."

At this point it should be noted that only by linguistic markers, or context, can we determine the sexes of the gods. Although most of the literature refers to Inyan as "he," there is no evidence that Inyan has any gender. What is clear is that out of this primal force, male (sky) and female (earth) properties are created.

After their creation (although the myths never tell why) the sky is considered supreme. After quarrels between Maka and Hanhepi, Maȟpiyato decrees that Hanhepi should be banished to the underworld and creates Anpetu 'daytime, light.' Maka is forever attached to Inyan, and to assuage Maka, who finds herself naked and cold, Maȟpiyato creates the Wi 'sun' or 'moon' and places it in the blue dome. Maka then becomes so hot that she pleads with Maȟpiyato to return the night to the blue dome. In acquiescing, Maȟpiyato commands Hanhepi Wi to follow Anpetu Wi around the universe, both alternately traveling from under the world through the blue dome.

We now find the Oglala universe divided into three major regions—the sky, the earth and waters, and the underworld. Maȟpiyato creates (though we are never told precisely how) humankind to be servants of the gods and places them in a subterranean region. There they are called Pte Oyate 'Buffalo People or Nation,' and their chief is Wazi 'Old Man' and his wife is Wakanka 'Old Woman'—literally, someone who is old.

Two points should be noted here. First, despite references to Wi as the sun, with a connotation that Anpetu 'day' is male and Hanhepi 'night' is female, the term Wi is essentially a female marker, and even today the term *wi* stands for both sun and moon, the two being distinguished by the qualifiers Anpetu Wi 'sun,' that is, day or light *wi*, and Hanhepi Wi 'moon,' that is, night or dark *wi*.[3] Here we see a symbolic replication: just as Inyan, in the beginning sexually undifferentiated, created out of itself both male and female properties, we later see in the origin myth, the creation of the sun and the moon, again out of an undifferentiated *wi*. But *wi* signifies female and is in fact terminologically related to *winyan* 'woman.'

The second point is concerned with the Buffalo nation, the metaphor for humans living in the subterranean world. In other myths and rituals we find that the Lakotas constantly equate women with buffalo; frequently they are interchangeable metaphors, symbolically representing both fecundity and nurture.[4] This relationship between woman and buffalo will be dealt with again later, but here let me emphasize that the very name by which humans living in the subterranean world are designated in the creation myth—"Buffalo People"—means that the Lakotas are a people *born of woman,* really and spiritually. In Lakota buffalo, along with other animals important to Lakota subsistence (elk and deer), are sexually differentiated by separate terms. While *tatanka* 'great ruminant' means 'buffalo bull' and serves as the generic term for buffalo, *pte* means 'buffalo cow' and is the term used when mythically or ritually addressing or referring to the buffalo, even though in English the distinction is never made.

Returning to the creation story, once the domains of the sky, earth and waters, and underworld have been established and humans and all the creatures of the world created, the cosmology begins to develop much like the classic Greek and Roman myths in that all of the major personae have human attributes. Much of the continuous development of the universe is contingent more upon the foibles of gods with humanlike weaknesses than upon godlike pronouncements upon the various constituents of the earth and sky. The second phase of the creation story begins "long, long ago when *Wazi* lived under the earth with his wife *Wakanka*. Their daughter, Ite (Face), grew up to be the most beautiful of all women, and even though she was not a god, *Tate* (Wind), who was a god, fell in love with her and married her. She gave birth to quadruplets, the Four Winds" (*Ehanni ohunkakan,* n.d.).

This phase of the cosmology has been equated with the creation of time and space. Judgments handed out by Maȟpiyato punish some of the gods and reward others. In the process they are rearranged throughout the universe so that their new locations on the earth and the four quarters of the universe symbolically represent time and space (Powers 1977, 166–71).

In the reorganization of the universe, a number of characters become important to understanding real Lakota social values. For example, Wazi, the Old Man, and his wife Wakanka are not satisfied with simply having a beautiful daughter, Ite 'face,' who marries the god Tate—'wind.' They seek power: they want to be gods. They conspire with Inktomi the trickster, who promises them power if they will help him make people look ridiculous, one of his chief missions in his godly and worldly pursuits. They agree, and Inktomi creates a scenario in which Anpetu Wi, who is married to Hanhepi Wi, becomes enchanted with Ite, who, as she becomes even more beautiful, begins to ignore her husband Tate and their four children (as well as fifth child, Yumni, with whom she is pregnant). At a critical part of the myth, Ite sits in Hanhepi Wi's place at a feast and insults her. Because all have conspired to shame Hanhepi Wi, Maȟpiyato intervenes and banishes Ite to the earth's surface, making one side of her face horribly ugly. She is then named Anukite 'Double Face' and plays an important role in the supernatural affairs of the Oglalas. Anukite is synonymous with Sinte Sapela Win 'black-tailed deer woman,' because Anukite "appears to men in visions, and in the real world, in the form of a deer, or two deer women, one black . . . and the other white. . . . The two faces of Double-Face and the two deer women represent proper and improper sexual conduct. . . . The product of an indiscriminate sexual union is *anukiya* 'cross-breed, hybrid.' . . . Men become disorderly or crazy when they . . . have sexual relations with the deer women" (Powers 1977, 197).

Women who dream of Anukite have unusual powers to seduce men. These women were not regarded as quite normal but were considered *wakan* 'sacred.' The Oglalas say that if a man meets a lone woman in the woods or on the prairie he must avoid her, for she may be a deer woman. The belief is that deer have a peculiar odor in their hooves that becomes fine perfume when a deer becomes a woman. This perfume acts as a medicine and works an evil spell on men. Sometimes even wishing to make love to the deer woman can be fatal (Wissler 1912, 94). After seducing men, these beautiful women turn into deer and run away. The men then go insane or die.

In the preceding story the deer woman represents a menstruating woman who is isolated from the group. A peculiar odor is emitted from the hoof. Having sexual relations with a deer woman (a menstruating woman) metaphorically can be fatal (to society). Many American Indian tribes believe that semen is finite, and "wasting" it on a woman who cannot conceive can be devastating in terms of reproducing and maintaining the population.

Wazi, Wakanka, and Inktomi are banished to the edge of the earth along with Anukite, and Tate is given custody of the four brothers (and Yumni, who is now born). The placement of Tate and the four brothers on the earth immediately establishes time and space, through the creation of the four seasons, which in Lakota are synonymous with the four quarters of the earth. Anpetu Wi and Hanhepi Wi are separated, and in so doing day and night are distinguished.

Anpetu Wi and Hanhepi Wi, before being separated by Maḣpiyato,[5] have a daughter named Woḣpe, usually translated 'Falling Star.' At the time the earth and the four directions are established, she falls to earth and takes up residence with one of the quadruplets, the South Wind. Each of the Four Winds has human attributes: the West Wind is cantankerous, the North Wind is pugnacious, the East Wind is lazy. But the South Wind represents all the idealized male characteristics: he is warm and friendly, and he likes to play with little children; thus the fifth brother Yumni, who never grows up and knows no place of his own, stays with the South Wind. Metaphorically, the seasons make their round as a result of the four brothers' fighting with each other. At the end of the cycle the East, West, and South winds unite against the North Wind and drive him back to his home, thus making the earth amenable to growing things. "The Four Winds are addressed as one god and have precedence over all gods except *Woḣpe,* the feminine."[6]

The woman Woḣpe is particularly important; in fact she is the most important of all characters in the myths so far, because it is this female, who after the emergence of the Pte Oyate, 'Buffalo Nation' from their subterranean homes will be transformed into the sacred Ptehincalasan Win 'White Buffalo Calf Woman.' It is this same woman who happens upon starving humans later in what are perceived to be historical times, with gifts of the sacred pipe and the Seven Sacred Rites. Thus the transformation of Woĥpe, the Falling Star of the cosmological past, into the White Buffalo Calf Woman of the historical past, represents a significant continuum from old to new, symbolized most dramatically in the appearance of a single woman.

The actual emergence myth begins with the desire of Anukite 'Double Face,' who was once the beautiful Ite 'Face,' to live once again with her people, the Buffalo Nation. She of course is a mortal who had been married to a god. Inktomi, meanwhile, is tired of playing pranks on the animals, so he and Anukite conspire to induce humans to come to the surface of the earth. They believe that if humans tasted meat, they would be drawn to the source of the food. And so Double Face prepares the food and gives it to Inktomi, who transforms himself into a wolf and takes the food and some clothing to the cave entrance that leads to the subterranean world.

It is told that the wolf found the Buffalo Nation and gave the food and clothing to the people. Despite the warning of an old woman not to follow the wolf, a human named Tokahe 'First' and three other men followed it to the earth's surface. There Anukite and Inktomi made themselves look attractive, telling the visitors that they were really very old but that buffalo meat kept them looking young. Tokahe and the others went back to the underworld, where they told the others the wonderful things they had seen on earth and coaxed them to follow. In all, Tokahe and his family plus six other men and their families ventured to the surface of the earth, where they came to be the original ancestors of the Seven Fireplaces.

But when they reached the surface Anukite showed them the ugly side of her face, and Inktomi laughed and made fun of them. Buffalo were difficult to find, and the humans grew cold, tired, and hungry. The beautiful sunny days of summer turned bitter cold. They could not find their way back home, and Tokahe, the first man, was ashamed. But Wazi and Wakanka, who had been banished to the edge of the earth, found them and taught them how to make clothing and tipis and how to hunt buffalo and prepare food. And the Buffalo nation soon became adjusted to the new life on the earth.

The Sacred Pipe

The single most important symbol of Oglala religion is the long-stemmed pipe called *cannunpa wakan* 'sacred pipe,' or more properly *ptehincala cannunpa* 'calf pipe.' As is true of any religious symbol so important to a group of people, there is much controversy about the sacred pipe. Its shape and size, for example, are contested. Some hold that the original pipe was the traditional long-stemmed "peace pipe" used by the Lakotas and other Indian people on ceremonial occasions at treaty councils held at the various forts. Others hold that it was a miniature long-stemmed pipe, like those made today and sometimes displayed inside a dwelling as a "house pipe," not to smoke but to remind people of their moral obligations. Others believe that the original sacred pipe was a "straight pipe" made from the femur of a deer and incised with geometric designs.

There is controversy over whether the original bowl made from catlinite was L-shaped or T-shaped, since both are common. And others argue over the proper decoration for the stem, ranging from the head of a mallard duck, a fan of eagle tail feathers, relief carvings of turtles and spiders, or something else. There is also disagreement on whether the sacred pipe that is currently kept by a sacred pipe keeper at Green Grass, South Dakota, on the Cheyenne River reservation is the original pipe, since there are reports that the original was stolen. It is also debated whether a single line of people has had the responsibility of keeping the pipe all these years.

But controversy over religious symbols tends to strengthen belief, not diminish it. What is not disputed and perhaps represents the most important agreement is that the sacred pipe was brought to the Lakota people by a sacred woman called Ptehincalasan Win 'White Buffalo Calf Woman.' It is also acknowledged that the White Buffalo Calf Woman and Woȟpe, Falling Star, are the same.

The coming of the sacred pipe is a story that is told frequently at Pine Ridge and other Lakota reservations. But as might be expected, just as there is controversy over the nature of the sacred pipe, a wide variety of stories are associated with its arrival among the Lakotas. A number of these stories have been collected and published. It is likely that some versions will therefore become dogma while others will fade into oblivion, largely because religious stories of this kind tend to reflect immediate and real needs. As these needs change, so does the myth, as long as it is viable. For example, one pipe story collected by the missionary Rev. Eugene Buechel, S.J., fails to consider that when the White Buffalo Calf Woman first appeared to the Lakota people she was nude, and one of the hunters who first saw her wanted to have sexual relations with her. Of course the teller of the story apparently knew the priest would not take well to the sexual references and simply omitted them. What follows then is a composite based on contemporary oral tradition as well as the literature.[7]

The Coming of the Pipe

Many winters ago the Lakota people were starving. The chief of the Itazipco 'No Bows,' also called Sans Arcs, sent two hunters out to see if they could find buffalo to help them lie over for the winter. They left early in the morning and headed west out onto the prairie. They decided to separate for a while and to meet at an appointed place. They searched all day, but when they met neither had found game.

As they began to plan what to do the next day, one of the hunters noticed a solitary creature advancing from the west. At first they thought it was a buffalo, but as it got closer it appeared to be human. It moved rapidly toward them. They in turn advanced toward it, hiding behind a hill in case it turned out to be an enemy. But as the human approached they saw it was a woman. As she got nearer, they saw that she was beautiful and wore no clothing; her long hair hung down and covered her like a robe except on the left side, where it was tied with a tuft of buffalo hair. She carried a flat fan made of sage in her left hand, and there was a bundle strapped to her back. Her face was painted with vertical red stripes. She spoke: "I am sent by the Buffalo Nation to visit your people. It is right that you are trying hard to fulfill the wishes of your people and find buffalo even though it is a difficult task. Go home to your people and tell them to erect a large lodge in the middle of the camp circle with the doorway facing west. Tell them to spread sage at the place of honor in the rear of the lodge, and let them prepare a small space of mellowed earth. Directly behind the altar tell them to build a small rack, and in front of the rack let them place a buffalo skull. I have something important to present to the tribe that will help them in the future. I shall be in camp at sunrise."

As she was speaking one of the men lusted for her. "Let us leap upon her," he said to his companion. "If she is good, I will take her to my tipi."

"No!" said the other. "She is one of the mysterious people. It is not well that you should do anything of that sort."

The first insisted, "I will attack her, for no one is around."

The other answered, "You may, but I will stand aside."

The woman, hearing them, said: "I do not come here to cause strife. I come from Wakantanka." With these words she took a filled pipe from her bundle and laid it on a buffalo chip with the stem pointing toward the east. Then she laughed and sat down.

The first attacked her and threw her to the ground. And as he began to ravage her, suddenly there was a rumbling in the heavens, and something like a snake flew down from above. A great mist descended upon them where they lay and lingered awhile. When the mist lifted the woman rose. Beside her was only the skeleton of the man who had attacked her.

Seeing what had happened to his companion, the other hunter became frightened, but the woman consoled him. She took up the pipe from the ground and approached him, saying: "I bring you this pipe. It is a calf pipe. I bring it to you because your people are starving. This pipe will bring you many buffalo."

She then told him to hurry back to his village and follow the instructions she had given. "A sacred pipe is coming to you, she said, "that will furnish you with abundance in the Spirit Land." She also told him that his people would know when she was about to arrive because they would see four puffs of smoke under the sun at midday. They must then prepare food and seat themselves in a circle for a feast. She instructed that all the men should bow their heads and look at the ground until she was in their midst. Only after she had served everyone the food could they look at her. Anyone who tried to harm her would meet the fate of the first hunter, but if the people obeyed her their prayers would be answered by Wakantanka and they would prosper.

Then she disappeared in a mist.

The hunter ran back to the camp in a zigzag course, as hunters do when they have found game. When he arrived he eagerly told the chief about the woman and gave the people her instructions. Quickly they began to construct a large lodge as she had ordered, and a camp crier circled the village telling the people to assemble on the next day and to ready themselves for this important occasion.

On the following day she could be seen standing on a hill, and lightning flashed around her. She came into the camp, and even the dogs were afraid to bark as she entered. The people were assembled, dressed in their finest clothing, the men with their heads bowed to the earth. She was now dressed in a beautiful fringed buckskin dress, leggings, and moccasins. She no longer carried the sage fan, but rather she held a large pipe, the bowl resting in her left hand and the stem in her right. As she entered the lodge she began to sing the following song:

> *Niya taninyan mawani ye*
> *Oyate le imawani*
> *Na hotaninyan mawani ye*
> *Niya taninyan mawani ye*
> *Waluta le imawani ye.*

> With a visible breath I am walking;
> I am walking toward a Buffalo Nation,
> And my voice is loud.
> With a visible breath I am walking;
> I am walking toward this sacred object.[8]

She walked in a circle clockwise, as the sun travels in the sky. The women seeing her beauty began to exclaim in admiration. One man curiously raised his head to behold her, and immediately a puff of black smoke blew into his eyes and a voice said, "You have disobeyed me, and there will be smoke in your eyes as long as you live." She then sat at the place of honor and laid the pipe against the specially made rack.

The chief then rose and addressed the woman as sister and

welcomed her to the camp. He acknowledged that Wakantanka had sent her to the people and that she had come to their rescue just when they were in great need. "Sister, we are glad you have come to us and trust that whatever message you have brought we may be able to abide by it. We are poor, but we have a great respect for visitors, especially relatives. Although it is our custom to serve our guests special foods, all we have is this water that falls from the clouds. Drink it and remember that we are poor."

The chief then dipped some sweet grass into a buffalo horn filled with water and gave it to the woman to drink. After she drank the chief said, "Sister, we are now ready to hear the good message you have brought."

"My relatives, brothers and sisters: Wakantanka has looked down and smiles upon us this day because we have met as belonging to one family. The best thing in a family is good feeling toward every member. I am proud to become part of your family—a sister to you all. The sun is your grandfather, and he is the same to me. Your tribe has the distinction of always being very faithful to promises, and of possessing great respect and reverence toward sacred things. It is known also that nothing but good feeling prevails and that whenever someone has been found guilty of any wrong, that member has been cast out and not allowed to mingle with the others in the tribe. For all these good qualities you have been chosen as worthy and deserving of all good gifts. I represent the Buffalo nation, who have sent you this pipe. You are to receive it in the name of all common people. Take it, and use it according to my directions" (Densmore 1918, 65).

Holding up the sacred pipe she said: "With this sacred pipe you will walk upon the Earth: for the Earth is your Grandmother and Mother, and She is sacred. Every step that is taken upon her should be as a prayer. The bowl of this pipe is of red stone; it is the Earth. Carved in the stone and facing the center is this buffalo calf who represents the four-leggeds who live upon your mother. The stem of the pipe is of wood, and this represents all that grows upon the Earth. And these twelve feathers that hang here where the stem fits into the bowl are from Wanbli Gleška, the Spotted Eagle, and they represent the eagle and all the wingeds of the air. All these peoples, and all the things of the universe, are joined to you who smoke the pipe—all send their voices to Wakantanka" (Brown 1971, 5–6).

"This pipe shall be used as a peacemaker. The time will come when you shall cease hostilities against other nations. Whenever peace is agreed upon between two tribes or parties this pipe shall be a binding instrument. By this pipe the medicine men shall be called to administer help to the sick" (Densmore 1918, 65).

Turning to the women, she said: "My dear sisters, the women: You have a hard life to live in this world, yet without you this life would not be what it is. Wakantanka intends that you shall bear much sorrow—comfort others in time of sorrow. By your hands the family moves. You have been given the knowledge of making clothing and of feeding the family. Wakantanka is with you in your sorrows and joins you in your griefs. He has given you the great gift of kindness toward every living creature on earth. You he has chosen to have a feeling for the dead who are gone. He knows that you remember the dead longer than do the men. He knows that you love your children dearly" (Densmore 1918, 65).

Then turning to the children: "My little brothers and sisters: Your parents were once little children like you, but in the course of time they became men and women. All living creatures were once small, but if no one took care of them they would never grow up. Your parents love you and have made many sacrifices for your sake in order that Wakantanka may listen to them, and that nothing but good may come to you as you grow up. I have brought this pipe for them, and you shall reap some benefit from it. Learn to respect and reverence this pipe, and above all, lead pure lives. Wakantanka is your great-grandfather" (Densmore 1918, 65–66).

Turning toward the men: "Now my dear brothers: in giving you this pipe you are expected to use it for nothing but good purposes. The tribe as a whole shall depend upon it for their necessary needs. You realize that all your necessities of life come from the earth below, the sky above, and the four winds. Whenever you do anything wrong against these elements they will always take some revenge upon you. You should reverence them. Offer sacrifices through this pipe and ask for what you need and it shall be granted you. On you it depends to be a strong help to the women in raising children. Share the women's sorrow. Wakantanka smiles on the man who has a kind feeling for a woman, because the woman is weak. Take this pipe and offer it to Wakantanka daily. Be good and kind to the little children" (Densmore 1918, 66).

Turning to the chief: "My older brother: You have been chosen by these people to receive this pipe in the name of the whole Sioux tribe. Wakantanka is pleased and glad this day because you have done what it is required and expected that every good leader should do. By this pipe the tribe shall live. It is your duty to see that this pipe is respected and reverenced. I am proud to be called a sister. May Wakantanka look down on us and take pity on us and provide us with what we need. Now we shall smoke the pipe" (Densmore 1918, 66).

Lighting the pipe with a glowing buffalo chip, she raised its stem to the sky and prayed to Wakantanka and all the good things that come from above. She then pointed the stem toward the earth and prayed to the place from which come all good gifts. Then, systematically, she pointed the stem of the pipe toward the Four Directions, beginning with the West Wind and turning slowly clockwise until all the directions had been prayed to, and then she passed the pipe to the chief and instructed him. And after he smoked, all the people assembled to smoke the pipe and pray accordingly, the pipe being passed clockwise from left to right around the seated assembly.

She then took a sacred stone from her bundle, inscribed with seven circles. These seven circles stood for seven very important rituals that would eventually be revealed to the people. She stayed with them four days, and during this time she taught them the first ritual, *wanagi wicagluha* 'spirit-keeping ritual.' The other six that she would teach them were *wiwanyang wacipi* 'sun gazing dance'; *hanbleceya* 'vision quest,' and *inikagapi* 'sweat lodge'—old ceremonies to which the ceremony of the pipe would be added; *išnati awicalowanpi* 'female puberty ceremony'; *hunka* 'the making of relatives'; and *tapa wankaiyeya* 'the sacred ball game.'

When she had finished instructing the people about the pipe and the seven sacred rituals, she told the chief to send two good runners to the top of the nearest hill to look for buffalo. She told the people to construct a buffalo drive. And she told them not to kill any buffalo before they entered the drive, because the buffalo might be followed by enemies.

The chief sent out the two runners, and presently the people saw a herd of buffalo running toward the drive following them. When the herd entered the drive the people fell upon them, slaughtering them. Just as the woman had predicted, the enemies also entered the drive after the buffalo, and they too were killed.

After the slaughter, the woman instructed the people to decorate the pipe with the scalps of their enemies and to feast on the buffalo meat. They were to end the feast with a victory dance.

At the end of the feast and the dance, she told the people to take a good look at her, because she was going to leave. As they bade her farewell she left the lodge, still walking clockwise. As she reached the edge of the camp the people were amazed to see her turn into first a red buffalo (north, where woman comes from), then brown (actually yellowish brown, representing the east—sunrise), then white (south—at the center), and finally a black buffalo as she passed over the hill (west—sunset). This represented the path of the sun. Symbolically her place was in the center, as a symbol of fecundity and of the birth of the Oglalas who emerged from the center of the earth just as the white buffalo is found at the center of the herd (universe). Then, as mysteriously as she had come, she disappeared.

The Calf Pipe in Cultural Context

What this long elaboration of the coming of the Calf Pipe tells us is that all the cultural values that are unequivocally Lakota were laid down by a supernatural woman, one who is perceived to be a mystical extension of the daughter of the sun and the moon, herself a prime mover in the cosmological plan. From a very real perspective, the sacred White Buffalo Calf Woman is most notably in her sexual prime. She attracts men, but at the same time she exudes virtue, which conquers all, even at the expense of the lustful man whose advances are thwarted by supernatural means, turning him into a pile of bones.

She is a seductive woman, but there are lessons here: the Sioux believed that if their women lost their virtue the buffalo would disappear and the people would starve. Romantically speaking, "To the Sioux not only the honor but the very existence of the tribe lay in the moccasin tracks of their women" (Sandoz 1961, 72–73). Thus the destruction of the man who was attempting to violate the sacred White Buffalo Calf Woman guarantees the survival of the Lakota people. Also, a man does not cohabit with someone he calls sister, a relationship between her and the rest of the Lakota nation made explicit when she entered the camp to address those assembled as relatives and to be addressed by the chief as "sister." So, as is true with other myths, the coming of the sacred pipe is not so much a fanciful story as a didactic one, and when the story is repeated the values associated with womanhood are reinforced as they are reiterated to each succeeding generation.

This is a story that touches upon the real-life problems that confront the Lakotas when they mythically enter the world from the subterranean depths, but it also deals with problems they face when they leave the relative abundance of the Great Lakes region and enter the inhospitable world of the Great Plains. The origin of this story may thus be in the recent history of the Oglalas rather than in the timeless past of cosmology. For example, the Oglalas probably did not reach the sacred Black Hills, where Wind Cave provided the opening into the world through which Tokahe and his followers entered the cultural world, until 1776. The famous winter counts of the Lakota people (and others), those pictographs that were used as mnemonic devices to record the most important events in the lives of the itinerant band members each winter, make reference to the winter of 1775–76[9] or of 1777–78[10] as the time when the Lakotas first discovered the Black Hills. Interestingly, both winter counts refer to a man named Standing Bull, who brought back a new species of tree (*ħante* 'cedar') to verify the discovery. One old man, Lone Man, claims that the person to whom the original Calf Pipe was given was Buffalo Stands Upward (Tatanka Woslal Najin), which is certainly the same name and same man even though the Lakota name is not provided in the two winter counts.[11]

Elsewhere there are references to *Wakantanka winyan wan iyeyapi* '[the winter that] they found the Wakantanka woman,' variously translated "god woman" or "Great Spirit" woman.[12] One Oglala account claims that "a mysterious woman was found, who it is claimed brought good news to the tribe."[13] According to another, 1797–98 was the "Took the God Woman Captive" winter; it adds that "a Dakota war party captured a woman of a tribe unknown, who, in order to gain their respect, cried out, I

am a *Wakan-Tanka* woman." There is also the cryptic note:
"This is the origin of their name for God (*Wakan-Tanka*), the
Great Holy, or Supernatural One, they having never heard of a
Supreme Being."[14]

A similar account for 1898 states:

> This year three young men went hunting. It was in
> the spring and very misty. They camped across the
> creek. At midnight came a woman, but where she
> entered they cannot say, for the enclosure was
> walled with logs like a stockade. There she stood
> by the fire. She gave them three words of advice:
> "Grow many and you will live"; "Pack up and run
> away, for two big gangs of the enemy will come
> after you"; "Go in that direction and I will bring
> many buffalo." Then she vanished they knew not
> where—up, down or where. The young men cried
> and prayed.[15]

Despite a discrepancy in some of the details, this appears to be an
attenuated version of the same Calf Pipe story.

Furthermore, there are other historical references that place
the sacred pipe and ceremonies, particularly the *Hunka,* in some
chronological order. All the winter counts cited above refer to
1804–5 or 1805 as the time of the Calumet Dance," otherwise
known in Lakota as *Tasinte un akicilowanpi* 'they sing over them
with tails,' described as "the *Hunka* ceremony when the candidates are made *Hunka* by the songs sung over them by the
officiating priest who at the same time waves a wand with pen-
dant horsehair."[16]

Although more research is required, evidence suggests that
the White Buffalo Calf Woman existed as a historical person,
though the interpretation given to her today by Oglalas and
anthropologists alike is that she was only of mythic importance.
By seeing her as historical, however, we reduce the imposed
chasm between myth and reality and thus demonstrate that the
values so highly considered by the Lakotas have been influenced
by a real woman whose dogma lives on in the form of myth.[17]

The period in which the historical White Buffalo Calf Woman
appears in the winter counts corresponds to a time when the
Lakotas are adjusting to the severities of the Great Plains environment, a hardship also stressed in the creation myth in which

Anukite (Double Face) and Inktomi forsake the tribe. Even a cursory examination of the winter counts shows that most winters are marked by reference to starvation, death, warfare, and a general preoccupation with doom. It is quite possible to view the coming of the Calf Pipe as a long-forgotten case of a group of people transforming a fragile woman, one susceptible to all human hardships, into a cosmic goddess in an attempt to construct a more satisfying culture that will permit them to survive against all odds.[18]

In short, despite history's past preoccupation with the importance of masculinity on the Great Plains, the newfound culture of the Oglalas, and presumably other tribes, and all the values entailed in such a life-style are rationalized through the prophetization and mystification of a woman.

3 *Wincincala:* Girlhood

Itokagata wicoti wan lila tanka na oiyokipi ca he. Tipi iyokihe el tima tunkašila eciyapi kin yankin na wicaša wan e na winyan wan wicakico ca nupin hiyotakapi.
  Lewicakiye "Ho wana oicimani wan yakagapi kta ca tanyan ecun po. Tokša anpetu wan el ake yakupi kte lo. Ho heci toške omayanipi kin hehanl oyaglakapi kte lo."
  "Ho iya po. Tka takuni akab yuhapi šni po."

Somewhere toward the south there is a large camp in which beauty and peace abide. There is a council lodge and inside sits one they call Grandfather. One day he calls out to a man and woman and both of them come and sit in his lodge.
  And he says to them, "You are now going to make a long journey, so do the best you can. Some day in the future you will come back here again. And then you will be asked to tell about how your journey fared."
  "So go now, both of you. But never own more than you need."[1]

Birth

According to Lakota belief, a certain aspect of a person's "soul" called *tun* lived forever and returned from the sky to invest itself in a newborn baby. Without this *tun* the baby could not live. Since the *tun* traveled from another place, when the baby was born the people said, *Hokšicala wan icimani hi* 'A baby traveler has arrived.'

All children, particularly during their first year, were considered *wakan* 'sacred.' People believed that during this time it was extremely important to treat the children properly lest they "return home." Twins were particularly sacred and somewhat picky about the homes they would ultimately choose. Twins were thought to wander around in the hills, frequently coming into camp and peeking into tipis until they found suitable parents to give them birth. Parents were concerned that both twins receive the same kinds of clothes and toys; if not, one of them would go back to the hills or perhaps die, as when a father gave one twin a buffalo robe but could not afford one for the other. The Lakotas believed that if one or both of the twins should die, they were sure to be born again, though perhaps into separate families. Only they had the power to recognize one another after being reborn. Medicine men often claimed their supernatural powers sprang from a previous existence as a twin (Dorsey 1889, 483). A general feeling prevailed that showing favoritism for one child, whether between twins or not, meant you would lose the less loved ones.

From birth on, children were not shielded from the realities of life and death. The sweat lodge and burial scaffold were as much a part of their environment as were relatives, other children, horses, and tipis. They were taught that they were merely passing through this life and that *maka kin ecela tehan yunke* 'only the earth lives forever.'

A number of beliefs surrounded the expectant mother. The pregnant woman was cautioned against traveling too far from home. If something frightened her, it could mark the baby. She should not be lazy and lie about the tipi, or the child would grow up to be fat. The woman should eat a lot of meat but should never prepare too much food, or she might lose the baby. Rabbit meat should be avoided lest the baby be born with a harelip, and she should not eat duck or the baby might have webbed feet. The woman should keep herself clean and while away the hours making clothing and a cradleboard for the baby, decorating the fawnskin clothes and moccasins with porcupine quillwork.

It was believed that medicine men could predict the sex of the baby by offering a child about two years old an awl with one hand and a bow and arrow with the other. If the child picked the awl, the baby would be a girl; if the bow and arrow, a boy. Also, if a little boy was shy in front of a pregnant woman the baby would be a girl, but if he was outgoing it would be a boy.

Inside a special tipi the pregnant women knelt on a freshly tanned deerskin and delivered into the hands of a matron, usually a kinswoman who herself had given birth and perhaps had overseen other births, thus earning a reputation as a reliable midwife, called *hokšiicu* 'takes the baby.'[2] Most frequently this woman was the grandmother or an aunt of the expectant mother, but the main requirement was experience.

A most important consideration was that the attending woman or women be of the highest character, because those surrounding the newborn had a profound influence on its life. If the baby was a girl, the midwife would watch her grow into womanhood and would call her daughter. The same woman would also more than likely attend to her at the time of her first menses.

At delivery the midwife cut the umbilical cord with a sharp knife and cleared the baby's mouth. It was also her duty to dispose of the placenta, which she wrapped in buckskin and placed high in a tree so that animals could not find it, lest they cast an evil influence over the growing child.

The grandparents of the new baby made a small buckskin container shaped like a sand lizard[3] and called *t'elanunwe* 'feigns death,' an animal respected for its longevity, and placed the cord in the container. Later the *t'elanunwe* would be tied to the infant's cradleboard and then to the female child's hair braid. It was believed that if the cord was discarded or was not in sight, the child would grow up too inquisitive. Adults would often ask a snoopy child, *Cekpa oyale he?* 'Are you looking for your navel cord?'

Early childhood was a grave period for both mother and baby. The grandparents stood by, and the old women were careful to check on women who came to visit the newborn. They were particularly on guard against those who were menstruating, because they believed the new mother might then not stop bleeding and might hemorrhage to death. Generally women were strong in the old days, but if the baby died the father would grieve and might cut off his little finger.

A woman's first child was cause for a great celebration in the camp. Her parents would announce it to the rest of the camp, and the father would be honored and encouraged by older men and women to be a good parent.

Little sexual distinction was made between toddling infants. The baby was wrapped in a diaper made from fawnskin lined with the hairy fruit of the cattail (*Typha latifolia*).[4] The baby was bathed frequently with soap made from soapweed (*Yucca glauca*)[5] and powdered with pulverized bracket fungi called locally *cannakpa* 'tree ears.' Its body was rubbed with a mixture of marrow and wild bergamot (*Monarda fistulosa*).[6]

When its mother was busy with household chores, the baby

spent a good deal of its early life swaddled in a cradleboard. It could be carried on its mother's back or hung in a tree where it swayed in the breeze. A sunshade attached to the cradleboard protected the baby's eyes, and feathers and other ornaments were hung from it to attract the child's attention. When the camp moved, the cradleboard was fastened to the saddle of a trusted horse or laid in the netting of a travois.

Although there were no structured lullabies, frequently a woman would *hokšikigna* 'soothe the baby' to sleep by humming or softly chanting such words as:

> *a wa wa wa*
> *Inila ištinma na*
>
> *a wa wa wa*
> Be still, sleep.
>   (Densmore 1918, 493)

The baby was nursed at once. If there was difficulty with lactating, the mother sought a young child with good teeth to cause the milk to flow, believing that good teeth were a sign the child had nursed a long time. The parents of such a child were given gifts by the grandparents of the newborn. On occasion, mothers without milk would chew the roots of slender milk vetch (*Astragalus gracilis*)[7] or drink a tea made from the skeleton plant (*Lygodesmia juncea*)[8] to cause the milk to flow.

Infants were also fed buffalo soup, cherry juice, and chopped meat. Often the mother would chew some meat and give it to her baby. To encourage babies to stop nursing, they were given meat and hard fat to suck on. Teething babies were also given a piece of buffalo ligament or a bone to gnaw.

Babies were taught not to cry lest they endanger the group by giving away its position to enemies or spoil a hunt by scaring off game. Every time the baby started to cry its mother gently cut off its breath by putting her hand over its mouth and nose, singing softly at the same time so as not to frighten it. When the baby struggled she let go, but this was repeated at the first sign of another cry.

Irritable, fussy babies were considered ill, and a number of treatments were used to relieve their distress. If a baby had difficulty breathing the mother would put drops of milk in its nose so that it would sneeze out the mucus. If it had a headache she would put her forehead next to the baby's in order to transfer the headache to herself. Common sicknesses were treated with a number of herbal medicines; matchbrush or broomweed (*Gutierrezia sarothrae*) for coughing;[9] mint (probably *Mentha arvensis*) made into a tea for diarrhea;[10] prairie mallow or scarlet mallow (*Sphaeralcea coccinea*) for open sores;[11] puffball or pasqueflower (*Anemone patens*) for rashes and blisters;[12] purple coneflower (*Echinacea angustifolia*) for toothache;[13] and sweet flag (*Acorus calamus*) for fever and also for a number of other ailments like headache and sore throat; this last is considered the Indian aspirin because of its wide use.[14] Powdered alum was also used for thrush.[15]

The best age for toilet training was two years. Little boys were sent out with their older brothers, and little girls went with their mothers. Children were discouraged from going outside the tipi at night for fear they might have nightmares when they returned.

The concept of illegitimacy was inappropriate in Lakota culture. All children were cared for. Neglect was unknown, and technically there was no such thing as an orphan. The term *wablenica* designated a child who had lost its mother and father, but there was always someone to assume responsibility for its care. Often these *wablenica* were showered with extraordinary kindness and attention. It was not unusual for them to receive fine horses and other gifts from a number of people as a sign of willingness to share the responsibility for their care (Standing Bear 1933, 84–88). Whether they were adopted formally, as in the *Hunka,* or informally, they were treated the same as biological kin.

As a little girl grew, she played with dolls and miniature tipis and made mud pies much like her non-Indian counterparts. When she was old enough to ride a horse, which could easily be at three or four, she was given women's accessories like her mother's: a knife sheath, awl case, strike-a-light bag, and hide scraper.

Childhood

A little girl could play most childhood games with boys as well as her girlhood chums, whom she would learn to call *maške,* a term of address and reference allocated to nonkin friends of the same generation. Other playmates would include her female siblings and certainly her younger brothers, as well as her female cross-cousins.

Of the numerous games and leisure activities available to children, only girls could play *škatapi cik'ala* 'small play,' in which "they imitate the actions of women, such as carrying dolls, women's work-bags, small tents, small tent-poles, wooden horses, etc., on their backs; they pitch tents, cook, nurse children, invite one another to feasts, etc." (Dorsey 1891, 329).

Little girls would frequently form a line in follow-the-leader style, touching the shoulder of the person in front, and zigzag their way through the camp, singing over and over, "the deer follow each other" (Densmore 1918, 492). Girls still joined with boys in playing many games:

Wak'inkiciciyapi 'making one another carry packs.' Children pretended they were horses or carried packs on their backs in imitation of their elders of the same sex (Dorsey 1891, 329).

Hohotela kic'unpi 'swinging.' A blanket was tied to four ropes to form a hammock and several children sat on it and were pushed; or one child sat in a swing made from two ropes. Those pushing shouted *Hohote, hohote, hohotela, hohotela* (Buechel 1970, 181; Dorsey 1891, 329).

Cab onaskiskita 'trample the beaver.' One child was the beaver, lying in the center of the circle with a blanket over him. Others circled chanting *Cab onaskiskita!* 'Trample the beaver!' When they stopped, the beaver rose and chased them. The ones he caught joined the beaver in the ring and covered their heads with their blankets (Dorsey 1891, 330).

Wonape kaga 'causing flight.' Seeing friends lying about listlessly, one child would say, "I'll wake you up," then throw something like an arrow or stone in the air for everyone to scramble after (Dorsey 1891, 330).

Hošišipa 'expression.' Children stood close to each other and pinched the tops of each other's hands with thumb and index finger, chanting *hošišipa*. Suddenly everyone let go, and they scrambled for one child, whom they tickled (Buechel 1970, 185; Dorsey 1891, 330).

Inahmekiciciyapi 'hide and seek.' The seeker was called *wawole*. The others hid and whistled when they were ready.

Those caught had to walk behind the seeker in the order in which they were found until all were caught (Buechel 1970, 334; Dorsey 1891, 331).

Matokiciyapi 'bear game.' One child dressed as a bear, with sticks fastened to his fingers for claws, lay down in a small hole. The others approached and called out *Tunkašila, mato pehin wan!* Grandfather bear, here is some of your hair! The bear sprang up and chased the players. The one caught was tickled until he or she stopped laughing (Buechel 1970, 334; Dorsey 1891, 333).

Wiokiciciya ecunpi 'they court each other.' An innocent pastime in which children pretended to engage in courtship at sunset (Buechel 1970, 588; Dorsey 1891, 330).

Partly through these games, the children became enculturated into the tribe and learned proper behavior toward fellow tribesman. But not all games were simply leisure activities. One of the most sacred rituals was called *Tapa wankayeyapi* 'ball throwing,' but the lesson was a religious one. The most important character in this game was a child who had not reached puberty. To begin the ball throwing, a man removed a piece of sod from the playing area, which symbolized the center of the universe. The child stood in the center, and the people took their places to the west, north, east, and south. The child was then given a ball made from buffalo hide stuffed with horsehair or grass and was told to throw it high into the sky; then all the people scrambled trying to catch it. When the ball was caught it was returned to the child, who again would throw the ball up.

This sacred ball game was taught to the people by the White Buffalo Calf Woman, who told them the ball represented Wakantanka in the act of moving away from the people, then coming back to join them. The ball's moving away was a symbol of ignorance—the people moving away from Wakantanka—and as the ball dropped back to earth they were united with Wakantanka and received knowledge.

Everyone tried to catch the ball as it dropped, because this good sign underscored one's responsibilities to one's children and to the tribe. It also supported the notion that if one neglected one's responsibilities some harm might befall a loved one, someone like the child who led the game. This dichotomy between ignorance and knowledge would be reiterated over and over, symbolized in the separation of light and darkness and in the Sun Dance, where the freedom from torture would be seen as a transition from disbelief to belief in the power of Wakantanka. A child was the appropriate one to throw the ball, because he or she was innocent of the deeper philosophical meanings of the game and therefore would not favor any particular direction where people would not have to try so hard to catch it.

In what appeared to be another simple game for children, the powers of Double Face were invoked. She was often represented by two women tied together with a two-foot cord from which hung a doll or ball. If a woman dreamed of this fabulous creature, she would take her child out to a lonely place and put it in a hammock made like a spiderweb. Swinging the child in the hammock brought it good fortune, and afterward a symbol of the spiderweb, which represented the whole world, would be painted on the child's robe so that everyone would know the ceremony had been performed (Wissler 1907, 49–50).

Both females and males usually were named for some important natural event, for a deceased relative or important person in the tribe, or for a historical occasion judged important to the *tiyošpaye*. Both also had a ritual name that would be used by the *eyapaha* 'announcer' at giveaways or inserted into the songs sung on such occasions as the Victory Dance.

The "firstborn" child was called *witokapa* if a girl and *wicatokapa* if a boy. The lastborn male or female was called *hakela* or *hakakta* 'the last.'

Female names were distinguished from male names only by the suffix *win*. Hence the man's name Maȟpiya Ska 'white cloud,' could be distinguished from the woman's name Maȟpiya Ska Win.

Naming often took place at one of the great ceremonies such as the Sun dance, where the children might also have their ears pierced:

> Even the children had a part in the Sun dance,
> which consisted in the piercing of the ears. Fre-
> quently this was done in fulfillment of a vow made
> by their parents. . . . The piercing of the ears was
> done by any experienced person [and] the parents
> of the child gave gifts varying according to their

means. . . . The piercing of the ear was originally done with a bone awl, this instrument being
replaced later by one of metal. After the puncture,
a piece of copper was inserted so that the wound
would heal rapidly. One or both ears might be
pierced, and if desired more than one hole was
made in each ear. . . . The children whose ears
were thus pierced were considered somewhat related in status to the men whose flesh was lacerated
in the Sun dance. (Densmore 1918, 137)

Little girls, like little boys, eagerly anticipated the storytellers
whose bedtime tales around the fire in the tipi served not only as
entertainment but as moral injunctions. In particular, the trickster tales called *ohunkankan* 'just for fun stories' (contrasted
with *wicooyake* 'legends') were negative reminders about proper
social conduct in the Oglala village. The most popular stories
centered on Inktomi 'spider,' who was both trickster and culture
hero for the Lakota people. If one acted in a way antithetical to
Inktomi's usual behavior, one would live in harmony with kin
and friends. Thus the didactic "trickster cycle"[16] taught how to
behave properly in Oglala society through stories dealing largely
with immorality and deception.

These popular tales were told by a man known as a good
storyteller. Often he teased the children huddled around the
winter fire by pretending he could not remember the stories.
Soon they would beg him and he, often as mischievous as Intomi
himself, would begin: "Once upon a time there was Inktomi,
who was walking around and came upon some white buffalo
dung. He looked at it and died." Died? retorted the children. . . . Tell us more! The storyteller quickly answered, "If
Inktomi has died, then that is the end of the story. There is
nothing more to tell." Finally he responded to their pleading
with a familiar tale.

Children dressed like their parents, little girls wearing deerskin dresses, leggings, and moccasins when they were old enough
to walk. In the winter they wore small robes and in the summer,
until they were three or four years old, they went naked.

As soon as they could walk, they rode horseback. In the spring
they helped forage for *tinpsila* 'wild turnip' or 'pomme blanche'

(*Psoralea esculenta*), and in the late summer groups of children picked *canpa* 'chokecherries' (*Prunus virginiana*).

As a girl grew she began to receive *wahohunkiye* 'counsel, advice' about values important to the Lakota. Foremost, she was taught to share. Of the four virtues that ranked most important—*wacantognaka* 'generosity,' *cante t 'inza* 'bravery,' *wacintanka* 'patience,' and *ksabyahan opiic'iya* 'wisdom' (literally, 'to behave wisely')—the first was the most representative of Lakota social values, and even small children were encouraged to give food and toys to others, training that would remain with them for the rest of their lives.

Kinship

The child was also taught to know her relations; the most important at her stage of life were:

Tunkašila 'grandfather.' This category included the fathers of both her parents and their male siblings; the father's fathers of both her parents and their male siblings; the husband of anyone she called grandmother; all the deceased males of the tribe; and any old man to whom respect should be shown, such as a chief or a medicine man.

Unci 'grandmother.' This included the mothers of both her parents and their female siblings and the mother's mothers of both her parents and their female siblings. Deceased women were known as *wicahunka*, a term based on the possessive form of the word for mother. *Unci* was also applied to any old woman to whom respect was to be shown.

Those a young girl (or boy) called grandfather and grandmother called her (or him) *takoja* 'grandchild.' *Takoja* was also a term older people applied to any young boy or girl whether related or not.

Ina 'mother.' This category included one's biological mother and all her sisters, and also wives of one's father's brothers. The term was also used to address the wife or wives of one's ritual father, or ritual mother, such as was obtained during a *Hunka* ceremony or in a private adoption.

Ate 'father.' This included one's biological father and all his brothers, and also the husbands of one's mother's sisters. The term was also used to address the husband of one's ritual mother.

Those one called father and mother called a daughter *cunkš* (or *cunkši*) and a son *cinkš* (or *cinkši*).

Tunwin 'aunt.' This included one's father's sisters and mother's brothers' wives.

Lekši 'uncle.' This included one's mother's brothers and father's sisters' husbands.

Those one called uncle and aunt called a niece *tunjan* and a nephew *tunškan*.

For the relatives above both males and females used the same terms, but for the following relationships there were separate terms for male and female speakers as well as for older and younger brothers and sisters.

Cuwe 'older sister.' Used by female speakers; this also included the daughters of one's mother's sisters and of one's father's brothers who were older than the speaker.

Tanka 'younger sister.' Used by female speakers; this also included the daughters of one's mother's sisters and of one's father's brothers who were younger than the speaker.

Males called their older sisters *tanke* and their younger sisters *tankši*.

Tiblo 'older brother.' Used by female speakers; this also included the sons of one's mother's sisters and those of one's father's brothers who were older than the speaker.

Males called their older brothers *ciye*.

Misun 'younger brother.' Both males and females used this same term to address and refer to their younger brothers, which also included the sons of one's mother's sisters and of one's father's brothers who were younger than the speaker.

Hakataka 'a male's sisters; a female's brothers.' A male's *hakataku* (possessive form) consisted of his older and younger sisters, including the daughters of his mother's sisters and of his father's brothers. A female's *hakataku* consisted of her older and younger brothers, including the sons of her mother's sisters and of her father's brothers.

Scepanši 'female cousin.' Used by female speakers; this included the daughter of anyone a female called uncle or aunt.

Šic 'eši 'male cousin.' Used by female speakers; this included the son of anyone a female called uncle or aunt.

Hankaši 'female cousin.' Used by male speakers; this included the daughter of anyone a male called uncle or aunt.

Tahanši 'male cousin.' Used by male speakers; this included the son of anyone a male called uncle or aunt. Often this cousin term was used by men when formally addressing all the members of their *tiyošpaye* at a public gathering.

Children were expected to show respect to all older adults, and particularly to their brothers as they grew older. Generally, older children took care of younger children and helped their parents with the household chores. It was the duty of the girl's *hakataku* to protect her, and in turn she honored them by making their clothing and cooking for them as she learned how. But as a sign of respect, as they grew up girls did not speak directly to their older brothers.

Throughout a girl's lifetime her parents sponsored ceremonies such as the *Hunka* to honor her and emphasize her place in society.

In the *Hunka* or adoption ceremony, two persons, an unrelated adult and child, publicly expressed a relationship stronger than friendship or family. A *hunka* gave preference to his *hunka* above all others. The *Hunka* was performed when a child was ten to twelve years of age unless she was sickly. Then it might be done earlier to give her strength.

The ceremony had to be conducted by a medicine man or another adult who had himself been *hunka*. Males and females of any age could become *hunka* if the prospective parties agreed to the relationship (Walker 1980, 218). Densmore (1918, 69) says, "Among the Sioux this ceremony was closely associated with the White Buffalo Calf Maiden, whose extraordinary good qualities were desired by parents as a model for their children's character."

The ceremony was also called *alowanpi* 'they sing over him/her' because the medicine man waved two wands tipped with horsehair over the principals. The ritual was conducted in a special lodge and was attended by everyone who had previously participated in it. It not only formed a bond between two people akin to a parent/child relationship but served to explain to the young person his or her responsibilities to the tribe. It was a way of formally incorporating the child into a level of social organization larger than the family. The *ate hunka* 'father *hunka*' was partly responsible for the child's future upbringing and therefore had to have a good reputation.

One of the most important ritual objects was another wand that was skewered into an ear of corn and laid on an altar inside the special lodge. The ear of corn also served as a symbol of the people's obligation to Mother Earth, the source of all food.

During the actual ceremony, a number of sets of *hunkayapi* 'they are *hunka* [to each other]' sat together in the tipi. The medicine man painted their faces and tied white plumes to their hair, and the wands were waved over them while the singers addressed the sky, earth, and four directions. Finally a buffalo robe was placed over each pair, and the medicine man crawled under each robe carrying a small bag with him. When he finished he moved to the west side of the lodge and told his helpers to remove the buffalo robes. Each pair were found sitting together with their adjacent arms and legs bound together. After the ceremony there was a large feast and the families of the older person and the child exchanged gifts.[17]

Children were taught about the great religious ceremonies such as the Sun Dance and witnessed them at an early age. They were admonished to treat the sacred pipe with respect, never to handle it foolishly or unwrap the bundle it was carried in, and never to show disrespect by stepping over it, for all these transgressions meant that some harm would befall a family member.

Girls were taught the stories about the emergence of the Lakotas and the importance of respecting nature. Their mothers and grandmothers kept careful watch over them as they began to mature. Soon their childhood would end and they would reach the stage of *tankake* 'becoming a woman';[18] their change in social status would then be announced to the entire *tiyošpaye*.

4 *Wikoškalaka:* Adolescence

O Mother Earth, who gives forth fruit, and who is a
mother to the generations, this young virgin who is here
today will be purified and made sacred; may she be like
You, and may her children and her children's children
walk the sacred path in a holy manner.[1]

Puberty

A change in the physiological functions of the Oglala female
initiated concomitant changes in her social and ritual status. The
transition from childhood to adolescence was decidedly marked
in a female's life; it was barely noticed in a male's.

As she grew, her mother and grandmother constantly reminded her that she must begin to pay respect to her *hakataku*—
her brothers and parallel cousins—by refraining from speaking
to them except through her younger siblings who, though members of her *hakataku*, were exempt from the injunction.

When she reached menarche, the young woman was secluded
in a new tipi set up outside the camp circle. An older kinswoman,
or another female chosen by the family for her impeccable reputation, usually attended to her needs and instructed her in her
new duties as a potential wife and mother. The Oglalas believed
that, just as when she was born, the influences surrounding a
young woman during her first menses had a profound effect on
her throughout her lifetime. And just as the placenta was carefully disposed of at birth, so were the first and subsequent menstrual bundles. The menstrual bundle was made of soft buckskin
lined with the soft down of the cattail (*Typha latifolia*), held in
place with a belt or breechclout.

Just as a boy might seek a vision as soon as his voice began to
change, a girl could do so by wrapping up her first menstrual flow
and putting it in a tree (Walker 1980, 79).

The announcement of the girl's reaching "womanhood" was

an important ritual sponsored by her parents—*išnati awicalo-wanpi* 'they sing over her first menses.' *Išnati* literally meant to dwell alone and referred both to the act of menstruation and to the isolation of women during their periods. It was also called the Buffalo Ceremony because it was performed to invoke the spirit of the buffalo and thereby secure for the initiate the virtues most desired by Oglala women—chasity, fecundity, industry, and hospitality—as well as to announce to the people that the girl was now a woman.[2]

The ceremony was conducted by a medicine man about ten days after the girl's first menstrual period, at the request of her father. The day before the ceremony the young woman's mother and her female relatives erected a tipi to serve as a ceremonial lodge for *išnati awicalowanpi*. The lodge was erected with its doorway toward the east. The women built a fire of cottonwood north of the lodge to protect the initiate from the evil influences of Anukite and Waziya, the Old Man. While the females were preparing the ceremonial lodge, the young woman took her menstrual bundle and placed it in a plum tree (a symbol of fruitfulness) to safeguard it from the evil influences of Inktomi.

When the lodge had been erected the young woman's father made an altar between the *catku* (place of honor—the west) and the fireplace (which was in the center of the tipi). He then placed the following ritual paraphernalia in the lodge: a buffalo skull with horns attached, a pipe, tobacco, a wooden bowl, sweet grass, sage, an eagle plume, a fire carrier, dried chokecherries, dried meat, a drum, two rattles, a breechclout, and a new dress for the young woman.

The medicine man wore a buffalo headdress with horns attached. On the rear of the headdress hung a shaggy strip of buffalo skin with a tail that hung below his knees. He wore only a breechclout, leggings, and moccasins. His hands, body, and face were painted red, and three vertical black stripes were painted on his right cheek. He carried a pipe and a staff made of chokecherry wood.

The people gathered in and around the lodge, and the medicine man began the ceremony. He prayed as he smoked the pipe, which he then passed around to the people. While they smoked he painted the right side of the buffalo skull red and then painted a red stripe from the occipital region to the middle of the forehead. He filled the nasal cavities with sage and blew smoke into them, thus symbolically imparting life to the skull, and prayed to the buffalo god and the four winds.

The young woman was brought into the lodge and instructed by the medicine man to sit cross-legged—as men and children sit—between the altar and the fireplace.

The medicine man continued to pray, this time to the Sun, the Moon, Mother Earth, and the Four Winds: "We are about to purify and to make sacred a virgin from whom will come the generations of our people" (Brown 1971, 119). He then said, "Bull buffalo, I have painted your woman's [the buffalo skull] forehead red and have given her a red robe. Her potency is in her horns. Command her to give her influence to this young woman so that she may be a true buffalo woman and bear many children" (Walker 1917, 146). He then turned to the young woman and said, "You have stayed alone for the first time. You are now a woman and should be ashamed to sit as a child. Sit as a woman sits" (Walker 1917, 146). She then moved her legs to one side and sat as women do.

Then the medicine man prayed that the young woman would be industrious like the spider, wise like the turtle, and cheerful like the meadowlark. With these attributes she would be chosen by a brave man who would provide for her. The medicine man recounted his vision, after which he said, "I am purifying one of my own people, for this virgin is that little buffalo calf I saw. I shall now take her to drink of the sacred water, and this water is life" (Brown 1971, 125). He began to act like a buffalo bull toward the initiate, saying, "I am the buffalo bull and you are a young buffalo cow" (Walker 1917, 147).

He bellowed, and red smoke (like the dust emitted by a buffalo giving birth to a calf) came out of his mouth. He blew the smoke on the girl until the tipi was filled with it. He danced toward the young woman lowing like a buffalo bull during the rutting season. He repeatedly sidled up to her like a buffalo performing a mating ritual. Each time he did this, her mother placed sage under her arms and in her lap.

The medicine man filled the wooden bowl with chokecherries and water. (The water was red and considered sacred, for it was meant for buffalo women.) He placed it on the ground to simulate a water hole on the plains and bade the young woman get on her hands and knees and drink like a buffalo with him.

The young woman was then told to remove her dress. The medicine man placed it over the buffalo skull, saying, "This young woman gives her dress to the buffalo women" (Walker 1917, 149).

After the young woman put on her new dress, her mother was instructed to arrange her hair so that it fell in front like a woman's. Then the medicine man painted the parting of her hair and the right side of her forehead red like the buffalo skull and said, "Red is a sacred color. Your first menstrual flow was red. Then you were sacred. This is to show that you are akin to the buffalo god and are his woman. You are now a buffalo woman— you are entitled to paint your face in this manner" (Walker 1917, 149). He tied an eagle plume in her hair and gave her a staff of cherrywood. Her mother removed the belt that had held the menstrual bundle, and the ceremony ended with giveaways and a feast in her honor.

The young woman was reminded that the buffalo was the most important of all animals. It provided food, clothing, shelter, and even fuel. It was a natural symbol of the universe, for it symbolically contained the totality of all manifest forms of life, including people. According to one story the buffalo originated under the earth like the Oglalas, who emerged from a subterranean place; this demonstrated that the buffalo and the Oglalas are one, the Buffalo Nation (Dorsey 1889).

Another story tells us the Oglalas believed that a man who dreamed of buffalo and thus acted like one had a buffalo inside him, and that a chrysalis lay near his shoulder blade so that no matter how often he was wounded he would not die. The chrysalis means that the buffalo (man/woman) has the power to renew himself (procreate).[3] There is constant metamorphosis, for there is a mechanism for revitalization within the organism.

There were other correspondences between woman and buffalo, both in myth and in ritual. For example, in a tipi the woman's place was at the north. *Tatanka* (buffalo bull) came from the north, but *pte* 'buffalo cow' is the term for buffalo in the ritual sense. In ritual, red is the color associated with the north.

The north was associated with winter *waniyetu* 'the place of the pines.' (The spirits live toward the pines.) The south, *itoko-gata*, is represented by *ska* 'white,' which is also associated with summer, *bloketu*. Bloka was an ideal Oglala male figure, *blo* is a potato (tuber) symbolizing the Oglalas emergence from a sub-terranean world.

When the universe was in harmony, the south was repre-sented by the center of the lodge over the fireplace and by the spot where the Oglalas emerged from their subterranean world. Thus the south was also a symbol of the creation of mankind. The Milky Way runs from north to south. The Oglalas believed that people go south to die, are rejuvenated, and then go north, where they wait to be reborn. Thus south was male, and north represented both female and buffalo. Both north and south represented life and death, depending on the context in which they were viewed (Powers 1977).

The ceremony also established the initiate's relationship with the White Buffalo Calf Woman, who in her sexual prime brought the sacred ceremonies to the Oglalas so they might live. There was a constant relationship between males and females (buffalo bull and buffalo cow), and sexual reproduction was emphasized, as was people's reliance on the buffalo for food. Both women and buffalo were associated with creating and sustaining life. The sexual nature of initiation ceremonies cannot be denied, since symbolically these rites transformed an individual into a man or woman. These, like all other rites of passage, are founded on a real change in the participants' social condition (Van Gennep 1960).

Išnati awicalowanpi was clearly a rite of separation from the asexual world and incorporation into the world of sexuality. Each month thereafter the young woman would be required to isolate herself in the *išnati*, where she would be waited on by her older female relatives. They would tell her to relax and to perfect her skills at quillwork and other crafts. There would then be less chance of *wekaluzapi* 'flowing hard' and *wenapopapi* 'hemor-rhaging.' The catamenial period was also accompanied by a number of proscriptions or "taboos" that forbade her to cook or touch food, to come near men or their weapons, and to deal with herbal medicines or ritual paraphernalia such as the pipe. If she were to come into direct contact with weapons or ritual objects, a medicine man would have to take them into a sweat lodge to be purified. The touch of a menstruating woman was thought to render such things impotent.

The young woman most of all learned about the evils of Anukite, Double Face, who lived with other supernaturals in the woods and could be hiding anywhere. Anukite was the bane of pregnant and menstruating women and of babies, causing stomach pains and cramps. She was cunning and had an acute sense of hearing, so women had to guard their speech lest she overhear them.[4]

The young women also learned about the virtues of the White Buffalo Calf Woman. To protect them from lecherous men who sneaked around the camp at night, crawling under the tipis to lie with the young women, mothers tied up their pubescent daughters in rawhide chastity belts.[5] The virginity of the young women was ensured by seeing that they were always in the company of a chaperone, usually a grandmother. When she was not walking with her granddaughter, she kept a watchful eye on her from inside a nearby tipi. The young woman was thus *witanšna* 'single woman,' that is, a virgin or metaphorically *winyan cokab ti win* 'a woman who lives in the midst of women' (Buechel 1970, 587), referring to her guardianship.

There was a story told in an Oglala winter count for 1853 in which *mato wan wišan manu hi* 'a bear came to steal a woman's vagina': "A man shot a bear in his tent. He woke suddenly from sleep and looked over at the horses. They were snorting. He saw a black object right under the tent. He took his gun and said, 'What are you doing over here?' No answer. The bear said '*Whi-h-u-u!*' It had pulled up two pickets of the tent and got inside" (Beckwith 1930, 361–62). Although this was meant as a joke, it referred to the notorious "tipi crawler," who could claim a woman if he saw her naked; if he was able to touch her vagina, she would have to surrender her virginity.

A young woman also had to be careful of a man who asked her one question with his lips but had another question in his mind. If she answered yes to the spoken (but not the intended) question, he could force her to consent to his sexual desires.

Young women were thus protected from seduction by being tied from the hips down into *tahasaka ojuha* 'rawhide containers' in anticipation of a tipi crawler's advances. Even though such a man was derided by the people because he obviously could not charm the young women, he still posed a threat to unsuspecting virgins, and as an extra precaution they were required to sleep with their feet toward the fire in the center of the tipi (Beckwith 1930, 361).

The young woman now concentrated on women's things, particularly cooking, tanning, and learning to sew buffalo hides together to make tipis. She still was permitted to ride horseback with her female friends. And she could play *tasihaunpi* 'deer bones,' in which a string of deer vertebrae was tossed in the air and skewered with an awl as it fell, or in winter, *paslohanpi* 'snow snake,'—sliding a wooden snake across the ice to see how far it would go.

But there were more important tasks for the *witanšna* that related to the Seven Sacred Rites brought to the Lakotas by the White Buffalo Calf Woman. One of the most important was the participation of virgins in the most sacred of all rites, the Sun Dance.

The Sun Dance was held in summer when all the Lakota bands gathered for the annual buffalo hunt. The purpose of the dance was to fulfill a vow taken in a time of duress—on the battlefield or during an illness. Often a person would pledge that if he survived an ordeal he would give thanks to Wakantanka by performing the Sun Dance. There were four forms of the dance: one might simply dance gazing toward the sun; one might be fastened by skewers of wood inserted through the breast to a tall cottonwood pole called *canwakan* 'sacred pole' and dance until the skewers broke through the flesh; one might be suspended off the ground from four posts by thongs attached to skewers inserted through the breast and the flesh over the scapulae; or one might pledge to drag one or several buffalo skulls attached to the flesh of the back by skewers and thongs.[6]

Although women did not pierce themselves in the same manner as men because of modesty, during a certain part of the dance they frequently offered flesh from their arms and legs, which was cut off in quarter-inch circles and placed in buckskin pouches. This was also the time when babies had their ears pierced in what might be regarded a miniature of this important ceremony.

Each part of the ceremony, which included several weeks of preparation before the actual buffalo hunt, was acted out with great drama. At the beginning the sacred cottonwood tree must be cut down by four virgins. Symbolically, the tree was regarded as an enemy. After being "stalked" by four young men chosen to find it, it was cut down by the girls. The first to strike the tree was treated as if she were counting coup on the enemy. In succession, each of the four first lifted her ax and feigned striking the tree while reciting a brave deed of one of her kinsmen. Then the virgins chopped at the tree, one after the other, making sure that it fell toward the south (Densmore 1918, 113).

The tree was then carried back to the Sun Dance camp and erected in the center of the dance area. Rawhide effigies of a buffalo and a man were hung from crossbars of chokecherry wood, and before the dance began warriors gathered to dance and stamp the grassy floor flat and at the same time to shoot their guns at the effigies. "Killing" the effigies was a guarantee that plenty of buffalo would be killed on the hunt and also that the enemy, symbolized by the human effigy, would not interfere with the chase.

Young women were also sought after by the male members of warrior societies, particularly to serve as singers. Good singers with loud, clear voices soaring strongly above those of the men were called *wicaglata*, a term signifying that the voices of the young women trail slightly behind when they sing as a mixed chorus. Although frequently one woman's voice was so strong that it could be heard over the loudest assembly of male voices, the Ihoka 'Badger Mouth' society employed four virgins to sing the warrior society's ritual songs. If these singers lost their virginity, they were dismissed. If they wanted to marry, they had to obtain the consent of the society members, who would then give them valuable presents. Their husbands would also be invested into the society (Wissler 1912, 32). Virgins were also members of other warrior societies, and though they frequently did not have curing visions as the men did, they were allowed to participate in the feasts of the Elk Dreamers and in the ceremonies of the Black-tailed Deer cult (Wissler 1912, 88–90).

Women's Sodalities

There were also sodalities exclusively designed for young women. The Wipata Okolakiciye was one whose female members learned quilling techniques through visionary instructions from Anukite or the Deer Woman. They were called together by an old woman and exhibited their work to each other at a feast. Similarly, those women who were profficient in tanning skins formed the Taha Kpanyanpi 'hide softeners' for cooperatively making tipis (Wissler 1912, 79).

Because virginity was important, a female (or a male) might be challenged to take part in a ritual to test her purity. One such ceremony was called *wimnašni*, a term connoting distrust. The common English translation is "biting the knife" or "biting the snake" (Walker 1980, 28). Before the ceremony began an eighteen-inch hole was dug, and in it were placed a knife and an arrow. A young man who wanted to assert that he had never touched the vulva of a woman reached into the hole, pulled out the arrow and bit it. A young woman wanting to prove her virginity reached into the hole, took the knife, and bit it. Frequently during the Sun Dance many virgins or young men in the camp would line up and file by the hole, each performing the act. They could be challenged by anyone who claimed to have been intimate with them. It was believed that if they lied they would be killed by the object bitten (Wissler 1912, 77).

Before courtship young men and women were lectured about the proper selection of a spouse, who was ideally from another *tiyošpaye*. Men would gather their grandchildren around them and admonish them, "Grandchildren, do not choose a wife from the corner of your household" (*Takoja, tiokaȟmi etan tawicutun sni po!*). The children were carefully taught their kinship terms so they would know who was eligible for marriage. The old men used to say to the young ones, "Climb to the top of a hill and look for a wife on the other side."

The term for incest was *wogluze*. Children born of incestuous relations were called *wicogluzewin* (girl) or *wicogluze hokšila* (boy). To be considered such was a disgrace. Many arguments in the camps centered on young people who married members of the same *tiyošpaye*, that is, "joined with one's own"—married a close relative (Powers 1977).

Courtship

For young women eager to meet young men, feasts and dances were held at night in the camp circle. Two popular dances were the Naslohan Wacipi 'dragging feet' or 'round' dance, in which young men and women moved clockwise in a circle, sometimes hugging each other, and the Hanwaci 'night dance,' said to be performed by unmarried males and females under the supervision of two married males (Wissler 1912, 79). Some times the couples danced under a blanket.

Although the girl "walked in the midst of women," there were times when she could escape the watchful eyes of her mother and grandmother and perchance meet a young man she fancied. The best occasion was when she was sent to draw water from a nearby creek or river. She made her way along a trail that was mainly concealed from the camp. If a young man was attracted to her, he would wait for her along the path and either reach out and tug at her dress or, perhaps more foolishly, throw pebbles to attract her attention. If the young woman welcomed his advances she might linger for a while and talk to him. If not, it was her perogative to continue with her chores.

Most courtship was not so informal. Known variously as *winole* 'seeking women,' *winokuwa* 'chasing women,' *wiiyape* 'waiting for women,' and *winokiya* 'talking with women,' the practice of courtship not only was formal but for the most part was entirely controlled by the young woman and her older female relatives.

The usual procedure was for the young woman to wait outside her tipi at sunset, perhaps talking with a female relative or a friend of her own age. Eager young men, and there might be scores of them, would slowly advance and form a queue a few feet in front of her. At this point her female companion would saunter away, leaving the young woman to talk with each aspiring suitor. Of course, her older kin remained in the tipi, placing themselves strategically to observe all the young men who approached her. These suitors would have equipped themselves with certain articles such as a headdress of antelope horns and, of particular importance, a courting blanket made by an older sister. As each walked or rode up to the tipi, he waited his turn. As he approached the young woman he would place his arms around her to envelop her in the courting blanket, a practice called *šina aopemni inajinpi* 'standing in the blanket' (W. Powers 1980a).

Each suitor in turn talked to his would-be sweetheart about

the important events of the day, the chase, a minor hunting trip; perhaps he recited some war stories he had heard, or he might even recount an exploit of his own. Chances are he would not be there talking to her had he not already distinguished himself in the hunt or on the warpath, because ultimately her selection of an appropriate spouse would be based on the young man's accomplishments, and his deeds would be carefully weighed by her whole family.

The success of his talk with the young woman was not left entirely to chance. Most young men came armed with elk medicine, a concoction made by a medicine man expressly to guarantee a liaison. Elk medicine was the male counterpart of Deer Woman medicine. Just as Anukite in the guise of the Deer Woman could drive men crazy, elk medicine was believed to place the young woman in the young man's power. The mythical elk man himself was considered irresistible to women, and so the most potent elk medicine was made for procuring women. On special occasions such as these, medicine men who had dreamed of the elk would "take the white part of the eye of an elk or part of the heart, the inside gristle from the projection of the fetlocks, or the hind feet, and mix it with medicine" (Wissler 1912, 88). The flageolet and a mirror were also acknowledged to be important tools of lovemaking. If a person's reflection could be "captured" in the mirror, then power could be exercised over her will.

The young man had limited time for this courtship procedure, since several others were waiting their turns behind him. He had to be brief yet convincing; if he took too long the other suitors might throw pebbles at him or even forcibly eject him.

The young woman had to be reserved during the meeting, and she chose her words cautiously. If she said something foolish the young man, particularly if rejected, might compose a song to sing about her in public. Although commonly translated as "love songs," *wiošte olowan* means 'idle talk' or 'insult' (W. Powers 1980a). The young man would sing these words later using the peculiar language of females as if she were repeating the unguarded remarks for all the camp to hear:

> You made me cry, you made me cry
> We were here together, and you made me cry!

Late at night, after all suitors had had their chance to speak to the young woman, one might hear echoing through the breezes the sound of the *šiyotanka* 'flageolet,' a five-toned flute on which love songs were played. Often a young woman recognized the player by the melody.

There is an old story about the origin of the courting flute. A young man was despondent, for the only woman he loved had rebuffed him because he was poor and she was a chief's daughter. Soon after she rejected him he left the camp in shame, not caring whether he lived or died. For four consecutive days, at dawn he shot an arrow northward and walked after it. Each arrow he shot killed a deer, which he roasted and ate. As he sat alone on the fourth evening he heard voices coming from a grove of trees. As he approached the spot he saw two exceedingly handsome men whose bodies seemed to glow. They had a long flute, which one man began to play with a sweet and piercing sound. They gave the young man the flute and told him to go home. They said that if he walked through the camp at midnight playing the flute, all the women would get up and follow him. Then the two handsome men turned around and changed into elks. The young man did as he was told, and as his music echoed through the camp all the women, including the chief's daughter, followed him. He ignored them all and heard only the sound of the flute. The only woman who did not join the crowd was the one he ultimately sought out and married. It is said that this young man was the original elk, the Dakota symbol of masculine beauty, virility, virtue, and charm (Deloria and Brandon 1961, 5–6).

When it was finally time for a woman in her teens to make her selection, there was great excitement in the camp. Usually her parents would consent to the marriage, as would the parents of the prospective groom. But there were occasions when marriages were arranged by the parents without consulting the couple. In this case lovers might run away, perhaps to another band of Lakotas. If the woman was not willing to go, the young man might capture her and carry her off to another camp.

A lonely young woman who suffered from unrequited love sometimes took her own life by jumping off a precipice. The following "Legend of Lover's Leap was told in many parts of Lakota country:

> A young woman had promised to marry a man,
> but he wished to "make a name" for himself be-

fore the marriage took place. He had been on the
warpath, but he wished to go again. . . . When the
war party returned they said that he had been
killed by the Crows. Sometime afterward . . . a
camp was made at the place where . . . the young
man had been killed. Dressing herself in her best
attire, the maiden went to the edge of the cliff,
and after singing the following song and giving the
shrill "women's tremolo," jumped into the river
below. (Densmore 1918, 494)

The words of the song went:

> *Zuya iyaye lo*
> *Ehapi k'un.*
> *He waštewalake*
> *Iyotiyewakiye.*

> You said that he went to war.
> That's why I'm having a hard time loving him.
> (Densmore 1918, 495)

And so the young woman learned about the world around her
and prepared herself for the day her parents would exchange
gifts with the parents of a suitable young man, when she would
leave the watchful eyes of mother and grandmother and move to
her husband's camp.

5 *Winyan:* Womanhood

My Indian mother, Pretty Face . . . in her humble way,
helped to make the history of her race. For it is the
mothers, not the warriors, who create a people and guide
their destiny.[1]

Marriage

Throughout her adolescence, the young woman continued to
learn the skills she would need as wife and mother. Her grandparents and parents continued to lecture her. Marriage would
bring new responsibilities and a host of new relationships; learning the proper relationship terms was important.

At the apex would be the uniting of her parents with the
parents of her husband, a relationship called *unmawahetun*, a
term of address used between the mothers and fathers of the
bride and groom. This term, which emphasized the bond between two families, can be glossed "co-parent-in-law" when
used as a term of address, or "relative by marriage," as a term of
reference. Each person distinguished all kin, consanguineal and
affinal, by the single term *otakuye* 'relationships.' After marriage, however, to distinguish between the bride's and groom's
relatives, each used the term *titakuye*, which corresponded to the
English "one's *side* of the family" and included both consan-
guines and affines already related to the bride and to the groom
before they were married.[2]

Kinship Terms

Although the woman continued the same relationships with her
consanguineal kin, marriage introduced a number of affinal kin
toward whom different kinds of behavior were required. There
were no older/younger distinctions in these new terms, but there
continued to be some male/female distinctions among men and

women of her own generation. Those kin now most important were:

Mihigna 'my husband' and *mitawicu* 'my wife.' These were the terms by which spouses addressed and referred to each other.

Tunkaši 'father-in-law.' This meant one's spouse's father.

Unciši 'mother-in-law.' This meant one's spouse's mother.

Šic'e 'brother-in-law.' Used by female speakers for a woman's husband's brother or a woman's sister's husband.

Tanhan 'brother-in-law.' Used by male speakers for a man's wife's brother or a man's sister's husband.

Scepan 'sister-in-law.' Used by female speakers for a woman's husband's sister or a woman's brother's wife.

Hanka 'sister-in-law.' Used by male speakers for a man's brother's wife or a man's wife's sister.

Takoš 'son-in-law,' 'daughter-in-law.' Used by male and female speakers for one's son's or daughter's spouse.

Whereas one showed great respect to one's consanguineal kin, there were different stylized behaviors between oneself and one's in-laws. For example, both a man and a woman expressed *wištelkiciyapi*, a term that connoted a wide range of meaning such as shyness toward one another or embarrassment and that underscored the fact that as a sign of respect one did not talk to, or even look directly at, one's mother-in-law or father-in-law. Thus, if a young man or young woman at home alone was visited by mother-in-law or father-in-law, the latter would not enter the tipi because it always required a third party to communicate between parents- and children-in-law.

On the other hand, one's behavior toward in-laws of one's own generation was quite different. Brothers- and sisters-in-law were required to engage in a *woiȟaȟa* 'joking' relationship. This was mandatory whenever brothers- and sisters-in-law met in public and usually took the form of obscene joking between brother- and sister-in-law and competitive joking between siblings-in-law of the same sex. Thus a brother-in-law might say his sister-in-law was to be pitied because she could not control her bladder and had the problem of urinating in public, or that he would not lend her robes anymore because she defecated on them. Perhaps he would accuse her of being a *witkowin* 'crazy woman,'[3] always looking for men, or make some derogatory reference to her anatomy—too fat, too skinny, not enough teeth.

The sister-in-law likewise would attack her brother-in-law's wife for being ugly, lazy, and generally incompetent.

Siblings-in-law of the same sex generally engaged in a constant patter of playful and good-natured insults, one trying to outdo the other's derogatory remarks, a litany of innuendos followed by outbursts of laughter that often lasted for hours. These competitions were not only one against one; people would gang up against other teams of in-laws in making humorous remarks. A man was expected to assist his brother if someone jokingly attacked the latter's wife, and everyone was always fair game for even the most outrageous verbal attacks that in any other circumstances would have led to violence.

Marriage was expressed by *okiciyuze* 'to join together' and largely involved a series of gift exchanges between the families of the bride and groom. Mothers said that when your daughter married she was gone forever, but when a son married you received a new daughter. Hence the marriage ceremony itself essentially marked a change in the wife's residence from her natal home to that of her husband. As the time neared for the daughter to prepare for the ceremonies and feasts, her mother would admonish her: "You are going to be a *wiwoȟ'a* 'buried woman,' so make the best of it because you are gone from me for good and you will die over there." This was another way of saying that the girl would live in the man's *wicoti* or hunting camp and move with him in search of the buffalo and other game. And it might be a long time before her husband's band and her father's band would meet. She would also be living with people who belonged to different *tiyošpaye*, those large divisions of the Oglalas in which people were related by birth though not by residence.[4]

In one major ritual, a woman was incorporated into the hunting band of her husband. First the husband's family would provide gifts for the wife's family. The gifts, including horses, robes, and other valuable things, would be given to the young woman, and she in turn would distribute them to her parents. She also took gifts accumulated by her own parents and gave them to the parents of her husband-to-be.[5] Once the gifts had been exchanged it was time for the *wiwoȟ'a hunka* 'adoption of the buried woman' and *šawicayapi* 'bestowal of gifts,' in which the family erected a special tipi and prepared things for the new daughter-in-law.[6] The husband's grandmother, mother, and sisters then dressed the new wife in a buckskin dress made by the husband's mother, painted the part in her hair, and then held a large feast for everyone.

The young woman was advised to learn to make moccasins well, for someday she would be asked to make a pair for her mother-in-law. Soon after her marriage the bride, eager to prove she was a capable wife, would make a pair of moccasins and present them to her mother-in-law. The mother-in-law's acceptance of the moccasins established the young woman as an industrious member of her husband's family (Standing Bear 1933, 110).

The young woman's grandmother was in charge of making the couple's tipi, which would remain the young wife's property, though the husband was required to furnish everything else. The woman owned her own horses, saddle, saddle blankets, cooking utensils, and clothing—in effect, everything in the household except the man's hunting and war implements.

Ideally, the new tipi would be set up near the husband's father's and brothers' tipis. Occasionally, if a man came from a poor family that could not provide his potential wife's parents with gifts, the man would leave his natal home and move into his wife's. When this happened the man was known as *wicawoȟ'a* 'buried man,' a man who lives with his wife's relatives. This condition was frowned upon, but it might be changed if he became a successful hunter or warrior.[7]

If a man was prosperous or came from a wealthy family, he was eligible to take more than one wife—usually two or three over a period of time. But he had to have substantial means, because each of his wives and the children born to her had to live in a separate tipi. The man also had to own many horses, because it required several to move each tipi and its contents and the children when the people moved camp in search of game or good winter campsites.

The most suitable co-wives were the first wife's sisters, hence sororal polygyny was the ideal form of plural marriage. The first wife remained in charge of the other wives, but they normally got along well together. They called each other by the special term *teya* 'co-wife.'[8]

Another marriage institution provided that if a spouse should die the survivor would automatically be taken care of. In the levirate, a man was expected to marry the wife of his deceased brother and also to assume the responsibility, with the help of his first wife (if he had one), of raising his deceased brother's children. Similarly, in the sororate, a woman married the husband of her deceased sister. In short, all siblings-in-law were potential spouses.[9]

The division of labor was such that men were in charge of hunting and defense and married women were in charge of the household and raising children. However, this division was not absolute, and both participated freely in all aspects of each other's work. If the husband was home for several days, he did what he could to lighten the woman's work. He cut wood, made or repaired saddles, cut meat into thin strips for drying, and gladly amused the baby. Men and women were expected to be considerate of one another. A wife was attentive to her husband, and every morning, as a sign of respect, he brushed and braided his wife's hair. For decoration he tied porcupine-quilled hair strings and eagle plumes on the ends of her braids and painted her part. Next he painted her cheeks red. Grease was sometimes mixed with the paint to protect her from the wind and sun (Standing Bear 1933, 94–95).

The woman was in charge of putting up and taking down the tipi, but she was aided in the chores by other women, children, and men. When it was time to move camp she packed the tipi, the bedding, clothing, cooking utensils, and food onto the travois and took general charge of moving all the household goods and the children so that the men would be left free to defend the group if necessary. Whenever the group traveled, the men preceded the women, children, and old people, so that if there was any danger, animal or human, they would be exposed first and could protect the others.

Women gathered foods such as chokecherries, buffalo berries, wild currants, wild plums, wild turnips, and wild beans, the last collected from the nests of field mice. Foods like these were packed into bladder bags and parfleche boxes when the camp moved.

The Lakota diet consisted mainly of buffalo, elk, and deer meat along with wild fruits and vegetables, but smaller game such as antelope, muskrat, prairie dog, raccoon, porcupine, skunk, wolf pup, fox pup, beaver, rabbit, wild duck, and prairie chicken were also eaten. Shelled corn was obtained through trade with other tribes.

The most common method of preparing meat was boiling it to make soup, but it was also roasted over an open fire. Soup made with *taniga* 'tripe' was preferred. Fresh raw tongue, liver, and kidneys seasoned with a little gall or bile were often eaten on the spot at a kill. Buffalo intestines were cleaned and roasted on a stick over an open fire.

Women accompanied their husbands and brothers on the buffalo hunt and helped them butcher the buffalo. The hide was removed and the meat was carried back to camp in it. At home, the fresh meat would be boiled in bags made from buffalo paunch, filled with water and heated stones. Other meat would be cut up into thin strips for drying into *papa* 'jerked meat' that, like dried fruits and turnips, would keep a long time. The Oglalas also ate *wakapapi*, meat cut thin and pounded together with marrow fat, and *wasna* 'pemmican,' dried meat pounded together with dried chokecherries and mixed with marrow fat. On special ritual occasions they served dog stew.[10]

The food supply varied with the success or failure of the hunt and the unpredictable Plains environment. When an abundance of food was available, people ate beyond satiety and then put the uneaten food in *wateca* 'new things' buckets (any container for leftovers) to keep for another time. If food was available, no one went hungry. People who could not provide for themselves went from camp to camp, a practice known as *tiole* 'to seek a house,' knowing that Oglala custom required any hungry person be fed, even a stranger. However, a person could wear out his welcome, and after too many visits with no attempt to reciprocate, he might be derogatorily referred to as *tuwe otakuye k'eyaš* 'anybody's relative.'

In addition to the meat, all the rest of the buffalo was used.[11] For example, the horns were made into ladles, cups, and spoons. The hair stuffed saddle pads and pillows. The ribs were used for sleds and other bones for games and toys. The skull was an important ceremonial object, and the bladder became a pouch to hold sinew, quills, water, or medicines.

Women tanned the hides with brains (which were also used to thicken soup) and sewed tipis and clothing with sinew—the long tendons of the back—which stiffened when dry. The tanned hides were used for tipi covers, moccasin tops, robes, dresses, leggings, pipe bags, pouches, breechclouts, shirts, bedding, and cradles. They were decorated with feathers, porcupine quill-work, and paints or dyes made from flowers, leaves, roots, berries, or minerals and other natural earth pigments. Later, articles were dyed by boiling them with blankets, causing the color to run.

Rawhide was used to make parfleche boxes for storage, moc-casin soles, shields, buckets, drums, rattles, splints, saddles, quirts, stirrups, cinches, horse masks, knife cases, and the circu-lar bull boats needed for fording rivers. Designs were painted on the rawhide items, and often sweet grass and leaves were placed in with stored goods to keep them smelling fresh.

Only men decorated the outside of the tipi, their shields, and their war implements. Designs were geometric and pictographic, mainly figures of men, animals, and natural objects that depicted historical events, battles, and other personal exploits.[12]

Though on special occasions men often changed their ordi-nary clothing for the spectacular feathered dance costumes, a woman's best was simply a dress and accessories that were more finely decorated than her everyday wear. Women's clothing was made from deerskin and elkskin, the latter being preferred for dresses because it required less piecing. Two skins were suf-ficient, sewn together along the sides and top with openings left for the head and arms. The same dress made out of deerskin would take about five skins.

This style of dress was replaced by one whose yoke was covered with quillwork or beadwork or both, some of the more elaborate ones weighing twenty pounds or more. The dresses were gathered with a belt that was quilled, beaded, or adorned with circular German silver conchos, its end dragging the ground. Attached to the belt were the woman's knife sheath, awl case, and strike-a-light pouch containing flint and steel. To com-plete her ensemble the woman wore moccasins and knee-length leggings held in place by buckskin garters. For dress occasions she added a long breastplate made from bone. In the winter she wore a buffalo robe and fur-lined moccasins like the men.

As the Oglalas received various materials through trade with other tribes and with the whites, dresses increasingly were made from dark blue wool stroud or, for summer, from calico. The yokes of the stroud dresses were often decorated with cowry shells, dentalium shells, or elk teeth, the last being extremely valuable because only the two front teeth were used. Thus some dresses bore the teeth of as many as fifty elks.

Sometimes children's dresses were fully beaded from neck to hem, but they were far too heavy for everyday wear.

The favorite design on the old dresses was a lizard motif, resembling the *t'elanuwe* or umbilical-cord containers made for newborns. This design was worn only by women and provided protection against female disorders and diseases.[13]

Men and women not only shared in providing food, clothing, and shelter, they participated together in leisure and ritual activities. Women joined the men in the gambling games such as *hanpaecunpi* 'moccasin game,' in which an object was hidden and its location guessed; or *kansukutepi* 'plum shooting,' in which dice made from plum stones were shaken in a wooden bowl and thrown for high score.

Sodalities

Just as warfare was an important part of a man's life, so was it important to the woman. Women often belonged to the warrior societies. In the Tokala 'Fox' and Cante T'inza 'Strong Heart' societies, women served as the singers. In the dances of the Napešni 'No Flight' societies, whose male members wore long sashes that were staked to the ground in the thick of a fight and could be removed only by a comrade, the sister of such a warrior would join in the circular dance holding on to her brother's sash.

Women were still highly respectful of their brothers even after they married, and they took great pride in celebrating victories. The whole village would turn out to feast and dance when their men returned from a successful foray against the Crows or Shoshonis or Pawnees. A number of dances were conducted by women in honor of their men, such as the *Iwakicipi* 'Victory Dance,' in which they carried the weapons and headdresses of their warrior husbands, brothers, and sons. They would also carry the scalps taken, stretched upon poles for everyone to see. During this "scalp dance" the singers sang praise songs about the brave warriors, and the female relatives responded with high-pitched ululations[14] when the singers mentioned the names of their menfolk.

There were also warrior societies made up of women whose male relatives had performed brave deeds. One such sodality, the Kat'ela 'Strike Dead' society, was organized by a woman whose husband, brother, or son triumphantly returned from killing an enemy. Its ceremonies stimulated the men to be brave so that when they returned from the warpath the women would glorify them by honoring their deeds (Wissler 1912, 76). The women danced carrying the weapons of their menfolk and those of the enemy as well. Often a man would be selected to represent the enemy. The women, dressed in their men's warbonnets, would dance around him, raising their arms and pretending to strike him dead—hence the name Kat'ela.

Women also had their own medicine societies, and one, the Wakan Okolakiciye, was an association made up of women who had dreamed of elk, buffalo, or horses. The women's main function was to supply war medicine, and though they were not paid, they shared in the spoils if their warriors were successful (Wissler, 1912, 28).

But not all women's activities were ritually oriented. In later years women participated in the secular *wacipi* 'dances.' Dressed in their finest buckskin-fringed dresses or in trade cloth dresses of dark blue decorated with elk teeth or dentalium shells, they would join in the *ipšica waci* 'jumping dance,' in which they stood around the periphery of the dance area hopping up and down in quick jerking movements imitating the prairie chicken, jumping slowly in an arc from left to right, then right to left, looking over the male dancers strutting inside the dance circle like prairie chickens displaying for their would-be mates. The women would also join in the *naslohan wacipi* 'dragging feet dance,' moving clockwise in a circle, each dancer first stepping out on her left foot, then dragging her right foot to meet it, in time to the accented beat of the three-quarter-time drumming and singing of the men seated on the ground in the center of the dance circle.

Although high value was placed on fidelity in marriage, there were occasions when a woman ran off with another man. This was called *wiinaȟme* 'to hide a woman'—that is, seduce or abscond with her. The couple would have to seek refuge with another band because a jealous husband had the prerogative of enlisting his male kin to track down the culprit and kill him. The woman might be beaten, and most frequently her husband would cut off her nose or ear so she would permanently carry the mark of an adulterous woman. Even the famous warrior chief Crazy Horse, after he surrendered to the United States government, eventually ran off with the wife of No Water. No Water chased Crazy Horse and, finding him with his wife, shot him in the face with a revolver. Although Crazy Horse survived, he forever carried the scar on his cheek.

For women who could affirm that they had been faithful to their husbands all their married lives, there was a special ceremony called *išnala kic'un* 'being alone,' that is, with no man other than her husband. Special feasts were held for women aged forty or older who had had only one husband—who had been sexually faithful to their spouses. Any women who desired it could take part in this special feast, and any man who wanted to challenge a woman's fidelity could do so by taking her feast bowl and throwing it away. The woman, however, could counter by demanding her challenger take an oath similar to the "biting the knife" ceremony. The man would have to swear that he had been intimate with the woman and then hold a gun barrel, knife, or arrow in his mouth. If he had falsely accused her it was believed he would be killed by the weapon. Most men were reluctant to take the oath unless the charges were true, and in most cases they would back down. But if the man did insist on taking the oath, those attending the feast would run the woman out of camp (Wissler 1912, 77).

Egalitarian principles held if there was to be a divorce. If a man wanted to part with his wife, he could announce publicly at a feast or dance that he was going to *wiiȟpeya* 'throw away the woman.' It is said that the custom originated with the Miwatani society and was later adopted by other warrior societies, the Tokala, Ihoka, Sotka, and Omaha societies (Wissler 1912, 70). At the appropriate time, a man wishing to divorce his wife would approach the drum, hit it with a drumstick, and throw the stick over his shoulder. The action was incontestable.

If a woman wanted to divorce her husband, she could *wicašaiṅpeyapi* 'throw away the man,' since it was she who owned the tipi. She would simply pack up all his belongings while he was away and leave them outside the doorway. When he came home, he had no choice but to take his things and leave.

After bearing her first child, the mature woman was committed to raising her children and overseeing the household. The ideal number of children in an Oglala family was five or six, though frequently a woman had fewer, since she nursed each child from two to four years. Nursing was stopped when the mother could no longer withstand the pain of her child's biting. It is agreed that Indian women were strong and robust and had less difficulty bearing and nursing children that their non-Indian counterparts; and though they were always busy attending to the needs of their families, their lives were neither overly laborious nor miserable.

A large family was valued for a number of reasons. Transporting the tipi and household belongings was an arduous task that could not be accomplished by one person. For example, the average tipi made from twelve buffalo hides could easily weigh several hundred pounds, and large tipis belonging to chiefs might comprise over thirty skins. The number of poles varied with the size of the tipi, but even a small tipi might require the women to maneuver one hundred to two hundred pounds of poles made from heavy lodgepole pine.

The more boys and young men there were in the family, the greater the chance of their providing enough food not only for the residential unit but for the extended group, including those who were too old or infirm to hunt or gather their own food. Young women too played a major role in butchering and preparing the meat as well as in foraging for wild fruits, berries, and vegetables. An amiable co-wife was an asset not only to the family at large but to the other co-wives who shared in the everyday household chores and in raising children.

As soon as young children could walk they were encouraged to take care of their younger brothers and sisters, and they shared in the hunting and gathering when they became skilled enough. It was their job to take care of the horses, watering them and guarding them against enemies while they grazed. Women had been charged with all these things, being recognized by the White Buffalo Calf Woman as those "who make the family move," blessed with a memory of the traditional ways that they would carry with them throughout their lifetimes.

6 *Winunȟcala:* Old Age

*Wicaȟcala na winunȟcala kin wowicala wan oyakapi s'a.
He wicaša otoiyohila icimani ahikiyapi. Na anpetu wan
ake unma wicoti ekta glapi kta keyapi.*

*Wicaša na winyan iyuha wiconi ekignakapi ehantanš
wanagi tacanku kin ogna itokagatakiya itoheyapi. Na
oehakita wicoti wan oiyokipiya winyeya he na tipi
iyokihe el tima Tunkašila eciyapi kin yanke. Ca ekta kipi
kin "Ho oicimani wan kagapi kin oglakapi kta keyapi."*

Old men and old women spend a lot of time talking
about their beliefs. They say that each person is just
here on a journey. And one day they will go back home
to that other camp.

When a man and woman are ready to lay away their
lives they start back toward the south along the Ghost
Road. And at the end of the road lies the camp ready to
receive them, and in the council lodge sits the one called
Grandfather. So they enter the lodge, and he says "Ho,
now it is time to talk about your journey."[1]

The Grandmothers

Old women, particularly those who reached menopause, were
respected for their knowledge, wisdom, and power. Grandmothers assumed most of the responsibility of caring for and
instructing female children, and in many respects they were more
important in this than the children's mothers. In addition to
teaching girls practical skills such as how to cook, sew, embroider
with porcupine quills, and tan hides, older women counseled
them on their spiritual and moral responsibilities. It was under
the tutelage of their grandmothers that Oglala children learned
about the world around them, sometimes explained in the somewhat cryptic language of old people. For example, children were
instructed that the *wakinyan* 'lightning beings' or 'thunder
beings' that lived in the hills to the west were related to *inktomi*
'spiders,' and that one should be careful not to step on a spider

because it would offend his powerful spirit. The only powers stronger were those of the thunder beings, so if one accidentally stepped on a spider, one should immediately address it and say, *Ho Tunkašila, wankiyan niktepi* 'Ho Grandfather, the thunder beings have killed you.' Thus a mere mortal would not be accused of killing the spider, and no retribution would come to him or his family for doing so. It was proper to blame the thunder beings because they were superior to the spider and had the right to kill it if they desired.

The grandmothers also began instructing the children in the sayings and admonitions of the Lakota people. Children were told not to gaze at the moon, because once long ago a woman who was carrying a child on her back looked at the moon for a long time and became weak and senseless (Dorsey 1889, 467). They were told not to point at a rainbow because *šake nitapa kte* 'your fingernail will grow into a ball' perhaps because the rainbow was considered a trap that held back the waters, and the finger might get stuck in it. They were told that refusing food might make the spirits angry so they would no longer provide it. Starvation was the greatest fear, and the loss of a child the greatest tragedy. Children also learned that the Lakotas believed one could in some circumstances induce mysterious things to happen. One must be careful not to turn around too fast or to wave one's arms frivolously, or one might attract the attention of a ghost that moved about on the wind. One should not travel at night because that was the special time when ghosts moved about. If one bumped into a ghost one could suffer from *wanagikte* 'ghost killing'—that is, a stroke. And the grandmothers also had a favorite expression, *cega wan ile ca tatamni ota kte* 'if you light the kettles there will be many buffalo placentas,' meaning that the act of cooking ensured that plenty of meat would be on hand.[2]

Children received knowledge and wisdom from their grandmothers, and, as the White Buffalo Calf Woman had promised, it was the women who would remember the things of value to the Lakotas. Old women would be the wisest, and perhaps because they were next to become the *wicahunka* 'female ancestors,' they were entrusted with all the rituals associated with death.

Imminent death, it was believed, was heralded by certain

omens. Some women could interpret just what these signs meant. A person could of course die on the battlefield or from wounds received in a fight. Someone might also die from an illness that manifested itself in some obvious way, such as the horrible diseases brought to the Lakotas by the white people, like measles, whooping cough, and smallpox.[3] There thus were causes for dying that could be regarded as empirical. On the other hand, when someone died of no explicable cause people believed it was because of the evil influences of ghosts, particularly the spirits of the deceased who were lonely and wanted their loved ones for company in the Spirit World. Such a lonely ghost—say, the spirit of a woman who longed to have a loved one with her—would announce itself in some mysterious way, such as the sound of an animal or bird at an appropriate time—perhaps the call of a bird at night or the cry of a coyote in the daytime. It was then necessary to frighten the ghost away, and this was most frequently done by burning sweetgrass, which was considered repugnant to spirits. Later, when the Oglalas received guns, men were told to fire them whenever they heard these strange sounds.

When a person died special things had to be done to the corpse, and this was entirely the purview of the older women. In fact, all the work associated with the preparation of the corpse and the burial itself was performed by the female relatives of the deceased.

The women painted the face of the corpse red. Occasionally, if a person had participated in the Hunka or Buffalo ceremonies, blue stripes or a blue V would be added to the face paint (Hassrick 1964, 298). The women then placed eagle feathers in the hair and dressed the deceased in his or her finest clothing, including moccasins with fully quilled or beaded soles. There were two times when moccasins were made in this way—when a newborn baby arrived, and when a person died—this underscoring the life cycle in a symbolic way. Next the body was wrapped in a buffalo robe and secured tightly with rawhide ropes. With the body would be placed the deceased's most valuable possessions. For a man there would be his lance, shield, and other weapons, his face paint, pipe, courting flute, and *wotawe* 'war charm.' A woman would have buried with her personal things such as her knife, awl case, strike-a-light bag, and favorite jewelry, as well as locks of hair from the mourners. Often extra moccasins would be placed with the dead since they were continuing on a long journey over the Wanagi Canku 'Ghost Road,' whose campfires could be seen on the Milky Way, running from north to south in the summer sky. The women made sure all the favorite belongings of the deceased were included, for fear that if anything of importance was withheld, the spirit would return to claim it.

A person could be buried in a number of ways, but the most important method was to elevate the corpse by placing it either in a tree or on top of a scaffold tall enough to discourage wild animals from profaning it. In the former case the wrapped body of the deceased was simply secured in a tree and those possessions that could not be wrapped with the body were placed below the branches supporting the body. Ideally a tree with four branches was sought, symbolizing the four directions.

The scaffold burial was called *canagnakapi hutopa* 'to place something on four wooden legs.' Again the four legs of the scaffold were symbolic of the four directions. The scaffold was made from forked posts set in the ground so that the top platform resting on crosspieces was eight to ten feet high. If the deceased had been a brave warrior who had counted many coups in his lifetime, the women would peel the bark from the posts and paint black bands around them (Hassrick 1964, 295).

Plenty of dried food would be placed under the scaffold, and if the person was important, his or her favorite riding horse would be shot and placed there. The Oglalas believed that the spirit of the horse could make the person's journey along the Ghost Road easier. The horse's tail would be cut off and hung from the top of the scaffold.

A prayer stick painted green at one end to symbolize the earth and yellow at the other to symbolize the sky, with an eagle plume attached, might be placed near the scaffold to help carry the deceased to the Spirit World in the south.

The remaining possessions of the deceased were given away or sometimes burned. Often the tipi would be given to some woman who had assisted with the burial (Bushnell 1927, 38).

In later times the body was often wrapped in a robe and put in a rough-hewn coffin made of pine, then placed in a tree or on a scaffold.

Friends and relatives expressed their grief in various ways. The wailing and lamenting of the women could be heard throughout the camp. This lamenting would be repeated over and over whenever people heard for the first time about the death of a relative. When one woman told another of the misfortune, the two would embrace each other, sobbing in drawn out descending tones for several moments, then depart along their way.

Often men who were grieving would insert sharpened wooden pegs into their thighs, knees, and calves, or their biceps and forearms. Women frequently slashed their arms and legs with knives or pieces of flint. Both men and women cut their hair ragged and short, and they might also cut off their little fingers as a sign of mourning (Hassrick 1964, 293–94).

The mother of the deceased stayed with the body all night for four days and nights, returning to her tipi each morning. The father stayed away from the scaffold and went to the top of a hill to pray. Other women were encouraged to stay home and be industrious, attending to their household duties and quillwork. They were warned by the elders not to go wandering around at this time or thereafter they would always be lazy.

The mourners, called *wašigla*, could not cook or even handle food for four days after the burial; therefore other relatives would perform *wašigla wowicak'u* 'feeding the mourners' until the grieving period was over.

Generally warriors who died on the battlefield were not buried. Their bodies were left there so that their spirits could haunt the enemy (Standing Bear 1933, 211). But they might have a symbolic funeral enacted for them. The immediate family erected a special tipi for the occasion, and on a rack placed in front of it they displayed the slain warrior's robes and other clothing. Mourners passed in review before the personal effects and scarified themselves to honor the deceased warrior and his family (Hassrick 1964, 293).

Very old people, usually at their own request, and those who had become infected with some deadly disease might be prepared for their funerals before they died. Old men or women, and sometimes an elderly husband and wife, would be dressed in their finest clothing and left alone in a tipi to die. People tell countless stories about preparing young people for burial because they had contracted *šabya* 'quick consumption.' Once a sixteen-year-old girl contracted cholera. She was dressed in a fine dress and leggings and new porcupine-quilled moccasins. She was then wrapped and tied in two buffalo robes and left in her tipi when the group moved on (Bushnell 1927, 41–42). It was common to leave anyone with such serious diseases alone to die, and it was expected that even the youngest of children would understand what was happening to them and not complain.

It remained the task of women to oversee burials with little aid from the men. It is said that after the people had been placed on the Great Sioux reservation, the Sicangu chief Spotted Tail insisted his daughter have an Indian burial. The body, bound in a deerskin shroud, was wrapped in a red blanket and placed in a coffin. The women gathered there passed by one at a time, whispering to her and placing remembrances in the coffin. Then they fastened the lid and raised the coffin up onto the scaffold. The men stood silently looking on, and none moved or offered any help (Bushnell 1927, 34).

Medicine Women

When a woman reached menopause she frequently received the power, from medicine men or from visions, to engage in various rituals. She was particularly adept at curing patients with herbal medicines. Such a woman was called *pejuta winyela* 'medicine woman' or *wapiye winyan* 'curing woman.' Those who had the power of witchcraft were known as *wiȟmunga* 'witch'—literally, someone who buzzes or hums, the idea being that certain powers could be sent long distances on something like sound waves and used to manipulate evil. Very few women practiced witchcraft, but all sacred women, like the medicine men, knew that acquiring power meant they must be extremely cautious for the rest of their lives. Misusing sacred power could cause the spirits to retaliate by taking the life of a loved one.

The medicine women specialized mainly in healing the sick through massage, through herbal medicines, especially teas, and through rituals that required them to suck out the illness through a bone tube. They were particularly good at finding "medicine"—various plants and minerals used in broths and teas—and it was believed they were guided by spirits who had control over each of the medicines. Medicine women also were midwives and prophets.[4]

Someone in need of the medicine woman's services sent a member of the family to her home with a filled pipe, the same way a medicine man was approached. The two discussed the nature of the illness, and if the medicine woman was willing to help the pipe was lighted and smoked, thus forming a kind of contract between her and the patient's relatives.

Most herbal medicines were boiled into teas and fed to the patient. Sometimes part of the brew would be massaged into the body. The number of herbs known by medicine men and women probably exceeded three hundred.[5] Some of the most popular were small ragweed (*Ambrosia artemisiifolia*), whose leaves were made into tea and drunk for troubles with urination, constipation, and childbirth or made into a compress to reduce swelling,[6] and sweet flag or calamus (*Acorus calamus*), whose roots were peeled and pulverized and chewed to alleviate headache, colds, and practically every internal ailment.[7]

The whole plant of daisy fleabane (*Erigeron annuus*) was made into tea and given to children with sore mouths. It was also used for urinary problems.[8] Wild bergamot (*Monarda fistulosa*) was used for a number of ailments. The chewed leaves of the plant were bandaged over a wound to stop bleeding; they were also boiled, strained through a soft cloth, and placed on sore eyes. The plant was also good for whooping cough and fainting spells. Often the fragrant leaves of another variety called *waĥpe wastemna* 'sweet-smelling leaves' were chewed by singers and dancers.[9] A delicious tea was made from the leaves of mountain mint (*Pycnanthemum virginanum*) and given to people with a cough,[10] as was broomweed or matchbrush (*Gutierrezia sarothrae*).[11]

Another multiple-use remedy was purple coneflower (*Echniacea angustifolia*), whose root was chewed for toothache, for bellyache, or to stop perspiration and quench thirst. The chewed root was also applied to swellings.[12] Slender milkweed (*Astragalus gracilis*) was made into tea in cases of amenorrhea.[13] The plants were under the control of the supernaturals, particularly the *wakinyan* 'thunder beings,' which manifested themselves in lightning. The medicine woman was required to go alone or with another woman who must not be menstruating. Often men and women searched for herbs together. The day had to be perfect—clear, with no clouds in sight. Once found, the plant could not be picked until the medicine woman made offerings to the spirits of the universe, praying to the sky and earth and to the four directions, beginning with the west wind and facing in each direction moving clockwise. The medicine woman might also offer a special prayer song, singing a separate stanza in honor of each of the four directions, sky, earth, and *wanbli gleška* 'spotted eagle,' who would carry her message to Wakantanka.

The plant was then usually wrapped in soft buckskin or, later, a red cloth and taken home, where it would be kept outside the tipi, usually tied to the branch of a tree where the medicine would be safe from menstruating women or marauding animals.

Since it was believed that the power of the plants was controlled by the *wakinyan*, if the medicine man or woman mishandled the plants or failed to observe the strictest adherence to the taboos associated with locating the herbs and properly preparing them, that person or some loved relative would be struck by lightning. The sacred persons were careful not only to pick a good day, but to leave offerings of tobacco for the spirits.

Ritual Participation

Old women participated in the Sun Dance and other important ceremonies as long as they were strong enough. Of all the ceremonies, the one that took the longest and required the most sacrifice was that called *wanagi wicagluhapi* 'to keep one's own ghost' or simply Ghost-Keeping Ceremony, referring to the spirit of a relative. The ritual was based on the belief that the spirit of the deceased lingered around the place of death for approximately a year. Such spirits could frighten people, harming them or even killing them, but they were also a source of knowledge about the spirit world from whom medicine men and women could learn much.

If the deceased was a child, either boy or girl, it was customary for the parents and other relatives to initiate the Ghost-Keeping Ceremony. At the time the child died, the father and mother announced that they were going to keep its spirit, and before the child was buried a lock of its hair was cut by a man with an impeccable reputation and was wrapped in a red cloth. An article owned by the deceased might be kept instead of a lock of hair, such as a piece of clothing or, for a little child, a toy or ornament.

The article became the central focus of the spirit bundle[14] that would represent the spirit for the next year and would be treated as if it were alive, being placed outside the special tipi[15] on pleasant days so it could enjoy the sun and breezes.

Keeping the spirit was a great sacrifice, in that both father and mother must forgo a normal life. The man could not hunt or go on the warpath, and the woman could not gather food or cook for her family. Thus it was a hardship not only for the parents but for those who helped them through the ordeal. One such person, usually a man, was in charge of providing the family with food and other things they needed, and he also accumulated various gifts such as pipes, awls, quillwork, and blankets and kept them until the final day of the ceremony, when they were distributed to those who had helped the most. This last day was particularly important because it marked the time the ghost was ritually fed for the last time and its spirit freed to travel along the ghost road.

When the ceremony began, the lock of hair or personal possession was placed in a buckskin bag and attached to a pine pole that stood in front of the ghost lodge for four days. After the fourth day a tripod painted red was set up inside the ghost lodge at the place of honor so its three legs were toward the west, north, and east, leaving open the south, the direction of the ghosts. If the dead person was a virgin the tripod and spirit bundle would be placed on a white buffalo robe. Those wishing to visit the ghost would have to be careful not to step between the spirit bundle and the fire and not to touch the robe or any of the sacred paraphernalia.[16] People coming into the ghost lodge entered and moved clockwise around it before exiting.

Every day for a year, the parents keeping the ghost had to feed the spirit by placing a little meat or soup in a bowl before it. At the end of each day the food would be buried or burned and some water would be thrown on the ground. It was a difficult ordeal because if the parents should forget to feed the spirit it might become dissatisfied with its treatment and leave the place or harm someone in camp.

When the camp moved, the ghost lodge and spirit bundle were carefully packed and taken along. During this period the parents had to be careful not to make any quick motions such as turning quickly or waving their arms or to engage in such activities as running or swimming, because the sudden stirring of the air might attract the ghost. Finally, at the end of the year when it was time to free the ghost, all the objects that had been accumulated were brought to the center of the camp and a great feast was prepared. A post whittled out of cottonwood, as tall as the dead child, was dressed to represent the child and then set in the ground. Anyone who was an orphan or was needy could approach the spirit post[17] and be assured of receiving food. The people gathered around and the men smoked the pipe, recalling the words of the White Buffalo Calf Woman who taught the Ghost-Keeping Ceremony when she arrived at their camp in the beginning.

The ghost was fed for the last time in front of all the people assembled, and the spirit bundle was slowly opened. As its contents were removed, it was believed that the spirit of the deceased finally departed.

This ritual was then followed by a great feast and giveaway in which all the belongings of the departed, as well as those of the parents, were given away to those who had helped them most during the year-long mourning period. Even the spirit lodge was given away or cut into pieces and the hides distributed among the needy. It was believed that if the spirit had been kept properly, four women would bear children the day it was released and the people would multiply.

The spirit post was left in the ground and later might be buried by the parents. Those who wanted special favors from the parents in the future would approach them saying they had cleaned the ground around the spirit post of their departed child, and the parents would reward them by giving them food.

The act of giving away everything was partly a response to the Oglala dictum that one should never have more than one needs and that one arrives on the earth as a traveler owning nothing and leaves the same way. But the family that gave everything away at the end of the Ghost-Keeping Ceremony would soon be pitied by other people of means, and soon all their possessions would be replaced at other giveaways.

The Ghost Road

At the end of a woman's life she was still useful to the tribe and the family. She was particularly rewarded if she remained with her husband until he died and then did not remarry. If she remarried, the people would gossip about her, saying she did not really love her husband.

Although people were afraid of losing their children, they had no fear of dying of old age, and frequently old couples would joke that when one died the survivor would immediately look for a younger spouse. But even an old man, if his wife preceded him, would be expected to live as a widower lest he be accused of not respecting her in life.[18]

It was perhaps appropriate, since it was the White Buffalo Calf Woman who provided the ceremonies enabling the people to live long with their relations, that the last person one encountered after death was also a woman. The Lakotas believed that at puberty everyone must be tattooed either on the wrist or on the forehead for this tattoo would enable the spirit to pass along the Ghost Road safely. Somewhere in the south the Ghost Road branched, and at the intersection was an old woman who inspected the tattoo of each spirit that passed. Those who possessed the tattoo were permitted to continue along the Ghost road until they reach Wanagiyata 'the place of the spirits,' which was perceived to be just like the earth except that one would see all one's deceased relatives as well as the abundant spirits of buffalo and other animals.

Those not wearing a tattoo the old woman pushed over the side of a cloud or a cliff. They would never be able to travel the Ghost Road again and would be condemned forever to roam the earth as ghosts, never finding a permanent home.[19]

Whether all the events that contribute symbolism to the life cycle of an Oglala female are true in the historical sense is not important. Those historical events surrounding childhood, puberty, womanhood, and old age, as well as the myths that glorify womanhood, have today been incorporated into a generalized Lakota belief system. In the need to establish an ideological foundation as well as a historical one, the Oglalas are no different from any other people: they constantly seek to validate their present existence, which is often perceived to be under the control of outsiders, by constructing a past that is more satisfying in myth than it could ever be in reality. The Oglalas, like other tribes, see themselves today facing a government that is largely unsympathetic, if not ignorant, about what it means to be an American Indian in the twentieth century. They constantly seek to reaffirm their identity first as Oglalas, second as Lakotas, third as Indians, and last as Americans.

But today the context in which one learns to be an Oglala is not much different than for the non-Indian. Oglala children grow up in an age of fast horses and faster cars. Teenagers wear the latest American fashions to rock and roll dances and the latest Indian fashions to powwows and other Indian events. Food is bought at supermarkets in small towns and large cities within a hundred-mile radius of the reservation. Families have radios and television sets, the only difference being that occasionally news stories are reported in the Lakota language. Pupils can attend parochial schools, federal schools, state schools, or private schools. People can be married or buried by practically any Christian denomination.

A number of things face an Oglala growing up at Pine Ridge, however, that do not apply to non-Indians or to Indians of other tribes. Because of the peculiar nature of treaty agreements, and American law as it affects American Indians, it is very likely that an Indian at Pine Ridge will be treated for illness by either a native practitioner or a public health doctor or nurse, but rarely by a private physician. It is likely that an Oglala who has committed certain offenses will have an untrained lawyer as his legal counsel and be sentenced by an equally untrained judge without formal education in the law. The Oglalas who govern the tribe and conduct its business are also likely not to have any formal education, particularly training in the law or public administration.

Although one is likely to find a few Oglala politicians, businessmen and businesswomen, or cowboys sipping martinis in an elegant hotel bar or at an Indian conference, it is likely that an Oglala growing up at Pine Ridge will be more aware of countless drunks whooping it up in the small town of White Clay, Nebraska, where they can legally buy "off sale" liquor (usually Budweiser beer and Gordon's muscatel wine) and of a significant number of young men and women dying at the public health hospital from cirrhosis of the liver.

Of course in the midst of crime, drunkenness, child abuse, drug addiction, and all the sordid crime that still is much more prevalent among non-Indians than among Indians, Oglalas grow up learning a host of values that any Americans would be happy to have their children espouse, whatever their color, ethnic origin, or religion. Oglala children are still taught above all things to be generous, to share food, clothing, shelter, and compassion with everyone—and this includes Indians from other tribes and non-Indians. They are taught to respect their elders, to learn the kinship terms and use them, to love their parents, to be loyal to friends, and most of all to cooperate rather than compete with fellow tribesmen, particularly kinsmen.

In short, Oglalas are in some ways very much like their non-Indian contemporaries, but in many ways they are different, and this holds for both men and women. The relationship between the sexes is not quite the same among the Oglalas as in the larger culture, because there continues to be an emphasis on a complementary or cooperative relationship between the sexes rather than a competitive one.

The Present

7 Growing up Oglala

Government Gravy

The Pine Ridge reservation is essentially the product of a number of treaties and acts of Congress whose objectives were to give whites access to Indian land for eventual exploitation and to promote programs, beginning during the Grant administration, to "civilize" the American Indian. To the average white bureaucrat civilization essentially meant teaching the Indians to work the land and to be Christians. Both programs were to be implemented within the confines of an Indian reservation, a parcel of land of varying dimensions that guaranteed both the Indians' isolation from the white man's culture and their dependency upon it.

The first act was the Treaty of Fort Laramie, signed in 1868 by all the Lakota divisions and the federal government. Its purpose was to end hostilities between Indians and whites and to establish the Great Sioux reservation, situated in Dakota Territory in what is now the western half of the state of South Dakota. Included in this area was the Black Hills, but owing to the discovery of gold there in 1874 and the subsequent attempt by the United States government to protect prospectors who were encroaching on Indian land, culminating with the annihilation of George Armstrong Custer on 25 June 1876, Congress passed the Black Hills Act of 1877, transferring ownership from the Lakotas to the federal government, clearly an abrogation of the original Fort Laramie treaty.

The civilization program emphasized teaching Indians to be useful human beings, and utility was largely measured by Calvinistic concepts of work. Farming was the occupation chosen by the federal government, but as long as the Indian had a reverential attitude toward the land and believed that "scratching the bowels" of Maka Ina, Mother Earth, with a plow was a heinous act, little progress was made. Also, farming and the labor of one's hands could not really be appreciated by people who did not own their land individually. Thus in 1887 the Dawes Act was passed by Congress, and ultimately Indian heads of households were allotted land in severalty. Since there was more land than there were heads of households, "surplus" lands were created out of the original treaty area and largely made available to the federal government, corporations, and other businesses.[1]

The original agency for the Oglalas was at Whetstone, Nebraska, but it was moved to Pine Ridge, South Dakota, in 1878. By 1879 another important civilizing agency, the Christian missionary, had located at Pine Ridge, and it is thus appropriate to say that missionaries have been at Pine Ridge as long as the Oglalas have. The Episcopalians came in 1879, followed by the Jesuits, who in 1888 built Holy Rosary Mission, a religious and educational retreat that figured prominently in the Ghost Dance movement and the Wounded Knee massacre of 1890.

The carving out of Pine Ridge as a separate reservation came in 1889 as a result of non-Indian pressure to break up the Great Sioux reservation. The ludicrously named Great Sioux agreement of 1889 was a result of Congress's passing an act that reduced the reservation by eleven million acres, forming six separate reservations, of which Pine Ridge is one. The act was passed on the advice of the military-led negotiating team, which convinced Congress that the Lakotas favored it. Only 10 percent of the Lakota males voted, though the original treaty of 1868 required a two-thirds majority for any modification (Pommersheim and Remerowiski 1979).

Growing up on the Pine Ridge reservation, for males or females, means being reminded almost every day that the United States reneged on a solemn treaty with the Lakota people and gave away Indian land, particularly the Black Hills, to non-Indian interests—mainly large corporations.

By the 1850s the traditional Sioux were forsaking their buffalo skin tipis for canvas ones, which were much easier to transport. The tipis themselves, except for ceremonial lodges, began to disappear at the turn of the century, and they were slowly replaced by log cabins, whose sagging timbers still dot the countryside around Pine Ridge, themselves later replaced by frame houses and split-levels. On the dusty rolling prairie that was the open range of the buffalo and the nomadic Oglalas, highlighted by magnificent pine-covered buttes, there sprang up the signs of bureaucracy. Red brick buildings began to encroach on both sides of wagon roads, forming the Pine Ridge Agency, the federal boarding school, district schools, ubiquitous churches, soon to represent over a dozen Christian denominations. But none were as powerful as the Catholics and Episcopalians, who between them controlled nearly all the souls of the prospective converts.

Early Education

Oglala children were taken from their homes and sent to boarding schools, either federal or denominational. Barbers cut the boys' hair short, and the girls soon sported the then voguish "Buster Brown" cut. The children were dressed like miniature white men and women and forced to speak English under penalty of a beating.

My oldest living respondent, who along with her sister and cousins went to boarding school in 1920, said:

> The boarding school was run military style. We used to wake up and go to bed by bugle call. We used to march to class and do calisthenics by companies. Company A was made up of the tallest girls, and Company F was the smallest.
>
> Girls wore "hickory dresses," black stockings, and "stogies" [high-top shoes]. One matron and her assistant took care of five hundred girls. One boys' adviser, or disciplinarian, took care of five hundred boys. The boys wore knee pants and caps.
>
> We lived in the dormitories. We got up at 6:00 A.M. and made our beds. They were inspected, and if they weren't made properly, they tore them up. We went to bed at 9:00 P.M.
>
> There was a place called the trunk room. That's where we kept our steamer trunks. They were filled with dried foods like *papa* and *wasna* because our parents thought that the white people wouldn't feed us right. After school—around 4:00 P.M., we would get the keys to our trunks from the matrons. And we'd go down and open our trunks and eat the Indian food.

The food made available by the federal government was considered laregly inferior. When the girls were out of earshot of the officials, they sang:

> Too much government gravy
> Makes me lazy.

The average school year ran from September to June. In the fall the parents brought their children to school in wagons or on horseback. In the spring they lined up outside the school waiting for their children to come out.

> It was like a parade outside waiting for us. All our parents were there in wagons, and there were riding horses with beaded saddle blankets standing all in a row.

Children attended three types of schools: federal boarding schools, where they stayed throughout the year except for Christmas vacation; "day" schools, which went only through the third grade; and "mission" schools, run by Jesuits, that were exclusively boarding schools. Holy Rosary Mission accommodated about five hundred students until the 1970s, when it became a day school, picking up students in the nearby area by school bus—a far cry from the time when

> We used to have our own "school bus." It was a horse. I would start off early in the morning and stop by each of the children's homes and pick them up. They would ride behind me, and sometimes that horse would carry as many as five of us little kids.

Another female respondent, a professional artist, had a similar experience, though she was three years younger than my eldest respondent:

> I went to school in a one-room schoolhouse. I was put into school at five, because the school had to have twelve [in order to open]. Two of us were too young, but they plunked us down anyway to make twelve.
> I went through the fourth grade, then I went to the Rapid City Indian School. And that's where my education really began. I found out who I was

and who I wasn't because it was an Indian school. There were no white students there. But there were white teachers and white matrons. That was a vicious school.

It was run like a military school. We wore uniforms, hickories—those little striped uniforms cut very straight—on weekdays and uniforms on Sundays, sailor uniforms, navy blue serge with a little red tie.

We woke up to bugles, and at night, taps. We fell into formations. We had officers for each company; each company had two officers, a captain and a major. The one who stood up and bossed everybody was a major, one of the bigger girls.

They would sound the bugle call and we would get in a line and march. And when we got up in the morning, after we dressed, we would stand up at attention and they would raise the flag. Then we would march into the dining room and stand behind our chairs. They gave the signal and everybody sat down. Old Yellow Horse was in charge. And she would tap on the bell and everybody would say grace. Tap on the bell, and everybody fell to.

We knew every drill there was to be known, right flank, left flank, forward march, and double time. And we had to salute the flag, and about face. Afterward we were back in the dorms, and we had a good hour of work. Everything had to shine, we cleaned up everything. We made the beds and we had to stand at attention while they had an inspection. Every morning.

Boys and girls were segregated in the mission school but sat together in the classrooms and dining room at the government schools. It was a welcome relief for some who could leave the reservation and attend one of the federal Indian schools such as Haskell Institute in Lawrence, Kansas, where there weren't quite as many regulations:

We didn't even march. They rang a great big gong and said breakfast was on and come on and get it. And if you didn't you were out of luck.

I was like a robot. Somebody would ring a bell,

or somebody would ring a gong, tell me where to
go, and I went.

Since the establishment of the schools at the turn of the
century, the emphasis had been on vocational training for the
boys and home economics for the girls. At Holy Rosary Mission,
where the Jesuits were assiduous in documenting their commitment to educating the Oglalas, a great deal is known about the
daily life of the schoolchildren.

"Mission" as it is locally known, estimates twenty-one
thousand Oglalas were educated between 1888 and 1963 (Red
Cloud Indian School 1963). The first class numbered twenty
children.

Under the careful and industrious administration of the Jesuit
fathers and brothers, boys were taught carpentry, shoemaking,
blacksmithing, baking, cattle ranching, farming, and dairying.
Girls received their training from the Sisters of the Order of
Saint Francis in cooking, hand and machine sewing, weaving,
spinning, and embroidery. Independence was the keynote of the
Jesuit order, and Holy Rosary Mission was different from the
other boarding schools in that it did not rely on government
funds to survive. The cattle ranch provided beef, the gardens
vegetables, and the dairy fresh milk and butter.

The girls, under the supervision of the sisters, did all the
cooking and kitchen work. They performed every chore related
to subsistence, from sorting eggs from the chicken coops to
canning foods. They learned to make their own clothing, quilts,
pillowcases, and all the things they would need for their personal
use. In class they learned to read and write, but it was never
suggested that their future held anything but becoming house-
wives and mothers.

Generally, school life mirrored American life in general, with
clothing and other styles lagging behind those of mainstream
America by several years.

At the turn of the century, clothing, aside from the hickory
dreses and stogies, reflected what white America perceived as
fashionable. Little Indian girls and young women alike wore long
skirts and high-necked dresses, with white starched aprons during chores, their high-topped shoes peeking from beneath their
skirts only when they sat in demure positions revealing womanly

restraint. The 1920s produced hosts of reservation flappers, complete with cloche hats fitted rakishly over bobbed hair, short skirts, dark stockings, and ankle-strap shoes (much to the chagrin of the grandmothers, who continued to wear their long calico dresses and deerskin moccasins). Often cardigan sweaters were thrown over their Sunday-best middies. The 1930s were an extension of the twenties with somewhat longer skirts.

As early as 1925, basketball became the essential athletic activity of the Pine Ridge schools, and Oglala girls, wearing letter sweaters and carrying pom-poms like their white sisters, led screaming fans in cheers to inspire their players. They were unique, however, in that most of their cheers were in Lakota, the language they were required to forget in everyday life but encouraged to cheer in, particularly when their teams played against white teams from off the reservation. As the boys dribbled down the floor shouting out plays to each other in Lakota, the girls lined up and led the fans in:

> *Ohiya, ohiya, ohiya po!*
> Rosary, Rosary, *Iya po!*
> *Hiyu po, hiyu po, luzahan*
> Will we win now. *Han, han, han!*
>
> *Tinpsilala, Tinpsilala ša ša ša*
> Shred em up, shred em up, rah, rah, rah.
> *Tapalala tapalala icu po!*
> Rosary, Rosary, *Iya po!*

The 1940s hit the reservation like the rest of the country. The war years found the young women wearing pompador hairdos and suits and jackets with padded shoulders; in the latter part of the decade hemlines plunged over popular cowboy-style boots trimmed with tassles, the kind worn by drum majorettes in every town in the United States.

In the late forties and early fifties, once the girls got away from the uniformity of the schools, they wore rolled-up jeans and boys' shirts, penny loafers and the popular bobby socks. Still the old women, mothers and grandmothers, continued to wear conservative long dresses, scarves over their graying braids, and fringed shawls. By the 1960s however, as the rest of the United States rebelled—the black power movement, flower children, and hippies—Indian girls and boys, particularly teenagers, began to let their hair grow long, decorating it with beads, feather hair strings, and headbands and generally mimicking the rest of the nation's youth, except that their ornaments were decidedly Indian.

Along with the clothing came the rest of the life-style so typical of non-indian America. Young women and men acted in school plays, usually religious vignettes at Holy Rosary extolling the virtues of Father Pierre DeSmet and the other early missionaries. There were also parades on traditional American holidays, first communions, confirmations, and later on the important school prom where in the forties and fifties Tommy Dorsey and Glenn Miller were as popular in the high-school gymnasium at the Pine Ridge Boarding School or Holy Rosary as in the crystal ballrooms of the big cities.

During World Wars I and II, Korea, and Vietnam, young men and women volunteered for the army. The canteen image of the woman waiting at home for her boyfriend or husband was very much part of the scene at Pine Ridge, except that Indian dimensions were added. Returning heroes were treated as warriors, and their names were celebrated in the old war songs and at victory dances that, except for the continuous stream of warfare during the twentieth century, might have become obsolete (Powers 1980b). Many of the values of the warrior society of the preservation days continued simply because the United States was at war, and many of the old society songs and dances, the victory celebrations, and the ceremonies in which women honored the deeds of their menfolk never had a chance to die out.

The idea that Indian men were still somehow destined to work with their hands and that women were needed at home also did not diminish. Even young people growing up in the 1950s and 1960s were encouraged to learn trades. Though there were few jobs on the reservation—a problem that still plagues Pine Ridge—young men and women often left to go to vocational schools. One woman became a nurse despite continual counseling that she should learn to work with her hands:

It was right after high school, and I went to vocational school. I think at that time [about 1963]

> they told us that Indians were good with their
> hands, so they pushed us into mechanical type
> things and secretarial training. They really didn't
> push college, and they should have. I took a sec-
> retarial course, and I was terrible in typing and
> shorthand, but the teachers kept pushing me, so
> that I just did it even though I wasn't interested
> in it.

Even though vocational training was promoted, education in
general has always been endorsed even by the most conservative
Oglalas. She continued:

> Our parents said that we had to have an education
> because that was a big trend and because we had
> to live with the white man, and we had to dwell in
> the white man's society.
> It's the same today. Even though we like it
> here, if we didn't think our kids were getting the
> proper education we would leave. We want them
> to be able to have the choice that we did—to be
> able to work on or off the reservation.
> I'd like my daughter to become a lawyer or a
> doctor, to settle on something better than I have.
> In fact, I know I will push my daughter more than
> my sons—she will have to do more—a whole lot
> more. I want to explain to her that it's up to her
> to excel. Look at my family—we lived in a three-
> room house, and when you grow up you say you
> don't want to live like this for the rest of your life.
> My father always had a thing for making some-
> thing of yourself and not owing anybody anything.
> He hated to see people living on welfare. He said,
> look around at other people and don't be afraid to
> be like them just cause they're well off.

She placed great importance on parental guidance:

> I think my mother was the one who would disci-
> pline me. She lectured me on proper behavior.
> She would verbally tell me things like "I don't
> want my daughter to grow up to be no good."
> That made me cry. It's funny though, now that I
> think back I think my father had the greatest in-

fluence on me. I always had to prove to him that I
could be something, because I think he said things
to me that made me feel like I wouldn't be anything. Whereas I think that my mother thought I
was good in some things; she was definitely supportive. I think that my mother was the stronger
person of the two, but I tried harder to prove to
my dad I could be something.

My mother never really told me about sex or
anything. It was just something she never spoke
about. But I picked up a lot of things from my
cousins and from my aunt, who was much younger
than my cousins. Mom used to tell me a lot of
things about growing up, but she never mentioned
anything about sex. All she would ever say is
offhand stuff like "You don't mess around with
boys!"

And when I got my menses, my grandmother
cried and I couldn't figure out why. It was so
scary, and I thought "What's happening to me?"
because they were crying and everything. But I
guess to them it was a tragic thing becoming a
woman because it meant that now I was going to
have babies, and they thought that I would have a
hard life after that. Which, you know, some of
them do.

Two Cultures

At one time one might have seen the socialization process of the
Oglala male and female as distinct from non-Indian socialization. Among the traditional Oglalas—those who believed in the
sacred pipe and generally subscribed to the precepts of Lakota
religion outlined in the life-cycle chapters—young people were
socialized simultaneously to two sets of standards. In the home
they learned the Lakota language and Lakota religion and participated in kinship behavior appropriate to Lakota standards.
There they listened to the old Inktomi stories and were reminded
by the old people not to forget who they were lest they marry a
close relation. By and large, when at home they behaved as they
perceived a proper Oglala should.

But when the young people went off to school, they were soon taught a whole new set of standards about speaking, praying, and generally getting along with their classmates and their kin. Missionaries and other teachers believed that one culture was being superimposed upon another and that in time the white man's culture would replace the Oglala's. But since the Pine Ridge reservation was established, the population has continued to increase, and with it Indian religion has flourished in a way that nobody believed could happen. There was a sudden tying back between grandchildren and grandparents.

This is the cultural state of affairs today, except that the socialization process in both Indian and white culture takes place both at home and in school. There is no longer a neat distinction about where proper values are imparted. One is as likely to find Indian children learning to speak Lakota in school as at home. Indians may go to a Christian church on Sunday and to a *Yuwipi* or other ritual on Wednesday night. Someone may be an accountant with the tribe by day and go into a sweat lodge in the evening to clear his head. An Oglala medical student in California may return home in the summer to be pierced in the Sun dance. A member of the Oglala Sioux tribal council may after a hard week of deliberations take the weekend off and go to Rapid City to place a few bets at the dog track. There seems to be no logic to how two cultures that allegedly are diametrically opposed can coexist so easily. Yet they do—in a mixture of Indian and white cultures whose rules are sometimes juggled to fit the convenience of the moment without people's forgetting that both have existed for a long time. The old people call this state of affairs *wojapi*, after a traditional food that is literally "all mixed up."

The Oglalas have been criticized for having been warriors and pagans in the past. But they too are good at handing out criticism whenever a white person believes that Euramerican culture is gaining control. As one middle-aged traditional woman told me about her recent visit to a church:

> One day we went to church and nobody was there.
> So some of the girls and I went in and we were
> sitting there, and when we came out the minister
> appeared and said, "What are you doing in
> there?" I said I understand this is a house of God,
> and I came to pay my respects.
> He said, "I've never seen you in church." I

said, "Yes, you've never seen me in church, but
I've never seen you out in God's country." He
said, "You are one of the lost sheep." I told him
that I was one of the lost sheep as far as his books
were concerned, but not as far as God was concerned. I said, "Your sheep won't come in there
by themselves. It's your job to go out and bring
them in." I said, "You might find them out at my
house. Come out and see." I told him to come out
there and meet the real creator.

Despite the defiant attitude, there is a general fear today that
Indian values are dying off and that no education in the world will
prevent that. Though the population is growing and there are
more native Lakota speakers today, there is still general concern:

What I see today in our culture, among our Indian
people, is very little. The language still exists, but
that's for the old people. When they're gone, the
language is going to be gone. You hear people say
that we Lakotas speak our language at home, but
only the parents do, not the children. I see families where the language is gone, and it is because
of the influence from the outside, and the number
one influence is that institution called school. The
children attend the whole week, for thirty-six
weeks, and then they come home on the weekends
and the summer, and that's when their families are
out having fun someplace.

The attitude that the white man's education is necessary to
survival conflicts with other attitudes that see modern education
as designed to erode Indian culture even when the emphasis is on
so-called Indian studies. Some traditional people believe that
Indian studies are essentially tailored for non-Indians who want
to come to the reservation and teach Indian children:

Indian kids are not learning as much as they
should because very little is required of Indian students. They are not being challenged in their abili-
ties or encouraged to try harder. Instead, they are
taught just enough to get by. We need teachers
who believe that Indian children have the same
ability to learn as their non-Indian counterparts.

These days too many people excuse inferior
work by saying that's the "Indian way." To me
that's a cop-out.

Since the beginning of the Indian school system, teachers have
come largely from white middle-class backgrounds, either military or missionary.

These non-Indian educators who come in here to
teach have usually attended some type of orientation or workshop first. The trouble is that what
they read or what they hear is some type of historical material on what the Indian is like, but what
they are learning is sometimes a hundred years
old. Actually our attitudes between a hundred
years ago and today are different. So when they
come here they don't experience what they expect
to find.

Most of the teachers today are white, but even when Indians
receive accreditation and decide to teach in reservation schools,
the feeling often expressed among traditionalists is that they are
bound to fail because:

Our Indian people who are educated and sent off
to get a college degree come back and want to
teach our children. But what really happens is that
they are oriented into the white man's way. So
when they come back, they isolate themselves in
some BIA compound, in their own little house,
and they start working on their career. They simply lose their Indian values and whatever they had
before they went away to school to get educated.
We can't go back to the traditional Indian way
of life, but the old values can be taught to our
children.

The same fear about the loss of language applies to relationships. Old people constantly decry the way young people not
only forget the language but forget their kinship terms and how
one is supposed to behave toward kin. The greatest criticism an
older person can level is that someone calls one person by more
than one kinship term. If kinship between ego and other can be
reckoned in more than one way, people have married others to

whom they are already related. In actuality, kinship lines are never easy to trace at Pine Ridge, mainly because of mutiple marriages. Although polygyny is no longer practiced, getting married "Indian style" is, and in fact more people share residences according to common-law practice than get married in either a civil or a church ceremony. For example, over the entire 1970s there were on average sixteen marriages a year in Shannon and Washbaugh counties, which are almost totally Indian, while there were slightly more than three hundred live births a year for the same period. Although over half of these each year were listed as "out-of-wedlock" births by state officials, it is not clear to what extent they reflect "Indian style" marriages.[2]

The children of these marriages are guaranteed a slot in a family of orientation even if they are abandoned. Traditional values persist, and children whose parents split up (whether married with "benefit of clergy" or "Indian style") are adopted into stable families, because there is no necessary correlation between type of marriage (or absence of it) and length or stability of the union.

Recently young people in their late teens and twenties are occasionally united in what is called a traditional wedding ceremony but that in fact does not resemble the exchange of gifts between parents and the move of residence to the husband's camp. The ceremony, conducted by a medicine man, is based much more on the Christian concept of exchanging vows, even when gifts are exchanged between the principal families.

Courtship

Older Oglala women today bemoan the fact that young women are no longer chaperoned as they should be. Young men no longer line up to stand in the blanket with the young women under the watchful eyes of grandmothers and mothers. Today the older traditional women say that everything happens too fast. Girls meet boys mainly at school, where there is no supervision. Like other Americans, they live in fear that their daughters, granddaughters, and nieces will become pregnant and that life will be hard for them. But when pregnancy occurs, the young woman is not chastised or humiliated by her kin. In fact she and the father, if he is present, along with the new baby are welcomed into the extended family, and the child is very much at home being cuddled by all members of the family.

Young people have many opportunities to meet, just as they do in a non-Indian community—school, games, movies, dances, and also rodeos, powwows, and various Indian celebrations such as Sun Dances. A long-standing joke has it that children are born nine months after the Sun Dance. This may not be so much of a joke since in the past it was at the large annual meetings that nonkin had the opportunity to meet and to develop friendships and intimacy.

In school, young people at one time were shy about talking to members of the opposite sex in public, always fearful of being embarrassed by their friends. But this is certainly not true today, except that a young person still does not confide in older people. Of particular concern among the older women is that they never know when their daughters have reached puberty and therefore cannot instruct them about becoming a woman. According to one women: "In the old days, when a girl got her period they would have a ceremony for her. But today nobody even knows. The girls start to grow up and nobody even knows it—and pretty soon they're having babies."

Young people meet each other at various events, but one of the most popular of Indian celebrations is the powwow, a term picked up from Oklahoma Indians in the mid-1950s. The Lakota term is *Omaha wacipi* 'Omaha dance,' a form of free-style dancing for man and women learned from the Omaha Indians in the middle to late nineteenth century. Today the dance is held outdoors in large shaded arbors called "boweries," and in the winter school and church gymnasiums and district meetinghouses are used. Males and females dress in Indian costume. The men wear feathered "bustles" and porcupine-hair headdresses, complete with beaded cuffs, armbands, suspenders, belts, and other accessories. Females are more conservative, dressing in the style of the early reservation period. The favorite woman's costume is a beaded buckskin dress or a cloth dress decorated with dentalium shells, elk teeth, or cowrie shells. The women also wear beaded leggings and moccasins and carry fancy long-fringed shawls. Sometimes street clothes are worn, particularly during the afternoon dances, but shawls are always required. Thus female dancers are called "shawl dancers," and during most celebrations far more women are seen dancing inside the arbor or on the gym floor than men.

Songs are provided by singers seated around large military-style bass drums, which they beat with soft-headed drumsticks. The singers are primarily males, but they are often joined by one or two female singers, the *wicaglata* of old. The presence of female singers at the drum lends prestige, because women will not sing for just any song group. Women who are out on the floor dancing will often dance up close to the drum and join in with the male singers while they dance in place. Older women, when they hear praise songs, join in with the *ungnahela hotun*, an ear-splitting tremolo each time the names of their kinsmen are mentioned.

Men and women dance separately during the Omaha. At one time the women simply performed the *ipšica waci* 'jumping dance,' made up of small hopping steps around the periphery of the dance area. This is regarded as the "real" Lakota form of dancing, and it has experienced a revival in the 1970s. Before the revival, men and women danced out in the middle of the arbor, the women dancing in the men's style, but more reservedly. But since the early part of the 1970s even the dancers' clothes, both male and female, are beginning to resemble the dance costumes of the turn of the century, a definite move away from the inter-tribal styles that were prevalent on the Plains and in urban areas during the 1950s and 1960s.

At some of the larger powwows, such as those held in conjunction with the sun dance at Pine Ridge, the dance arbors are large and can accommodate a thousand dancers or more. Several groups of drummers sit under the arbor and take their turns singing. Outside the arbor industrious families set up booths where they sell traditional Indian foods like fried bread and "Indian tacos," a new type of food imported from the Southwest, and modern foods such as hamburgers, hot dogs, and cold pop. Men and women, boys and girls, and little children constantly mill about outside the arbor near the stands looking for friends and new acquaintances while the dancing is going on inside. Each year, during the day, an all-Indian rodeo sponsored by the Oglala Sioux Rodeo Cowboys Association takes place a few hundred yards from the powwow grounds, and young people scurry back and forth from one attraction to the other. Indian rodeos have events for women, as do the white rodeos. Occasionally a traveling carnival is set up near the powwow grounds, and parents and children ride merry-go-rounds and ferris wheels while in the background the old Lakota songs can be heard, as can the crack of the rodeo announcer's voice over the loudspeaker.

Women and girls as well as men and boys participate in dance competitions, with cash prizes sometimes reaching hundreds of dollars. Dance contests are held in all the districts of the reservation and also in cities where there are large Indian populations. Often Indians from Pine Ridge travel to these cities as well as to other reservations to camp out and attend the powwows sponsored by other tribes. Some young women have abandoned the traditional buckskin and cloth dresses for the girls' and women's contests and wear modified male costumes and even participate in the boys' and men's contests. Although this is regarded as unusual, they are welcomed in those traditionally male contests, and some have even won first prize.

Young women and girls have also begun to sing traditional men's songs around the drum. Although this is frowned upon by some of the elders, modern Indians like to hear women singing men's songs, particularly because the women can sing much higher, which is highly valued in Indian songs. The female singers also accompany themselves with drumsticks around the drum. This is regarded as another very unusual feature because traditionally all the drumming was done by men. Groups of female singers have been organized on a number of Northern Plains reservations. And though it is recognized as novel behavior, they are always asked to sing at large celebrations.

Some of the contemporary powwows are modeled after rodeos, complete with parades, grand entrances, and the institution of the "powwow princess" who, like her counterpart the "rodeo queen," officiates at the daily events. These young women are generally chosen from traditional families, and one requirement is that they own and wear traditional beaded dresses and accessories.

College

The possibility of choosing between Oglala and white culture is extended over a longer period today at Pine Ridge. Whereas most adults went to grade school and some attended high school, with the establishment in 1970 of the Oglala Sioux Community College (now called Oglala Lakota College), administered by the Black Hills State College in Spearfish, South Dakota, young Oglalas can now obtain higher education without leaving the reservation.

Much of the program is like that offered at any other community college in the country, but at Pine Ridge there is a strong emphasis on Lakota studies, a subject offered as a major. Not only are the courses themselves taught by Oglala educators, but commencements are highlighted by powwows, feasts, and the conferring of sacred "wheels," which are tied to the graduates' hair, usually by a medicine man.

What is particularly interesting about the college is that women graduates outnumber men overwhelmingly: Roughly 90 percent of graduates are women. For example, the graduating class of June 1979 comprised thirty-four women and three men. Some male administrators believe something should be done about the "changing" roles of men in today's world, attributing this in part to men's shying away from activities where they might fail. A young Oglala woman writing in the college newspaper *Lakota Eyapaha* voiced the following comment:

> There is no reason why men could not be just as effective as women, working as housewives while their wives are in the work force, but realistically it is culturally unacceptable. In the Indian society, men were always the brave warriors and hunters.
> I often hear the male members of my family say that women are weak and feeble. . . . The irony of all this is that women are much more flexible to do male-dominated work such as carpentry, construction, police-duty . . . but men refuse to do housework or care for their children.[3]

One interesting point here is that all the women I interviewed who have achieved high-status roles were expected to do things that normally would be considered male. For example, one woman said:

> When I was growing up my grandma told me that

> I had to learn to do everything. I had to do all the
> things that a woman had to do, like take care of
> the kids and cook. But she told me that I also had
> to be able to do just about everything that a man
> had to do. That's why I can ride a horse or drive a
> tractor as well as any man.

And another, who had grown up with six uncles, had to
babysit for the youngest and compete with the oldest:

> I always had to prove myself as good as the boys,
> and that's one of the things that my father made
> me do. He would say, "If you can't ride a horse
> right, just get the hell off the horse." So I had to
> do what I did right or not do it at all. And of
> course I always had to be better than my youngest
> uncle.

There is a general concern today, expressed by women and
men alike, that women are more capable and industrious than
men. The traditional excuse for men's idleness is general frustration over identity:

> People don't really know what they are going to
> be. Are they going to be Indian? Are they going
> to be white? Or do they fall somewhere in be-
> tween?

Some also believe that the Oglalas can survive by maintaining
an equilibrium between the two cultures. But there is growing
consensus that women have an advantage over men when it
comes to getting an education and finding a job, and some
Oglalas are adept at analyzing why. For example:

> I think that women are taking a more responsible
> position as far as family life is concerned. As far as
> thinking we have to get ahead, we do because we
> have to feed our families. While the men are just
> sitting back and saying "Man, this is bad and
> there's nothing we can do about it," women feel
> that they have a responsibility to the family. *She*
> has to take care of the kids. On top of that, there
> are not too many women sitting home. Everyone I
> know is working.

Part of this responsibility is expressed in occupations that are traditionally female, such as teaching, nursing, and clerical and secretarial work, but more women are also beginning to apply the management skills required to run a household and raise a family to occupations and professions of some authority. But the newfound power being entrusted to women is not being leveled against Oglala men. There is no competition as such between males and females over occupations such as police (though certainly there are more men on the Oglala Sioux Tribal Police Force), judges (an elected post; most judges have always been women), tribal administrators, or district leaders. And in business, women have taken up arts and crafts, become directors of cultural programs and college professors, and gone into newspaper publishing, law, and politics.

Organizations

Women have also banded together to form a number of reservationwide organizations such as the Sacred Shawl Society, founded in 1979 to deal with the problem of domestic violence, and the Lakota Indian Women's Council,[4] which addresses problems of discrimination in employment, social service needs, alcohol and drug abuse, and the training of women, particularly in medicine, to name a few. Another organization, Women of All Red Nations (WARN),[5] founded in 1978 in Rapid City by women representing thirty Indian nations, has become a national and then an international organization whose purpose is to fight for equal rights for all American Indians (not only females).

These organizations, plus others formed by Indian women on college campuses and at Indian centers in various urban areas where Indians have relocated, are modeled closely after the prereservation sodalities. And though women frequently fight for women's issues exclusively, on larger social, political, and economic issues they often band together with their menfolk against the manipulative measures of the United States government.

In summary, the socialization process today can be analyzed from a number of perspectives. One is the issue of traditionalism versus modernism. Some Oglalas feel they are more traditional or more modern, yet they are capable of being both to a certain degree, depending on the situation. As one woman said: "I want my kids to be aware of the old Lakota ways as well as what goes on today. I want them to have the benefit of both cultures."

White versus Oglala does not necessarily coincide with modern versus traditional. Some *iyeska* 'mixed bloods' speak Lakota better than "full bloods," despite the constant criticism that there is something inherently superior in being a mixed blood. There is, as any biologist knows, only an ideological basis for such racist thinking.

Finally, males and females governed by traditional values see a complementarity between the sexes that manifests itself in the reality that women are taking on more important roles in the tribe and that it may not be long before a woman becomes president of the Oglala Sioux Tribe.[6]

The socialization of the Oglala woman—and man—thus occurs along three essential but flexible continua: traditional versus modern; white versus Indian; and male versus female. The successful female finds herself capable of operating at both ends of each continuum, but at the same time she sees herself cooperating, not competing, with males on each continuum— even at the sexual level, where she is required to participate in the man's sphere but he is not expected to be part of hers.

8 Making the Mark

From Buffalo to Beef

Between Oglala men and women it has always been conceded
that the men took a turn for the worse once confined to the
reservation. One expert stated:

> I am sure that the Indian man was the real victim
> of reservation policy. When the soldiers herded a
> tribe into a reservation the Indian men joined the
> ranks of the unemployed and went on relief. They
> would gladly have hunted, followed the war path
> and engaged in all the occupations they had been
> trained for, but there was no chance. So they sat
> around in idleness. On the other hand, the Indian
> woman had no time to loaf. As of old, she was the
> housekeeper, gathered the wood, reared the chil-
> dren, cared for the sick and made most of the
> clothing. Then it was her job to gather whatever
> vegetable food was to be used.
> Any day in camp would reveal the females toil-
> ing early and late. To see so many useless males
> around frequently aroused my resentment, but the
> women never complained about it. True, they
> were often vociferous in demanding the return of
> the old times but not with the idea that they would
> have less to do. So far as I could see, the morale
> of the women was far less shattered and it was
> they who saved tribal life from complete collapse.
> (Wissler 1938, 239)

The Treaty of Fort Laramie guaranteed in perpetuity that the
Oglala and other Lakotas would be fed—hardly a proper compensation for the annihilation of the American bison. Nevertheless, according to article 10, the United States would deliver the
following to any Indian over four years of age who settled on the
reservation and complied with the stipulations of the treaty:

128

"one pound of meat and one pound of flour per day, provided the Indians cannot furnish their own subsistence at an earlier date. And it is further stipulated that the United States will furnish and deliver to each lodge of Indians or family of persons legally incorporated with them, who shall remove to the reservation herein described and commence farming, one good American cow" (Pommersheim and Remerowiski 1979, 103).

The treaty was weighted so that more benefits would accrue to the Oglala family that began farming. But given the technology of the day, the land was not suitable for cultivation except in the southeastern part of the reservation, in what is now Bennett County. This more desirable land was the first to be invaded by white farmers and ranchers, so that today this section is considered the "ceded" portion of the reservation, though it is still the home of many Indians. Recently it is no longer being designated as part of the Pine Ridge reservation on most maps.

The earliest annuities were distributed at the agency town, now called Pine Ridge Village (to distinguish it from the rest of the reservation). The reservation was then divided into ration districts, each having a central location where its residents could procure such commodities as bacon, flour, coffee, lard, beans, sugar, and occasionally other staples. Most important, the ration district centers were where people received their beef allotment.[1]

At first the Oglalas regarded beef as inedible because of the terrible odor that came from the corrals where cattle were kept. Finally the heads of households were told to kill the "spotted buffalo," as the cattle were called, in the same way they had once killed real buffalo. This was great sport for the Oglala men, and every ration day a steer would be let out of the corral and an Indian's name called. The Indian set out after the steer on horseback, carrying a rifle, and brought it down some way from the corral. The women quickly followed butchering the meat and loading it into wagons as they had butchered buffalo in the past (Powers and Powers 1984).

Ranching was also encouraged, but most Oglalas did not have the capital to start a herd. Those who were successful at running steers and horses were usually children of the *iyeska* 'mixed bloods,' derogatorily called "half-breeds," mainly the sons and daughters of white men who had married Oglala women. These men came to the area as traders, trappers, and soldiers, the last fresh from the Civil War, seeking adventure on the Great Plains. Most of the earliest were French, men with names like Janis, Pourier, Coltier, Bordeau, Shangreaux, and Richards (Reeshaw), and today most of the non-Indian-sounding surnames are French. To these were added Mexican and Irish cowboys who drove the cattle up from Texas, some of them also marrying Indian women. Finally there were the galvanized Yankees of the Civil War, sent to the Plains to fight Indians.

Soon trading posts began to dot the reservation, with one major post in each ration district. Here Indians could trade for—or buy when they had cash—things the treaty did not provide. When Indians were expecting income from the popular practice of leasing lands they owned in severalty to prosperous white ranchers and farmers, the traders, in order to stay in business, offered credit until their white lessees paid them—often once a year. Thus sprang up what many Oglalas feel was the downfall of the Pine Ridge economy: *icazopi*, literally 'to make a mark,' derived from the fact that illiterate Oglalas who bought on credit made their marks on the bill of sale.[2]

Earning a Living

The Bureau of Indian Affairs was organized to oversee the federal government's part of the treaty bargain. Most Oglalas believe it has failed for a number of reasons, the essential one being that it has exercised a paternal influence, doing what Indians normally would have done for themselves in earlier days. According to treaty rights, Indians received food, clothing, shelter, and perhaps most important, land to live on. Not only were there few jobs in the early reservation days, there was no need for them. The government provided everything. At Pine Ridge, as well as on other reservations,

> The government agency is used as an extension of the person in many areas of living. It's as if the person has few capabilities of his own when in relation to the government agency. If he has some problem it is not infrequent that he thinks first of going to the government agency before attempting to attack the problem himself. In effect, the relationship is symbiotic but only in some areas, so that it is a focal symbiosis. (Mindell 1967)

Thus businesses at Pine Ridge have been almost nonexistent. Moreover, any enterprising Oglala man or woman who wanted to become an entrepreneur was criticized by fellow tribesmen for "selling out to the white man," for the only way anyone can make a living on the reservation is at the expense of the Indian. Since the establishment of the reservation, particularly after the turn of the century, various businesses have come and gone: hotels, motels, gas stations, cafés, pool halls, drugstores, grocery stores, laundromats, and today even supermarkets. Some large industries have tried to locate on the reservation but have had little success. Since there had never been a need for jobs, there had never been a need for workers. And it has been only over the past twenty years that development has provided regular jobs, particularly the white-collar jobs generated by government programs. According to one respondent:

> There is no economic growth on this reservation
> even though 55 million dollars comes in here every
> year for economic development. I only know of a
> couple of families that have prospered, but their
> businesses don't employ more than one or two
> people. The United States government has a lot of
> background briefs going around that state that In-
> dians should be equal to non-Indians to engage in
> free enterprise, but when someone like our family
> comes along and wants to be capitalistic they
> throw all kinds of roadblocks up, not only the
> United States government but the tribe. I think
> they are trying to perpetuate Indian dependency to
> keep the jobs for the federal employees. I think
> the government wants to keep Indians on the dole.

Not surprisingly, most of the people at Pine Ridge are unemployed. According to one official:

> The 8.2% figure of unemployment on the National
> labor front is minimal compared to the unemploy-
> ment rate on the reservation. According to esti-
> mates given by the BIA in Pine Ridge, the
> September 1980 unemployment figure is close to
> 57% (later estimates place the unemployment
> figure at 65%). The glaring injustice of this astro-
> nomical figure has been camouflaged by an iniq-
> uitous welfare program that breeds dependency,

corrupts integrity, and mercilessly destroys healthy
personal pride.

Of those who have an income, most still earn it by leasing their
precious individually owned land to white tenant ranchers and to
a lesser degree to farmers. Moreover, 67 percent of the Indian
households have a self-reported income of under $3,500 annu-
ally, placing them well below the poverty level.[3]

Indians often must wait a whole year before they are paid
lease money, and during this time they are forced to go to the
stores that give them *icazopi*. If the white traders and grocers are
to extend credit on this scale, they must increase the price of their
goods, often to twice as high as stores fifty or sixty miles away off
the reservation.

Those Oglalas who have a steady income, like those who work
for the Bureau of Indian Affairs, the major provider of jobs,
venture farther away to spend their money. An average Oglala
family living on the south side of the reservation usually drives
into one of a number of small Nebraska towns to buy necessities.
Most families travel within a hundred-mile radius to towns such
as Rushville (twenty-eight miles), Gordon (forty-five miles), or
Chadron (sixty miles). The farther away, the lower the prices,
but also the less the likelihood of getting credit. On the north side
of the reservation families travel to Hot Springs (sixty miles) to
buy groceries or even to do their weekly laundry at the laundro-
mat. On the east side of the Pine Ridge people go to Martin,
South Dakota. The point is that most money, no matter what its
source, is spent off the reservation.

Those establishments closest to the reservation that trade with
Indians cannot survive without extending credit. The most-
frequented town servicing the reservation is White Clay, Nebraska. White Clay, two miles south of Pine Ridge Village, is in
what is sometimes called the "contested" area, land that was
initially established as a buffer zone between the reservation and
local white homesteaders.

White Clay—which has a population of forty-one, of whom 25
percent are reputed to be millionaires—is the major distribution
center for alcoholic beverages near the Pine Ridge reservation. It
is estimated that Indians from Pine Ridge spend $200,000 a
month there on beer and wine, placing White Clay second in

sales only to Omaha, Nebraska's largest city.[4] This figure does not include money spent on the reservation, where, because it is illegal to sell alcohol, a thriving business is conducted by bootleggers. Although it has always been against the law to buy, transport, or sell alcohol at Pine Ridge—a legacy from earlier times when it was a federal crime to sell liquor to an Indian— there has always been an unlimited supply of beer, wine, and whiskey (in that order of preference). It has never been seriously considered that anyone be arrested for violating this law, particularly in a part of the United States where an unusually great number of people historically have been thrown into the local jail for drunkenness as an adolescent rite of passage.

Economically, the average Oglala is faced with traveling long distances and spending less money on food and clothing or traveling a short distance and paying more. Either way Oglalas spend much more money than should be required, but this is in part by choice. The obvious solution is to create a viable reservation economy, but so far no one in tribal or federal government has been able to keep even the most likely projects in operation for any length of time.

This is so not only because the government originally provided all the Oglalas' needs, but because they have never had a work culture or ethic that in any way reflects mainstream American attitudes. There is no history of wage labor or salaried jobs, and there are no cultural conventions associated with work. Thus, when industries such as the moccasin factory or Wright-McGill came to the reservation they had difficulty recruiting and maintaining a work force. People were eager to get jobs, but there was high absenteeism, particularly during the summer when people traveled around on and off the reservation to attend religious and secular celebrations such as Sun Dances or pow-wows and Indian fairs. Finally the companies went to nearby off-reservation towns to recruit non-Indian employees.

There was, however, a different response to employment from males and females. When men, for whatever reason, discontinued their employment with these companies, they simply quit. But women were able to maintain their jobs by agreeing to do their work at home. Men often helped their wives at home lacing moccasins, and so on, but essentially the woman was the one employed. Thus women were more flexible because they could continue working in what was regarded as their "natural" environment, the household, while men could not.

This is still the case today, except for the white-collar jobs that have sprung up on the reservation since the Kennedy administration, particularly during the Johnson administration's War on Poverty. The Pine Ridge reservation has been a recipient of all of the important programs designed to stimulate the economy since then. These have included welfare, aid to dependent children, and community action as well as programs sponsored by the National Endowments to stimulate interest in the arts and the humanities and by the Department of Health, Education, and Welfare to combat problems in public and mental health.

Small Business

At least a few Oglalas have in the recent past attempted to start their own businesses, ranging from cattle ranching and horse breeding to smaller enterprises like general stores, groceries, and arts and crafts outlets. But the general attitude of traditional Oglalas is that people entering the private business sector have sold out to the whites or are somehow exploiting other Oglalas even when these businesses prove that they can support workers and therefore at least minimally improve the economy.

The attitude of the people who start such enterprises is that they get no support from the rest of the Indian people, particularly the tribal council, which stands to receive the greatest benefit, since campaign pledges of local politicians always include increasing employment. A great deal of frustration is felt, particularly by those individuals and families who, after receiving aid from organizations like the Small Business Administration, must rely on final approval from tribal council committees such as public health or zoning boards. The sad fate of many Oglalas who aspire to own and operate their own business, whether a gas station or a café, is that they eventually give up. A successful businesswoman at Pine Ridge commented:

> Most people look at the tribe as a corporate body
> that would help out its members, but instead
> there's a deliberate attempt to thwart growth.
> That's why you see limited economic growth here.
> That's why our people who have the talent and

ability to run their own businesses don't. They get
too bogged down in the bureaucratic bungle of the
bureau.

Growth has diminished since twenty years ago, when a number of relatively stable businesses lined the main street of Pine
Ridge Village. Another woman who had served in various high
administrative positions in the tribe said:

All those original store owners either moved out
or passed away. Now the Pine Ridge city council,
as they call themselves, exists, but they don't try
to help people start these businesses back up.

The likelihood of new growth is questioned:

If a person could start a business, even if they
don't have any financial backing, but they are
starting out with money they already have, or
money they saved up, or have borrowed from their
relatives, they still can't afford the big insurance
that goes with it—to insure the goods they sell.
They also may get harassed, or burned out, or
closed up. So playing around with the white man's
culture—you have to have the bucks to do it, or at
least the backing.

Some fear that businessmen and business women, in fact all
who are in the limelight, are somehow more closely scrutinized
by members of the tribal government. One woman ran a successful special-education program that was well funded by a state
agency and approvingly evaluated by a team of academics after
the first year. Yet one day:

I walked into the tribal offices for some reason,
and there was a monitoring meeting going on. I
walked in just as they were discussing *me*. They
had been discussing me for a whole week and I
didn't know about it. "Who's going to put a bell
on that cat's neck?" That's how they were talking
about me. They didn't have the nerve to come to
me and tell me about it. Instead they were trying
to build each other up to see who would do it. So
they said, "Come in, we want to talk to you."

> What they were concerned about was that I was
> doing something without the authority of the tribal
> council.
>   But I don't need their authority, so I told them
> that they were invading my privacy. I said, "I'm
> not going to stand here and explain anything to
> you." I told them it was none of their business. I
> was operating independently, and I didn't need
> their approval. I don't need their authority or any-
> one's permission for anything. People like that try
> to tear people like me down. Just like a group of
> little kids. If there's an outsider they don't ask
> them to play.

This woman was addressing a tribal council committee made
up entirely of men. It is generally agreed that a man would not be
so aggressive with other men, and chances are that a man,
confronted like this, would agree with the council or give up his
enterprise. According to another professional woman:

> I think men are a lot more prone not to say any-
> thing. If something happens [like this], someone
> will say, "Hey, you're an Indian, and you're not
> the same." Whereas women are more aggressive
> these days, and probably would say something.

As entrepreneurs Oglala women have been at least as successful as Oglala men. The first private corporation on the Pine
Ridge reservation, organized so that those involved could do
business directly with outside agencies rather than relying on the
tribal council to intercede, was started by two women and one
man. Women have operated their own newspapers, laundromats, cafés, gas stations, beauty parlors, and educational programs—in short, the whole range of services available at Pine
Ridge have been run by women as often as by men. But in one
area women have been able to excel, for the dual reason that
their ability is regarded as underscoring their Indianness from
both the traditional and the modern points of view. This area of
expertise is arts and crafts.

Arts and Crafts

Arts and crafts permit women, and to a lesser degree men—

whose labors are confined to featherwork, and recently silver-smithing—to engage in an enterprise that often provides a mea-ger income; but they also serve as a means of expressing rela-tionships and values considered traditional.

Craftwork such as traditional buckskin tanning—almost a dy-ing art—quillwork, beadwork, ribbonwork, and making shawls and quilts, as well as making Indian clothing and costumes for males and females are ways women can gain high status along strictly traditional lines. Although it is possible to sell such items through local trading posts, and in some cases larger chain stores, no Indian woman or man has ever been able to make a very good living at the traditional arts, though some women have made a steady income by manufacturing shawls and quilts, which are popular on the larger American market.

Most of the traditional articles, which include beaded belts, armbands, cuffs, leg bands, headbands, hair strings, breech-clouts, and dresses, are simply too exotic for the larger market or too expensive as tourist items.[5] These are made by Indian women for other Indians, mainly relatives, to wear at secular and reli-gious events regarded as traditional. Thus old kinship ties are still strengthened through exchanges by brothers and sisters or cousins, and these relationships are still highly valued though frequently difficult to express through the institutions introduced by the white man. Some women are known to be proficient beadworkers, and they are often asked to make things for their nieces, nephews, and grandchildren to wear on special occa-sions. Infants when they are christened are usually given beaded moccasins, beaded bonnets, and star quilts. At every major life stage today, something is given to the principals that has some sentimental—and that means traditional—value.

Oglalas constantly fear that the old arts and crafts, like the language, are disappearing. In fact fewer items are being made today, but that is largely because school and other jobs occupy women's time. When the reservation was first established and up through the 1940s, traditional costuming flourished. It is often said that the Lakota people, once they no longer had to hunt for game and retired to the annuity system of the United States government, began beading in great quantity simply because they had the time and the materials to do it. The common joke is that if anything didn't move, an Oglala woman would bead it.

Today, as a result of this florescent period, one still can find beaded book covers, cigarette cases, covers for cigarette lighters, watch fobs, watchbands, sneakers, bow ties, and numerous similar objects. Before 1950 every family had amassed great quantities of beadwork that was worn in the great secular dances such as the *Omaha* dance, for which both men and women decked themselves in traditional costumes replete with heavy beadwork. After that time collectors ravaged the reservation, and the quantity of traditional costuming diminished.

With the advent of schools, churches, and later jobs for women, it was only the older women who were proficient in beadwork and sometimes quillwork. As they began to die off, it appeared that so would the traditional crafts. However, now that schools such as Red Cloud Indian School and Oglala Lakota College have begun offering courses in traditional Lakota arts and crafts, increasing numbers of women and men are taking them up, though for the most part the style of beadwork is somewhat modified and decidedly more "costume" jewelry is made in proportion to the fine accessories that enhance a male or female dancer's apparel. The items now made include earrings, pendants, handbags, change purses, high-top moccasins, belts, and vests, and even skirts, blouses, and dresses for everyday wear.[6]

Oglalas recognize the difference between old-time and modern-day beadwork. In the old days the Lakotas were known to produce exquisite articles rivaled by none. But today larger beads are used, and there is a predominance of loomwork, the white man's innovation, instead of the favored appliqué work known as hump stitch, in which beads were sewn directly to buckskin so they formed arched rows.

Another form of art is the *wicaȟpi šina* 'star quilt.' Although quilts of various kinds have been used on the Lakota reservations since they were established, this particular form features a configuration of eight-pointed stars known in Pennsylvania as the Star of Bethlehem design. There is a strong possibility that quilting techniques and this particular design were taught to Lakota girls when they attended Carlisle Indian School in Carlisle, Pennsylvania, at the end of the nineteenth century.

Until twenty years ago, most people made crazy quilts, pieced together from random bits of cloth. However, over the past two decades there has been a trend toward star quilts made from small pieces of solid and calico print cotton cut into diamond shapes and then sewed together to form designs that feature some special variation on an eight-pointed star. This northern star, as it is sometimes called on the reservations, is also a favorite beadwork design and is particularly important because it echoes geometric patterns that are felt to be traditional because of their relation to older craft techniques.

Star quilts are used whenever people hold celebrations perceived as traditional. Often they are made from the cloth offerings used in *Yuwipi* ceremonies. People suffering from respiratory ailments are told to drape these sacred quilts over their heads to make inhalants more effective. Small star quilts are given as gifts at baby showers. Women spend the whole year making star quilts to be given away at memorial feasts, graduations, confirmations, and marriages. Today it is common to drape the coffin with a star quilt during a wake. One or more star quilts and matching pillows are wrapped and tied around a new tombstone until it is unveiled. Quilt tops are often spread on the ground at large gatherings and systematically given away by the sponsors to their relatives and friends, particularly those who have traveled great distances. In effect the star quilt, though made from raw materials exclusively traded for and now bought from whites, has become the singular piece of craftwork that is the symbol of being Lakota in the modern world. Thus the traditional role of the woman as artist and craftsman is still important because all Oglalas require an abundance of star quilts over their lifetimes.

Today quillwork is highly prized, but few still practice this ancient technique of appliqúe with porcupine quills on buckskin or rawhide. Some of the older women continue to make traditional costume pieces, which underwent a revival in the 1970s, but most modern quillwork is done on accessories for everyday wear: necklaces, watchbands, earrings, and the like. Some old women still decorate pipe stems or make items such as decorations for tipis and old-time costumes that are in great demand by collectors off the reservation.[7]

Oglala women have continued to be involved in sodalities much like the ones they joined before the reservation period. They now form craft guilds called cooperatives, in which they join together to buy certain materials such as beads and buckskin in order to reduce the cost. Co-ops tend to change regularly as people leave one to form or join another, not unlike the way sodalities changed membership in earlier times.

One such co-op run by the tribe encourages women to make traditional craft items, which it sells at Indian powwows and other events. The advantage of these co-ops is that Indian women are guaranteed a ready market for their products and in turn receive abundant materials, sometimes on credit. Thus even poor people can benefit from this program, which is more like the old Oglala idea of barter than like the modern market economy. The co-op acts as an agent, constantly commissioning Indian craftwork and turning the finished articles into immediate profits.

In summary, the reservation provides few work opportunities for the Oglala people. It is possible for some to survive by manufacturing craft items, but despite their popularity few can make a living from this. Most people still obtain the bulk of their income from leasing their lands to white ranchers and farmers. Those who do practice arts and crafts, a domain restricted mostly to women, carry on the Lakota tradition. The work force today is largely underwritten by bureaucratic jobs provided by various government agencies, and even these jobs are held mostly by women. By and large, men and women are elected or appointed to jobs on the tribal council or work for the Bureau of Indian Affairs, the tribe, or the state of South Dakota. Most of the wage workers and entrepreneurs, however, are women.

9   It's the Men Who Are the Chiefs

The Tribal Council

With the demise of the buffalo-hunting economy, the policy making aspects of traditional Oglala political organization fell prey to federal control, rendering self-government largely a myth. In 1934, under Roosevelt's New Deal, attempts were made to place more political and economic control into the hands of the Indians with passage of the Indian Reorganization Act (IRA).[1] This act was drafted to give Indians more control over their destiny—or that was the intent. However, most Oglalas today believe that their fathers and grandfathers were railroaded into agreeing to its conditions and that a majority never did accept it, as happened earlier in the signing of the Sioux benefits bill. Despite this, the IRA was put into effect, and the Oglalas, like other Indian tribes, have since been governed by what was legally incorporated as the Oglala Sioux Tribe. This political New Deal had broad implications for tribal leadership, changing the original system—one governed by warriors and hunters known as *wicašitancan*, today still glossed "chief"—into one governed by a legalistic body modeled straightforwardly after the federal government. The Bureau of Indian Affairs continued its vigilance over the Indian tribes, and the superintendent still wielded incontestable control over the newly designated tribal government. Nevertheless, there was some semblance of self-government, restricted mainly to reservation matters of little consequence to the American citizenry. The emphasis was placed on the structure of the Oglala Sioux Tribe, with little concern for what background tribal leaders needed to be effective administrators. Hence, as in all colonial societies, the old chiefs who had proved themselves as the hunters and warriors of an earlier period became the new politicians, running a bureaucracy with the help of their kin. The most successful were those who could get along with the white man as well as their own people, and many chiefs were appointed by the local superintendents because they would sign important documents that the government required. This procedure gave rise to the derogatory term "paper chief," a leader who served his people most effectively by following the white man's orders.

Today, as a result of the IRA, the area under tribal government includes all of Shannon and Washabaugh counties except land that has passed out of Indian ownership. There are thirty-two members of the council, which includes a president and vice-president (elected reservationwide), a secretary, and a treasurer as well as representatives from the nine districts. Besides district representation, three communities are represented separately on the council—Pine Ridge Village, Red Shirt Table, and Oglala Jr. Of the thirty-two members, five are from Pine Ridge Village.

Council members must be at least twenty-five years old. They are elected for two-year terms, and all terms expire at the same time, leaving very little continuity in programs from one council to the next (article 3, sec. 6, Oglala Sioux tribal constitution; Oglala Sioux Tribe 1935). All tribal members at least twenty-one years old who have lived on the reservation for at least a year are eligible to vote in tribal elections.

The council is required by the tribal constitution to meet at least four times a year, in January, April, July, and October. Actually they meet more frequently owing to the volume of tribal business (Grinnell 1967). The executive committee consists of the president, vice-president, secretary, and treasurer, a "fifth" member (elected from the council, by the council), and the BIA superintendent. This committee meets once a week and carries on tribal business between council meetings. There is considerable controversy over the existence of the executive committee because the tribal president and BIA superintendent are ex officio members.

Members of the tribal council and other tribal officials may be removed by impeachment and two-thirds vote of the council after a proper hearing or if convicted of a felony or any offense in which their honesty is questioned. In either case, automatic forfeiture of office is the result (article 3, secs. 1 and 2, constitution). There is no provision for recall of an official or council member by a vote of the electorate (Grinnell 1967).

An election board of three to six members appointed by the

executive committee is responsible for administering the primary
and general elections. The election board prepares and posts all
ballots and has "absolute power of the final counting of votes,
investigating complaints of illegal voting, and for maintaining
order at the polling place. They must publish the results of the
election no later than two days after the election."[2]

The tribal government exists not so much to make decisions
for the Sioux as to harness resources from the federal government: "Tribal councilmen are elected to 'get something from the
BIA.' . . . The criterion for selection is not that the tribal
councilman can represent them or their opinion but because they
[the electorate] feels a particular person knows how to handle
whites and can 'get something for the Sioux'" (Thomas 1966–67,
3). Thus council members may be competent or incompetent,
responsible or irresponsible—invariably, though, they are marginal to the community and sometimes even personally disliked.

This is also why, though the country Sioux view the tribal
government as "the tribe," they do not see the council as representing them or making decisions for them. The council stands
between the tribal members and the United States government.
The Oglalas have never fully accepted the council, and the
United States government has never accorded it real power or
authority.

The tribal councils powers are delineated in some detail.
Policymaking power of considerable breadth is delegated to it,
but subject to the limitations imposed by the Oglala tribal constitution (Grinnell 1967, 34). Under the tribal constitution the
council has the power to negotiate with federal, state, and local
governments; legislate economic, social, educational, and domestic affairs of the tribe; establish a tribal court; maintain a
law-and-order code; control domestic relations; charter subordinate tribal enterprises; and regulate the appointment of
guardians for minors and mental incompetents (Burnette and
Koster 1974, 184).

The tribal council also has the power to restrict undesirables
from the reservation; assign tribal land to members; employ legal
counsel for the advancement and protection of the tribe; purchase land that becomes available; govern the inheritance of real
and personal property; and execute leases on tribal land. In
addition it may veto any action that threatens to destroy tribal

property; expend tribal funds; advise the secretary of the interior of budget estimates; and regulate tribal elections (Burnette and Koster 1974).

While the list of powers may seem impressive, the fact is that the Oglala tribal government is without real power because the tribal constitution states that all the tribal council's decisions are subject to the approval of the secretary of the interior. The tribal government then, operates in subordination to national law as well as to the provisions of treaties the Oglalas are party to. At the micro level there is no de facto political authority—the United States government is in charge: "It is quite clear that the acts of the tribal authorities are subject to a federal veto, exercised primarily under the authority of the Secretary of the Interior" (Grinnell 1967, 36).

The constitution further states that the superintendent is the representative of the secretary of the interior and as such his approval must be obtained in tribal matters. Although he does not have direct veto power over tribal decisions, he makes recommendations to the secretary of the interior. Thus most day-to-day decisions about Oglala life, such as those having to do with education and relief, are made by BIA personnel. In a larger sense one might say that the tribal government is merely an arm of the BIA, since BIA superintendents maintain almost absolute power over newly elected tribal councils.

Political life at Pine Ridge is characterized by a cleavage between one group seeking to preserve the traditional values and another seeking to adopt the white man's ways. The former, "full bloods," are particularly sensitive to the fact that the contemporary political system is essentially alien to the traditional Oglala culture, and they tend to emphasize the rights of Oglalas as guaranteed by the treaties. The latter group, "mixed bloods," represent a more acculturated view and attempt to solve problems of the reservation within the framework of the 1935 constitution, in terms of non-Indian values. To this group, concern for treaty rights is less important than it is to the full bloods. The terms "full blood" and "mixed blood" are cultural rather than biological designations; that is, they are based not on blood quantum but rather on the group a person identifies with socially and culturally.

The years since 1935 have been turbulent ones at Pine Ridge. Tribal officials have frequently been charged with misuse of funds, nepotism, and acting in non-Indian ways, though no action has ever been taken to change the situation.

During the 1960s Indians began to be more demonstrative. Organizations sprang up to work toward Indian rights. Tribes demonstrated to protect their federal treaty rights and the sources of their livelihood. In some cases they won—but whether they won or lost, other Indians were beginning to stand up for their rights. Whereas earlier Indian groups had essentially followed a nonviolent strategy and the concept of red power had been largely verbal, things were slowly changing. Indian voices were beginning to be heard. Indian political goals were not assimilation and integration—those were the goals of the United States government. What the Indians wanted was the right to their own tribal identities and recognition as sovereign nations.

Women Chiefs

Within this broader historical context we find that one of the effects of the Indian Reorganization Act was to make education available to more women. The New Deal also led to a dramatic change in women's participation in tribal government. According to one woman:

> At the beginning, we [women] didn't know we
> could go to school. When the IRA came about, we
> were told that we could do the same things that
> the men could, so we started to make applications
> and we started to get involved.

Although men were reluctant to admit women to the leadership circle, there was little they could do. She continued:

> The men didn't like it—and sometimes I think
> they still don't like it—when women got elected to
> the council. And it wasn't too hard to do that be-
> cause out in the districts all their relatives helped
> them.

Currently the reservation is divided into nine districts, the last comprising exclusively Pine Ridge Village. Each district has a meetinghouse and is administered by an elected official called the district representative. The district representative sits on the tribal council and serves as an intermediary between the district and the council. However, the real decision making is at the district level, because it is the district that most nearly represents the old *tiyošpaye* formation. Thus nearly everyone is related, people are willing to help out their kin, men or women. The tribal council, though the official representative body instituted by Congress, in effect represents an artificial construct. Since all the people live in the districts, the tribe, in effect, has no people to represent.

During the 1981 run-off election for tribal council representatives, an unusually large number of women ran. Table 2 shows the proportions of women and men running for the tribal council from each district.

It will be interesting to see to what extent women are involved in tribal politics in the future. However, these figures certainly indicate that the tribe is not run by males alone and that, since the reservation was established, increasing numbers of women feel quite confident about gaining leadership roles.[3]

In addition to the district candidates, in 1981 for the first time one of the six candidates for tribal president was a woman— Shirley Plume from Manderson, a community in Wounded Knee district.

Mrs. Plume had been involved in Indian politics for twenty years before deciding to run for tribal president. She had served

Table 2 Proportions of Women and Men Running for Tribal Council

District	Women	Men
White Clay	9	20
Pine Ridge Village	7	30
La Creek	0	4
Porcupine	7	18
Medicine Root	5	17
Pass Creek	3	8
Wounded Knee	4	20
Wakpamni	9	24
Eagle Nest	3	13
Total	47	154

as superintendent of the Standing Rock reservation for six years, after holding a number of positions with the Bureau of Indian Affairs in Oklahoma, in South Dakota, and at Pine Ridge. In one campaign speech she talked about the prejudices and precedents she would have to overcome as a woman:

> These may be the most challenging times that In-
> dian tribes have faced in many years, but I have
> great faith in our Lakota Nation and every con-
> fidence that we will endure. There is a loyal seg-
> ment of our tribe, really the remaining element of
> what once was the Lakota Nation, who choose
> above all to remain steadfast in their identity; who
> have never fully participated in the good times,
> even when our tribe was showered with programs
> and great amounts of money—but they have sur-
> vived, awaiting better times, better leadership and
> opportunities which truly serve their needs and
> purposes. I feel a great affinity for these of my
> relations, in-laws and friends. I hope that I can
> continue to learn real purpose, patience, and true
> Indian perspectives from these the real Lakota
> people on the reservation and combine it with the
> experience and skills that I have accumulated over
> the years for the greater good of our people.
> I enjoyed many wonderful years of help and
> support from a strong and gentle person during my
> life and career, from my late husband, Paul, and I
> learned from him that real accomplishment may
> have to come from what we instill in our children
> and what they accomplish. I call on all my old
> friends, the new friends I hope to make and to my
> relations, to support my candidacy for the office of
> President of the Oglala Sioux Tribe.[4]

Part of the fragmentation on the Pine Ridge reservation arose because the United States government felt a centralized govern-ment would be best. But the Oglalas have no allegiance to the tribal council, except to the extent that temporary alliances with council officials may serve the immediate interests of individuals, because the true allegiance is between kinsmen whose locus of organization is out in the districts.

Although women participate in the tribal council and many

women represent their districts during council meetings, most of their political activity—that is, most decision making that affects people directly—is found in their work in district or community politics.

The community, a less stable entity than the district, closely resembles the hunting bands of the prereservation and early reservation periods. These communities tend to be fissiparous; people move in and out of them situationally. For example, a person dies, leaving a house vacant; new people move in for a while, perhaps until the husband or wife gets employment elsewhere, then they leave the community and someone else moves in. A few families may be lifetime residents, but often entire communities become extinct or combine with others.

Like the districts, each community is run by a president who presides over a membership that in theory comprises all who want to belong. Meetings are held regularly to decide issues that directly affect local families.

Issues include things like deciding how to spend block grants that are awarded to the communities in each district by the tribal council. Money normally is spent on improving roads, buying fertilizer for individual gardens or feed for cattle, repairing fences, and hundreds of other day-to-day needs.

Upon visiting these community meetings one soon finds they are attended mostly by women, who often outnumber the men ten to one. In some communities the meetings are regarded as hen parties by the men, who stay home waiting for the women to bring them news of what went on but seldom attend and exercise their votes. Said one man: "The women make the decisions anyway, and then they let me know what's happening."

Women see other women as being more aggressive than men in politics and more vociferous at meetings at all levels of tribal government. Women are also aware that they are capable of using their femininity when they have to motivate the men: "I think I always considered myself not a bra-burner, because I think that you can use men to your advantage." A woman can pretend to be weak and men will come to her aid. But men cannot timidity lest they be criticized by other men.

When a woman won over a traditional male leader in one recent community election, the men complained that a woman could not be forceful. Yet according to another woman, when the newly elected female president was out picking up wood one

day, "all the men were falling over themselves to help her."
Women do not discuss their strategies in public because males
would be intimidated, but women themselves recognize that they
have the best of both worlds.

Women contribute at all levels of government, holding membership on key committees such as the health board, credit
board, and numerous school boards. Since 1934 they have been
increasingly active in every segment of the tribal bureaucracy,
including law and order and the tribal courts. But women are
perhaps less active and less vocal in those political dramas in
which the tribe issues challenges and debates questions of national import, such as the Black Hills claim.

Regularly the Oglala tribal council, particularly the males, has
found it necessary to take issue over Indian affairs with none
other than the president of the United States and various cabinet
officers. The irony here is that although it is extremely difficult, if
not impossible, to manage the everyday affairs of the reservation—public health, homicide and suicide, poverty, unwanted
pregnancies, jobs, housing, law and order, sanitation, education—it is perfectly acceptable to verbally attack the United
States government over historical issues like the Fort Laramie
treaty. Various Oglala representatives meet regularly with high
government officials over the Black Hills claim. Currently the
tribe is suing the United States, the state of South Dakota, and
several counties for $11 billion.[5]

Council members spend a great deal of money traveling between Pine Ridge and Washington, D.C., for countless meetings
over problems that are never resolved. While the men are engaged in what they perceive to be higher-level politics, it is left
mainly to the women to try to solve the everyday problems for
which there are possible solutions.

Activist Women

One essential way Oglala women, and Indian women in general,
differ from activist women in mainstream America is that Oglala
women are supportive of their men. As one Oglala poet writes:

> So we are standing up next to our men
> We are standing up and taking up the battle.

Here and now
To protect our young so their unborn can
know the freedom
Our Grandparents knew.

The future of our young and unborn is buried
in the past.
We are today who will bring the rebirth of
Spiritualism, dignity and sovereignty.

We are Native American Women.[6]

What makes an Oglala woman militant is that she organizes
with other women to help Oglala men face contemporary issues,
such as land claims and water rights. But some issues are considered more important to women than to men. For example, the
adoption of children, health care, sterilization, and abuse are
seen primarily as women's issues. But along with the men they
fight against the constant erosion of the land base, energy resources development, and multinational corporations that plan
to encroach on Indian land.

Activist women are quite likely to join their men in armed
conflict like that which erupted at Wounded Knee in 1973 on the
Pine Ridge reservation, the site of the original massacre of 1890.
The "occupation," as it is called, was led by men and women
belonging to the radical American Indian Movement (AIM).
AIM was founded in Minneapolis in 1968 as a means of helping
Indians adjust to city life, particularly harassment by local police,
but in 1970 when AIM members first came to Pine Ridge and
tried to organize the young people of the reservation, the older,
traditional Indians were intimidated, and most were critical of
AIM's militant tactics. Yet only two years later the same traditionalists were calling on AIM to help them fight discrimination.
Perhaps the change occurred in part because the traditionalists
were impressed by AIM's takeover of the BIA in the "Trail of
Broken Treaties" demonstration in Washington, D.C., on 3–9
November 1972. (They viewed the demonstration as a major
victory for Indian rights.) Or perhaps it was a last desperate
attempt to be free of what they perceived as a corrupt tribal
president and his supporters and the tribal council form of government. Whatever the reasons, two groups—the older tradi-

tional, reservation Indians and the younger urban, educated Indians—with differing world views but with common goals and a common dislike of colonial power—joined forces.[7]

On 27 February 1973, to dramatize the poverty, corruption, and oppression at Pine Ridge and call the situation to national attention, armed members of the Oglala Sioux tribe and of the American Indian Movement invaded the village of Wounded Knee, South Dakota, site of the 1890 massacre, and took eleven hostages. The United States government responded by sending in hundreds of FBI agents and United States marshals to confront the Indians.

The occupation of Wounded Knee lasted seventy days. The Sioux demanded that the government agree to honor the treaty of 1868 before they would withdraw from the hamlet. The government promised to investigate the charges against the BIA's tribal government and several other AIM grievances. But in the interim two persons were killed and one was paralyzed for life. Wounded Knee hamlet was in shambles, and none of the political issues were resolved.[8]

The American Indian Movement is no longer as popular as it was in the 1970s, but some of its radical ideals have been carried over into other organizations. One such organization in which the Oglalas are active is Women of All Red Nations (WARN), organized in Rapid City, South Dakota, in September 1978. Like other Indian organizations, the women of WARN, representing over thirty Indian nations, address issues that are of concern to all tribal members, not just women. Like men and women of the New Left, these young people tend to identify with what they perceive to be the traditional way of life. Their heroes are people like Agnes Lamont, an old Indian woman whose son was killed by federal marshals during the Wounded Knee occupation.

But what is most significant about activist Lakota women is that they generally do not belong to any organization. AIM and WARN tend to attract young women who are for the most part college-educated. Much of their strategy has been learned in the cities, on college campuses and in urban Indian communities where Indians have been subjected to the same treatment other minorities receive in low-income neighborhoods. But most of the older women who have positions in the tribe, district, or community, or even women who have no particular interest in tribal politics, often spontaneously become active in influencing legislation and in protests about issues that affect the community or the tribe.

Mrs. Lamont as a traditional woman, enjoyed attending Indian celebrations, visiting relatives and friends, and joining in feasts. She was not active at all until her son was killed at the Wounded Knee occupation. After that time she represented traditional people in protests over the Black Hills and gave expert testimony in the courts on and off the reservation. She traveled around the country speaking at Indian rallies and soon became a cause célèbre in her own right.

When the tribe appealed a Black Hills decision in Saint Louis at the Eighth Circuit Court of Appeals, tribal officials scoured the outlying communities for traditional people who would take the eight-hundred-mile bus trip to Saint Louis so their voices could be heard. Almost all the traditionalists were women, and most were grandmothers, who dressed for the occasion in shawls and blankets, mainly because they understood that was how the white people expected them to dress. Before the court sessions they paraded in front of the court carrying signs that stated, "Reagan: Take Your Honkies out of Our Black Hills." Although some young women were present, most of the activists ranged from seventy-five to eighty-six years of age. They gave the appearance of being organized by a group well trained in protest.

Much of the image the Indian women as associated with organized movements stems from the naive way the press reports Indian affairs, both locally and nationally. It should be stressed that most white people in the states of South Dakota and Nebraska not only do not visit the Pine Ridge reservation but often go to extremes to avoid it, especially since the Wounded Knee occupation. Knowledge of what goes on at Pine Ridge thus is largely based on hearsay reports from the surrounding whites. Even those white people who live in the border towns are almost entirely ignorant of Indian culture, since their only contact with Indians is in the course of everyday business. Hence most Indians and whites meet for trade or exchange and credit. The stereotype of the Indian therefore tends to be based on whether he pays his bills and whether he gets drunk. Indian women are not excluded from this image.

1   Zona Fills the Pipe and her granddaughter, Vanessa Shortbull, 1983. Photo by Thomas C. Casey, Jr.

2   Agnes Yellow Boy and Chrisi, 1983. Photo by James Strzok, S.J.

3 Liz Chase Alone and her granddaughter, 1983. Photo by James Strzok, S.J.

4 Rhea Two Bulls, 1983. Photo by James Strzok, S.J.

5 View of the Pine Ridge Reservation near Oglala, South Dakota. Photo by James Strzok, S.J.

6 (*Left*) Wife of Dreaming Bear. Photo 15841, Field Museum of Natural History, Chicago.

7 (*Right*) Mrs. Kills Ree and her grandson, 1945. Photo courtesy of the Heritage Center, Inc.

8 Powwow at Oglala, South Dakota, 1985. Photo by William K. Powers.

12 Naming ceremony at Payabya community, 1984. Photo by
James Strzok, S.J.

13 Annual Sun Dance at Pine Ridge, about 1960. Photo courtesy
of the Heritage Center, Inc.

14 Making *papa* and *tašupe* (jerky and Indian sausage), 1916.
Bates-Foster photo, courtesy of the Heritage Center, Inc.

15 Indian women cooking, about 1940. Photo courtesy of the
Heritage Center, Inc.

16   Making *wasna* (pemmican), 1945. Photo courtesy of
the Heritage Center, Inc.

17   Mr. and Mrs. Clement Sands and Stephen at Spring Creek,
1955. Photo courtesy of the Heritage Center, Inc.

18   Four generations, about 1940. Photo courtesy of the Heritage
Center, Inc.

19   Family outing about 1930. Photo courtesy of the Heritage
Center, Inc.

20 Isaac Crow and family. Photo courtesy of the Heritage Center, Inc.

21 During World War II, Oglala women entered the military. Photo courtesy of the Heritage Center, Inc.

22 Senior prom at Holy Rosary Mission, 1960. Photo courtesy of the Heritage Center, Inc.

23 Girls' basketball team, Holy Rosary Mission, 1930. Photo courtesy of the Heritage Center, Inc.

24 (*Left*) Flappers at Holy Rosary Mission, about 1920. Photo courtesy of the Heritage Center, Inc.

25 (*Right*) Riding around the campground, about 1940. Photo courtesy of the Heritage Center, Inc.

26 Varsity cheerleaders, Holy Rosary Mission, about 1950. Photo courtesy of the Heritage Center, Inc.

27 Etta Youngman, associate judge of the Oglala Sioux tribal court and mother of six, 1983. Photo by Lisa Clifford.

28 Bessie Cornelius, artist and designer, Lakota Studios, Wounded Knee, South Dakota, and mother of six. Photo by Thomas C. Casey, Jr.

29 Emma "Pinky" Iron Plume (*left*), owner of a small business in Manderson, South Dakota, and member of the Shannon County school board. Daughter of Shirley Plume (*right*), member of the Oglala Sioux tribal council, member of the board of trustees of Oglala Lakota College, and mother of three. Photo by Thomas C. Casey, Jr.

30 Judi Cornelius, designer and writer, founder of the *Oglala Nation News*. She is currently a management analyst in Washington, D.C., and mother of two. Photo by William K. Powers.

31   Darlene Shortbull, R.N., supervisor of the Outpatient Department, United States Public Health Hospital, Pine Ridge, South Dakota, and mother of three. Photo by William K. Powers.

32   Lily Shangreaux, director of research and development, American Indian Center, Lincoln, Nebraska, and mother of one.

33   Sadie Janis, housewife and craftswoman. She has spent her entire life on the reservation and is a reservoir of information on Lakota language and culture, which she learned from the old people. Photo by William K. Powers.

34   Nancy and Bill Horn Cloud. Nancy is the daughter of Laura Red Cloud, who was an herbalist. Before her death Laura passed on her knowledge of Lakota medicine to Nancy. Nancy's husband Bill is a well-known singer and has made a number of recordings that are popular both on and off the reservation. They have raised three children and numerous grandchildren. Photo by William K. Powers.

35   Zona Fills the Pipe. Zona graduated from Flandreau Indian School in 1929. Before her retirement she was director of the Red Cloud Arts and Crafts Cooperative. She is the mother of two and has also raised a number of foster children. She is active in church and community affairs and is well known and respected both on and off the reservation. Photo by William K. Powers.

Another example of the media's naiveté regarding Indians occurred in the summer of 1980 when a meeting was held at Pine Ridge about the Black Hills claim. A local white stringer for Associated Press filed a story in which he described a seventy-five-year-old woman who attended the meeting:

> Among the aged militants at the Pine Ridge meeting Friday was Zona Fills the Pipe. She stood quietly in a neat cotton dress, her long silver hair braided down her back, but her brown eyes snapped when she talked about the proposed settlement.
> And she told friends she would make a sign to carry saying "The Black Hills are not for sale."[9]

The article was published in a local paper, to the surprise of the "aged militant," who in fact spent most of her time at Pine Ridge teaching young people beadwork and making home visits to women on welfare to help them manage their budgets. It was a great embarrassment to her, so she went to Legal Services and had an attorney write a letter to the newspaper stating that she had been falsely accused of being a miliant and that the story was libelous. The point here is that this woman, like most Oglala women at Pine Ridge, was not part of an organization. However, she was able and willing to participate in demonstrations over matters that affected her tribe and community.

In a similar vein, when the best-selling novel *Hanta Yo* was published in 1979 it met outrage from the Indian community because it depicted Indian men and women in a way they considered unfair and in fact obscene. One woman, Hildegarde Catches, also known as Red Warbonnet Woman, reacted strongly against the novel, particularly its portrayal of Indian women. She told me:

> Growing up here on Pine Ridge reservation, I believe that I know what Lakota life and culture is. I have a strong faith in Indian religion and the Indian people. My Lakota values are my strength today for everyday living. Without those values, life's frustrations would destroy me.

On the basis of her belief that the novel had defamed her people, she sued the author, the publisher, a television producer, and the network (who were involved in a proposed television miniseries adaptation) for $2 million. Although the suit was thrown out of court on a technicality, the miniseries was canceled temporarily, partly on the strength of her convictions and actions.[10]

Law and Order

In the traditional past, law and order was maintained by warrior societies and the *akicita*, particularly when bands came together to hunt buffalo in the summer and participate in the Sun Dance. The major occupation of the *akicita* was to prevent enthusiastic young men from charging the buffalo herds prematurely and thus stampeding them before the rest of the hunters were assembled. Anyone who broke rank and thus diminished the possibility of killing many buffalo was severely dealt with. The *akicita* had the power to make judgments against offenders, going so far as to punish them by slashing their tipis, destroying their weapons, or even killing them.

A kind of retributive law also existed at the level of the smaller hunting bands. Persons convicted of theft or adultery were dealt with by both male and female members of the victim's family in what was sometimes a long-lasting feud.

Today, particularly with access to education made possible by the New Deal, women play a remarkable part in the judicial process at Pine Ridge. In fact there were periods in the 1970s when the Oglala Sioux tribal court was administered exclusively by women.

In law enforcement, authority is divided between the federal and the tribal governments. The jurisdiction of the federal court extends to ten major crimes defined by national law, which include murder, manslaughter, rape, assault with a deadly weapon, arson, burglary, larceny, robbery, incest, and assault with intent to kill. In such cases tribal jurisdiction is expressly denied. In addition federal courts have exclusive jurisdiction in cases involving counterfeiting, draft evasion, smuggling, and the like. Furthermore, the federal courts have exclusive jurisdiction in cases involving violation of statutes for the special protection of Indians (Grinnell 1967, 59).

The tribal council determines the organization of the tribal courts, the qualifications and tenure of judges, and other matters pertaining to judicial functions. No legal training is needed to be a judge or lawyer in the tribal court.

Many Oglalas believe that under white control law enforcement has deteriorated from a sound functional system where the morality of the tribe was preserved by public opinion to a complex maze of technicalities. The present system, like other tribal institutions, represents Anglo-American concepts and often conflicts with traditional Oglala practices. The critics are essentially suspicious and resentful toward the tribal law and the courts under the 1935 constitution, since these laws clearly place the individual Oglala in conflict with his heritage. This remains true even though the officials administering justice are Oglalas themselves.

The Oglala tribal constitution has serious omissions in terms of protecting the people's rights. For example, there is no bill of rights. Apparently those who drafted the constitution did not recognize the need for safeguarding individual rights against the actions of tribal authorities.

In addition there are no conflict of interest laws for tribal officials who are suddenly dealing in millions of dollars; no laws to hold officials accountable to either the federal government or tribal constituents; no laws to keep tribal elections honest; no laws prohibiting use of federal funds to reelect incumbents; and no laws to provide for jurisdiction of tribal courts over tribal officials who may have exceeded their authority. This total lack of protective laws placed every Indian at the mercy of any elected officials unscrupulous enough to take advantage of their own people. Once in office, dishonorable officials could corrupt elections, bribe voters, and coerce people dependent on them for jobs into voting them into office again and again.

Though Pine Ridge is a federal reservation and jurisdiction over the ten most serious crimes is under the control of the Federal Bureau of Investigation, most everyday ajudication is handled by the chief judge and associate judges and revolves around domestic cases, drunkenness, disorderly conduct, and child custody. Other cases involving juveniles are handled by the juvenile judge. Plaintiffs and defendants may be represented by lawyers, of whom some have been trained at law school and others have no formal training but often have an uncanny ability

to cogently argue the facts of each case. Since the judges themselves are frequently not formally trained, there is a belief that
some cases are better argued by local lawyers without training
than by those who have law degrees.

Judges and lawyers are assessed by their ability to understand
the traditional background to some of the crimes, an understanding few white lawyers possess. Many of the cases, for example,
require some knowledge of traditional Lakota culture in order to
be properly argued. The following dialogue comes from the
observations of an anthropologist who visited the Pine Ridge
reservation at the turn of the century and witnessed the tribal
court in operation. In one case where a woman was accused of
beating another over the head with a pail, the following exchange
occurred:

> JUDGE: "Did you beat this woman over the head with a
> water pail?"
> STANDING WOMAN: "I did."
> JUDGE: "Why?"
> STANDING WOMAN: "She came around making a fuss. I
> told her to go away, to leave me alone. She con-
> tinued until I beat her over the head with the water
> pail."
> JUDGE: "Are you living with the husband of this
> woman?"
> STANDING WOMAN: "Yes."
> JUDGE: "Why?"
> STANDING WOMAN: "She had a good man who worked
> hard, but she was always nagging. I am a good
> woman and work hard; I needed a good man so I
> took him into my house. Then this woman came
> around making a disturbance, so I beat her over the
> head with a water pail."

> There was a deliberate pause then a second judge
> asked: "Standing Woman, did you have a previous hus-
> band?"

> STANDING WOMAN: "Yes."
> JUDGE: "Where is he?"
> STANDING WOMAN: "He was lazy, no good, quarrelsome,
> so I ran him away."
> JUDGE: "Where did he go?"

STANDING WOMAN: "To live with this woman," pointing
to the one with the bandaged head.

The four judges wen into a huddle . . . the two men
were brought in. . . . The four stood in a row and after
all agreeing that they were content with their new
arrangements, the judges again went into consultation.
After lecturing the four culprits and admonishing them
to live in peace, the judges entered into the agency record two divorces and two marriages. (Wissler 1938, 131)

People generally agree that women make good judges because they are accustomed to making unpopular decisions with
their children. Not only do they make these decisions, they stick
to them. It is believed that men strive for consensus and are likely
to change their minds if they can find a sense of agreement among
their fellows.

One Oglala woman who was a judge and had served in other
important tribal jobs, including the tribal council, explained how
she got into politics and law:

They needed someone who could make decisions.
Nobody cared if I was a woman. In fact, I went to
Washington and I was spokesman for the group of
us. I appeared before congressional committees to
obtain funds for tribal projects, and I met with
senators and congressmen. But I would give it up
to stay home, because that's where a woman has
her real responsibility. It's the men who are the
chiefs.

Women who are judges are also outspoken about the conditions at Pine Ridge and about what they believe are the greatest
problems facing the Indian today. According to one female
judge:

The people who hurt most on the reservation are
the young people, the children, because they suffer
the results of their parents, the adults, who are so
involved in their jobs or no jobs, and who are
under state welfare or receiving some title assistance or aid, or who lose control of their home because of alcoholism. These are the most severe
problems.

Although some tribal politicians believe liquor should be sold on the reservation so its sale can be controlled and so the revenue it produces can support tribal programs, the same judge said:

> For several years they have had a law covering liquor violation. It stems from way back, and as far as the reservation is concerned it's still a violation if anybody has liquor. My opinion of the whole thing is this. In my experience if a non-Indian is arrested with liquor on the reservation, he is automatically transferred to Fall River County. But the state does not honor *our* laws, our liquor violation law. So when they go to court the case is dismissed because they don't honor our laws, so there is a conflict there. If an Indian is caught with liquor on the reservation the judge would have to enforce the law. As a mother and a member of the tribe, I'm concerned. Everywhere you go, to White Clay or Rushville, you can go to a bar, sit there, and drink openly. Now if these Indian people had a place they could go and drink openly—not behind a barn or in a ditch and drink up all the liquor they had—if they had some place they could walk in, where nobody would bother them, without looking behind them for a cop, their attitude, their behavior would have to change.
>
> Another thing, we have to have some kind of institute to detox people, for treatment. We have to have these types of institutions to help those who are already sick. A lot of our people are sick right now. They're not drunks, their minds are destroyed mentally by the alcohol. It's just a merry-go-round for them and they are the ones who are in jail all the time.

That alcohol plays a significant part in serious crimes and accidents at Pine Ridge cannot be denied. For example, in 1981, 86 percent of all accidental killings were alcohol related. Of 125 natural deaths recorded between 1977 and 1980, 99 involved alcohol. According to the Oglala Sioux Insurance Program Report, during this same period, eighteen homicides and five suicides were caused by people's drinking excessively. Alcohol-related deaths exceeded those caused by cardiac arrest, cancer, and pure accident. Furthermore, 100 percent of the cases of assault and battery against women involved drunken men, and 50 percent of staff absenteeism in the schools was attributed to drinking. Of all persons arrested in Sheridan County, Nebraska, just south of the reservation line, 28 percent were Indians, and 53 percent of these committed crimes that were alcohol related. Finally, over 90 percent of all cases involving physical abuse, neglect, sexual assault, maternal neglect, and family abandonment were caused by alcohol.[11]

Although there is some disagreement over just what the most serious crimes are, all concur that two issues must be resolved. The first is who controls the police force—the tribe or the Bureau of Indian Affairs. The second is who has jurisdiction over Indians and non-Indians on the reservation and in the state of South Dakota.

Both the tribe and the Bureau of Indian Affairs have had an opportunity to run the law-and-order operation, and this includes hiring and training police officers, establishing police board reviews, and forming a police commission. The Oglalas face all the problems confronting any police force anywhere in the United States. But what is distinctive about Pine Ridge is that the kinship rules also affect matters of law and order. A policeman is not likely to arrest someone to whom he is related. On the other hand, when outside policemen are employed they are apt to cause problems, particularly if they are members of other tribes or non-Indians. As with any police force anywhere, complaints are made against the Pine Ridge police—they are never around when you want them, they are untrained and corrupt. But the distinctive problem centers on just who the police have jurisdiction over and to what extent the rules that govern the state of South Dakota also cover the reservation. In particular, if an Indian breaks a law off the reservation, he can be arrested by state or local law enforcement officers. But if a white man breaks a law at Pine Ridge, technically the Oglala police are powerless. Occasionally whites are incarcerated because, owing to "sunburn," the local officers cannot determine the offenders' race, but normally the job of dealing with non-Indian offenders on the reservation is the business of state, local, or federal agents.

The problem of law and order has not been fully worked out, but the Oglalas agree that one of the major reasons the criminal justice system does not work on the reservation is that it is based on ideas relevant to Euramerican culture but not traditional Lakota culture, where kinship still takes precedence over bureaucracy.

These problems are not likely to be resolved in a place where there is constant need to interpret not one law of the land, but a mixture of treaty, federal, state, and local reservation laws. It should be emphasized again that women participate fully in the judicial system and are regarded as equal, if not superior, to men in evaluating and pronouncing judgment in most cases.

10 Hard Times

Sickness and Health

The Oglalas continue to distinguish between sickness perceived to be common before the white man's arrival, called "Indian sickness," and that brought by the white man, called "white man's sickness." Generally, medicine men cure the former, physicians the latter, though today physicians often try to collaborate with medicine men, mainly by permitting them to conduct ceremonies at patients' bedsides. At the same time, a few medicine men have been attempting to treat, through ritual curing, diabetes and cancer that have been diagnosed by physicians but deemed incurable or treatable only by a long-range program.

Partly as a provision of the Fort Laramie treaty, which placed the health, education, and welfare of the Oglalas in the hands of the United States government, the government has overseen Indian health since the establishment of the reservation. The first physicians, including Dr. Charles A. Eastman, a Santee, worked at Pine Ridge out of the farm districts, where nurses were also assigned. Physicians also doubled as agents or schoolteachers. In 1930 the Bureau of Indian Affairs built a hospital on the north ridge of Pine Ridge Village, and in 1955 the hospital came under the jurisdiction of United States Public Health Service, Division of Indian Health. The hospital was expanded in 1959 and now has fifty-eight beds, with seven physicians, thirty-four nurses,[1] and miscellaneous staff members including a dentist. In 1965 a community mental health program was initiated, and for a time there was a resident psychiatrist.

There are alternatives to the Public Health hospital, such as the Veterans Administration hospital in nearby Hot Springs and numerous private physicians and hospitals off the reservation. There are no private practitioners on the reservation, and surgery is usually performed by contracted physicians at off-reservation hospitals.

The Public Health hospital is in many ways the hub of activity at Pine Ridge. It is where children are born and people die, and it is essential to know what is going on at the hospital on any given day to fully understand what is happening on the reservation at large.

Although the number of admissions has generally declined because surgical cases are sent to other hospitals, the out-patient clinic, which is open twenty-four hours a day, has had a dramatic increase, reaching thirty-thousand patients in some years. Most of the patients are women and children, and a well-baby clinic and a prenatal clinic for expectant mothers have decreased infant mortality over the years (Maynard and Twiss 1970, 106).

The most common illnesses treated today are arthritis, diabetes, and heart trouble; there has been a sharp decline in impetigo and in tuberculosis and other serious diseases owing to improved medical and sanitation programs. It appears that the greatest amount of disability on the reservation is found among full-blood males, mixed-blood males, and full-blood females in descending order. Mixed-blood females and non-Indian males[2] tie for next to last, and non-Indian females exhibit the least physical disability treated at the Public Health hospital (Maynard and Twiss 1970, 107). Of course the distinction between "full blood" and "mixed blood" is never clear. Often an Indian-sounding or non-Indian-sounding surname is the only criterion considered. Generally speaking, Indians on the reservation have twice as many complaints as non-Indians about physical disorders, but the statistics do not differentiate between types of illness—for example, somatic as opposed to psychosomatic disorders. It would be useful to know, because most full bloods suffering from psychosomatic disorders would be likely to consult a medicine man rather than a public health physician, and this reemphasizes that health and illness are not absolute categories, cross-culturally speaking, and that hard statistics do not tell us much about people's attitudes toward well-being.

Clearly, Oglala attitudes toward treatment at the Public Health hospital have changed little over time. A large number of people attend clinics, and most agree that the hospital could reduce the time they wait. This problem has been partly alleviated by clinics out in the districts and by field health nurses who travel about the districts to give postoperative care.

Most feel that physicians at the hospital are second-rate. This stems from the unfortunate historical fact, associated with public health not only on reservations but wherever these facilities exist, that originally doctors performed tours of duty at Public Health Service hospitals in lieu of military service. Similarly today, young physicians may recieve government loans for medical school that can be paid back by performing public health services, usually for two years. The net effect is that the Public Health Service doctors are young, in a society that equates wisdom with age, and they are perceived as beginners, if not students. The Indian people have always held the opinion that these doctors are at the hospital to learn on Indians until they become skillful enough to work with whites, at which time they return home to a more lucrative practice.

The physicians, on the other hand, mostly men, serve such short terms of duty that they never really get to know the people they treat. Often there is a language barrier, and usually a culture barrier that, along with the unpredictable Plains environment, is strange and frustrating to physicians who generally come from East or West Coast cities.

A general mistrust of the physicians leads to a strained doctor/patient relationship. Whereas off the reservation most physicians are treated with great deference and respect, at Pine Ridge they are treated as second-class citizens, if not rank amateurs. They are regarded as youngsters who are there because the treaty requires it and because they can use Indian patients to learn how to practice medicine.[3]

In such a situation, exacerbated because medical help often is impeded by irate patients, who have even gone so far as to attack physicians, Indian nurses—particularly those born at Pine Ridge who speak Lakota—are the most valuable assets to the entire Public Health program. The problem, however, is that most nurses are white, and according to one Indian nurse: "White nurses and Indian nurses hassle each other. And they hassle the aides, and even the doctors. Most of the aides and LPNs are Indian, and when a white nurse is on duty, most of them don't want to take orders from them." Similarly, when a white nurse was frightened by two drunken Indian males and demanded better security, she was told by those in charge that they couldn't help her being white; it would not have happened to an Indian nurse.[4]

In recent years even physicians who enjoyed their work at

Pine Ridge have left the reservation because of these adverse conditions, which the Public Health Service is incapable of ameliorating. One doctor was shot at while he jogged around the compound where the physicians live, and others left suffering from what is generally called Pine Ridge "burnout," a sudden overwhelming feeling that the bureaucracy has such a stranglehold on the Indian people that there will never be a sense of normality there. Then general uncontrollable frustration sets in.

But the Indian nurses for the most part stay on and are useful in training each new cadre of doctors as they arrive to begin their tour of duty. But mostly the nurses are important in reducing fear and anxiety in patients, particularly the traditional Indians, who may never have been in a hospital and find the entire experience alarming.

But such reliance on the Indian nursing staff often puts these women in an uncomfortable position. They must use enough strategy not to threaten the new physicians, who feel some insecurity, not knowing the people and their language. On the other hand, they must also deal with Oglala males who are working in subordinate positions and must defer to the nurses' judgment even though "women aren't supposed to boss men around." According to one Indian nurse:

> When I was pregnant the janitors were always
> there to roll up the bedding and move patients for
> men, and I don't think they felt bad because they
> are the janitors and I am the nurse, because I
> think in that type of situation we are all equal. But
> I think that a lot of the maintenance crew have re-
> sented the fact that I can call down and say get up
> here and fix this or that, because it's not equal
> terms in that situation. Maybe I won't be well
> liked, but I feel like that is my position and I
> should be telling them what to do.

Furthermore:

> I would like to change a few things if I could just
> get in a better position, and then I get scared be-
> cause I think maybe when I get to a higher posi-
> tion I won't do such a good job, and being Indian
> maybe I would have to do a better job—because

of who I am. And it's my husband who pushes me
and says I can do it. Even if I don't—he knows I
can.

The Oglala nurse, who is also traditional, has difficulty dealing with other Oglala women, particularly activists who charge
the Public Health physicians with sterilizing young women either
without their permission or without their fully understanding the
consequences. This is highly unlikely, since it is illegal to sterilize
a woman at the time of delivery even if she requests it before
being admitted to the hospital. She must be discharged, then wait
four to six weeks and be readmitted for the procedure, a practice
that, while no doubt a relief to some, is annoying to others since it
requires an additional surgical procedure.

Another source of frustration in dealing with activist women
springs from the rhetoric of young AIM members who mistakenly believe there was no prenatal care in "the old days."[5] Thus
they try to discourage pregnant women from receiving prenatal
care because "real" Indians did not require any.

Although there is no empirical evidence that sterilization is
going on (the population has increased by 50 percent in ten
years) and though stillbirths are increasing owing to rejection of
prenatal care, the Indian nurse must use her traditional background both to alleviate patients' pain and to combat the charges
of activists who, though few in number, cry out for a return to the
old way of life.

Sometimes being a traditional woman causes frustration despite the training of one's profession. One nurse who was pregnant wanted her husband present at the delivery, but tradition
suggested she might have done something to "mark" her baby;
thus she was afraid to have him there lest he see a deformed
child. She told me:

> Talk about tradition—we had a baby here in the
> hospital that had a cleft palate. And I avoided
> looking at him for a long time because they tell
> you not to look at things like that. And I never
> did look at it. Then one day I heard the baby
> crying, and I walked in. I saw the cleft palate and
> I was so taken back and frightened and I couldn't
> forget that baby. And that was my biggest worry

when I was pregnant. I guess that's why I kicked
my husband out of the delivery room.

The Compound

With the exception of the Indian nurses who live at Pine Ridge,
all the doctors and nurses stay in what is called the compound, a
cluster of single-family ranch-style homes within walking distance of the hospital. This is convenient in that doctors on call
can quickly get to the hospital for emergencies, but the convenience is overshadowed by the doctors' isolation from the rest of
the reservation. Occasionally some visit the country to see sick
people, but generally their only association with Indians is in the
context of the hospital.

This detachment also makes it harder for Indians to get to
know the doctors and reinforces the accusation that the physicians are not really interested in the Indians except as a stepping-
stone in their careers. Although there is some socialization between Indians and whites at parties and picnics in the compound,
it is only a select few Indians who are invited, and most, though
not all, either are employed at the hospital or work in some area
of responsibility. Thus the compound, through no conscious
effort by the physicians, serves as the center for what may be
regarded as elitist activities on the reservation.

But there is a great deal to learn about Indian health on the
reservation and to some extent the Indians' accusation that the
white doctors are there only to study them and get practice is
borne out, though for different reasons. For example, to attract
young doctors to the Pine Ridge staff, resident physicians ac-
tively recruit. Pine Ridge is not the easiest place to staff because
of its reputation as the most volatile reservation in the country,
which is well known in Public Health circles. One of the drawing
cards, however, which partly compensates for what some doctors
see as a real risk to their lives, is that at Pine Ridge one can treat a
host of diseases not found in the average urban or suburban
clinic. These include various forms of tuberculosis, impetigo,
and advanced cirrhosis of the liver as well as more common
illnesses and conditions requiring immediate medical attention,
such as broken bones, gunshot wounds, stab wounds, and of
course childbirth.

The advantage to the Indian patients is that most doctors curious enough to serve in Public Health at Pine Ridge, with all its risks, have a high degree of commitment to people badly in need of good medical care. However, the almost forced detachment created by the conditions of the compound and the need for doctors to attend patients nearly all their working hours makes it impossible to quash rampant myths about the white physicians' lack of interest and expertise.

Another problem is that if medical doctors are not experimenting on Indian people, nearly everybody else is. At almost any time one can find a host of medical, psychological, psychiatric, educational, and social work experts conducting some kind of study of the reservation population, using the hospital as their headquarters. Every new bureaucratic plan dealing with juvenile delinquency, alcoholism, teenage pregnancy, drug abuse, or battered women can be tested at Pine Ridge and usually is. Every type of service is made available to the Oglalas, including group psychotherapy, alcoholism counseling, community development—a list that goes on and on and neatly mirrors all current programs being run in every major city of the United States. The problem is that hardly any program tried out at Pine Ridge has any relevance to the people there, traditional or modern.

Take mental health. The program at the Pine Ridge hospital requires a certain faith in Euramerican notions about mental health and illness. Not the least of this faith is the assumption that a relationship, particularly a talking relationship, between a psychiatrist and a patient can lead to the cure of such presumed incapacities as acute depression, personality disorders, character disorders, schizophrenia, and various psychoneurotic disorders. It is also assumed that such meetings between doctors and patients, and the records of these meetings, are kept confidential. But at Pine Ridge, particularly with the hospital serving as the nexus for all important gossip, it is impossible to maintain confidentiality about any kind of disorder. As one woman said:

> Those who are having mental health problems are really out of luck. There is no place for them to go. They won't go to the Public Health hospital here because if they did that they would hear

everything they told the doctors on the street corner in the morning. The only thing to do is to refer them to outside psychiatrists.

Physicians in staff meetings also talk freely about their Indian
nurses and aides, often in condescending ways, without giving
thought that word will get back to the subjects of discussion and
be considered an assault on their character. For example, during
one staff meeting the name of an Indian aide was brought up.
Doctors recommended that she be admonished because every
time there was a powwow going on she called in sick. The
physicians concluded that though she was Indian and a good
nurse's aide, she would have to be reprimanded. One suggested
that if she continued to be absent she should be fired. Unfortu-
nately no one thought to simply set up a schedule at the hospital
so that white nurses, who were generally not interested in powwows, could work when Indian nurses wanted free time. This
could easily have been worked out, because everyone knew in
advance just when Indian events were going to be held.

Indian people are very much aware that they are constantly
being studied, and while some criticize the various federal and
state agencies, others blame the Indians who participate in these
programs. According to one older woman:

> I get offended because I feel that Indians who get
> involved in the study of Indians just use it as a cop
> out—an excuse. I really don't trust their motives. I
> don't trust all of them anyway. I think very few of
> them are really looking to see why we behave the
> way we do.

For example, while federal and state agencies are studying
how to alleviate the problems of school dropouts, young traditional Indians are telling the experts that Oglala people do not
like to send their children to schools that militate against Lakota
culture. According to this same woman:

> I hear Indians saying that they don't want to send
> their children to school because they love them.
> They say that if their children go to school they
> will be severely disciplined by white teachers, or
> because they value their children too much, but I

really don't trust their motives. It's just part of the game of playing Indian. We would never come up with these answers if the government didn't send people out here to solve our problems.

Many of the accusations against the physicians and the agencies are a continuation of what this woman calls "playing Indian"—that is, inventing a life-style supposedly based on traditional life to explain why Indians do not participate in white American culture.

For example, a number of rumors deal with teenage pregnancies and the abandonment of babies. One tells of a thirteen-year-old girl carrying a tiny baby who walked into the state welfare office and wanted to exchange the baby for money because she thought the welfare office provided this "service." Another story relates how a teenage girl who had just obtained her driver's license wanted to trade her newborn baby for a Chrysler. An Oglala woman hearing the story quipped: "Automatic or standard shift?" suggesting that such stories were rampant on the reservation. But at least some of the stories are true. According to one woman:

> When I was young and got married, I never heard of anyone giving up their children, and I don't personally know of anybody who did. But now I hear of it all the time.

Upon being asked why it happens, she said:

> I think that many times they just give up their kids because they just don't want the responsibility. The way we were taught by our own parents and by our churches was that we were completely and totally responsible for our children, and I think putting this responsibility on unstable or unmarried young people is hard. Maybe they're married, maybe divorced, but it's no different than any other society. On TV this morning, I just caught snatches of it, it was children of divorced parents and how they were adapting to a whole new way of life and going to a school and realizing that they are probably 30 or 40 percent of the school. They are children of divorced parents who are living

either with a single parent or a state parent. And
their natural parent somewhere else may be with a
complete family, so I think it's just easier all way
round to just give up the children. The social service department here makes it easy because they
are involved in the welfare of the child, and any
day anyone can go in there and say this child is
sorely neglected and should be taken from the
mother. I think that in the white society too many
young mothers are intimidated by their children.

The young traditionalists who claim that the physicians at the
Public Health hospital are operating a wholesale sterilization
program do not distinguish between surgical sterilization and
birth control in general. Most women do not believe that sterilization takes place. According to one:

I think the doctors would perform it if the woman
wanted it. But this wholesale sterilization that I
hear some of those radicals talking about, I just
don't believe it. If there is so much going on, how
come there are so many children being born?

Public Health Service nurses who have the most contact with
pregnancies generally agree that women between thirteen and
twenty-eight are having the most babies (South Dakota Department of Health 1970–78), and that this is the age range where one
also finds the highest incidence of drinking. It is this generation
that sees itself as somehow returning to another era. According
to one woman:

Yes, I think that though they say they're going
back to the old ways, they—like their parents—
don't really know what that's all about. It's mainly
the girls and women who are not doing very much
but running around and drinking that want to be
traditional, and they don't really know what that
means; they're not really very realistic about
things.

But working women agree that it is possible to maintain a
balance between being Indian and living in a white man's world.

I think that people are more frustrated these days,
and people really don't know what they want to

be. They ask themselves, Are they going to be Indian or are they going to be white? Or do they fall
somewhere in between? I think that I am lucky because I grew up in a family that was kind of middle of the road. We didn't lean over to be Indian,
but we also didn't lean over to be white.

But you have to know who you are, and I think
that's what's missing. It's really too bad for those
Indians who don't know who they are. I feel that
I'm just as good as any white person, and I also
feel that I'm as good as any other Indian. But I
don't think that most people here have that kind
of confidence.

Unwanted children also lead to programs promoting adoption. Although there are strong negative values associated with
having children out of wedlock (children of couples who cohabit
in what is considered to be Indian-style marriage are not included
in this category) or too soon, before girls are out of high school,
once a pregnancy and birth occurs in a family the baby, whether
there is a willing father or not, is generally adopted by the
mother's family with little stigma. One woman brought her
daughter's baby into her own family because:

We knew who the father was, but his father
thought the baby would be better off with us.
They knew we worked hard and were better off
than he and his son were, and we would just do a
better job of taking care of the child.

Active young traditionalists have voiced concern over the
adoption of Oglala children, believing they should not be
adopted off the reservation. According to one woman:

There is an adoption agency and right now there is
a group of women in Pine Ridge, I don't know
what they call their program, but they take unwanted children and care for them. And they are
trying to prevent all adoptions off the reservation.
They say that people have no right to adopt children off the reservation, so their program is
geared to keeping them here.

But not all women are certain Indian children might not have a
better chance if adopted by white families. According to one:

Well, we were involved in a situation like that. We
have a doctor friend, he and his wife, she was
white, and the adoption agency just wouldn't deal
with him. This was twenty years ago. So we told
him we would look for a baby for him, so he came
home here. We found out there was a baby up for
adoption on another reservation. We told the doctor, and the doctor talked to a judge here on the
reservation and to the parents of the baby. The
guardian was a white woman, and they talked to
her and got it all squared away with the court and
the parents, and the baby was given to them. He is
now twenty-one years old and a graduate of one of
the large eastern universities, but he was taken
from a shack on the reservation terribly ill, left in
the hospital five months. At fifteen months he was
maybe a pound or two over his birthweight, so his
foster mother took him and said she would keep
him until he was found some parents, and this doctor got him.

Many are concerned over where sex education should be
taught, but the answer is not so easily split along traditional or
modern lines. One modern woman believes most people on the
reservation equate sex education with birth control, and she
doubts that any young people know very much about sex:

I don't think it's taught at the schools to that extent. I have a friend who is a nurse, and I ask her
if the kids come in and ask her anything, and she
says yes they do. Young girls come in and they do
ask her if there is such a thing, can we get the pill,
and she says, not from me. You have to discuss it
with your mother and a doctor. Then maybe the
doctor will allow me to dispense them. She lets
them know it's available.

Planned Parenthood will provide birth control pills, but the girls
must see a doctor first:

She could go to the doctor very easily, but I
understand at Public Health the doctor will not
prescribe them without the parents' consent. One
friend of mine, that was a doctor here, he's gone

now, said he met a few parents who said, oh yes,
give them to them, I don't want any grandchildren
coming unless she's married. Others are real angry
at the school system because they feel they
shouldn't be teaching them this because of morals.

Upon being asked about male sterlization, most respondents
expressed puzzlement, and one commented:

I have never heard of any such cases. Here on the
reservation it's so "macho." It's the women who
have it done.

Battered Women

Despite any ideology of complementarity between the sexes, the
Pine Ridge reservation has not escaped a concern of national
import: the abusive treatment of women. Complementarity does
add a particular dimension at Pine Ridge, however, that has not
been a major concern among white and black Americans, and
that is the abusive treatment of women by other women—frequently aggravated by the presence of a man—and to a lesser
degree the abuse of men by women.[6] Pine Ridge men are tough,
and so are Pine Ridge women.

Oglala women generally believe that the abuse of females is
decidedly a male problem, stemming from the Oglala male's
emasculation by the reservation system: no job, no prospects for
one, and no possibility of achieving dignity in a white culture.
Already frustrated by his own impotence, a man finds his rage
magnified by drinking. It is agreed that 100 percent of cases of
abuse, whether to women, children, or men are alcohol related.

Alcoholism, though generally attributed more to males, is
empirically as bad or perhaps worse among females, if statistics
on death from cirrhosis of the liver are any guide. From the late
1960s throughout the 1970s more white males and females than
Indians died of this alcohol-related problem in the state of South
Dakota. Of the Indians, however, more females than males died
of it.

Although these statistics alone do not necessarily tell us about
drinking patterns of Oglala males and females, there is no question that women drink as frequently as males and as fast. They

are also thrown into jail for drunkenness and consider it no more a stigma than men do. A high-ranking female council member once told me casually: "I know that old woman really well. Why we go back a long way. I can remember sharing a cell with her one Saturday night."

Ideologically, however, everyone at Pine Ridge is against drinking and abuse, particularly those who follow what they believe to be a traditional life, whether full blood or mixed blood. And drinking and abuse are probably two areas of reservation life-style that defy categorizing by blood quantum or sex. Ironically, even though statistics show that whites in the state of South Dakota have more problems related to alcohol, Indians as well as whites generally believe that Indians have a greater problem.

Although men, women, and children suffer from alcohol-related difficulties, domestic violence is not easy to assess on the reservation. Some women are hesitant to call wife beating unusual (and this would hold for whites as well as Indians). As one stated:

> I consider it wife abuse [among the Indians] when
> they would paint their wife red and drag her
> through the brush because she would not obey her
> husband, and cut off her nose, and stuff like that.
> *That's* abuse.

This of course referred to the husband's treatment of a wife found having sexual relations with another man.

> But on the other hand, what I think they're talking
> about today when they say abuse of women is in-
> tolerable abuse—you know, the abuse of someone
> who can't fight back. I think that people don't like
> to see brutality against people. They would rather
> see them ridiculed because that keeps everybody
> in line—when they're ridiculed—you know, teased.
> That would keep a man or a woman more in line
> than if you abused them. When you live close in
> an extended family ridicule is better than hitting or
> spanking.[7]

Some women feel that domestic violence has always occurred, even in the historical past, but that what is now being experienced at Pine Ridge is a symptom of a situation that is being recognized nationwide:

> I think we see a lot of abused women in this day
> and age. I think we're just keeping up with the
> times. It's not only on the reservation. But here
> everybody is physical and aggressive—and I think
> that's part of it. Even in my father's day people
> abused each other—but it wasn't as common then.

Others believe that domestic violence at Pine Ridge is really foreign to the Lakota people and is a product of white culture. Lily Shangreaux, an Oglala woman, states:

> On the Pine Ridge Reservation, as elsewhere,
> some people believe that it's normal for violence
> to occur in the home. Some also believe that it is
> "traditional" to beat your woman, but the idea
> that it is man's right to beat his wife stems from
> the belief, held by European settlers, that when a
> woman married she became her husband's prop-
> erty. Unlike her European counterpart, a Lakota
> woman was not considered her husband's property
> to do with as he pleased. She often enjoyed a
> greater amount of freedom and exercised more in-
> fluence in social and political matters. Contrary to
> the belief that the Indian woman was a subservient
> drudge, she was often a strong (physically), inde-
> pendent, free-thinking individual.
> A Lakota woman who suffered abuse at the
> hands of her husband had more alternatives than
> women in white society. He could expect a beating
> from her family or she could obtain a divorce
> simply by placing all her husband's personal pos-
> sessions outside the lodge, and no one would criti-
> cize her for having failed at her marriage.[8]

Whether or not abuse is a product of white contact, the pattern of abuse is known from surveys conducted by the Public Health Service. The average abused woman is twenty-six years old; in 85 percent of cases the aggressor is male, but in only 51 percent is he the victim's spouse. Oglala females are abused equally by male friends and other family members, and in at least 4 percent of cases the woman is abused by a female acquaintance.

Whether they were married or not, in 69 percent of cases the abuse took place while a woman was living with the male, and 61 percent of the time she was abused in her home. The act was carried out about equally often (6 percent of the time) in an automobile, on the streets of Pine Ridge Village, or in a friend's house.

Almost half of the female victims live in Pine Ridge Village, and almost half live in cluster homes—housing developments akin to projects—which are beginning to proliferate on the reservation and which are also the location for other crimes, particularly homicide and suicide. Cluster housing was originally proposed for the safety and convenience of unmarried and widowed women with dependent children, but Indians generally believe it was devised by the federal government to lure landowners off their individual sections of land by making available houses with running water and electricity. The name arose because, relative to their spacious surroundings out in the country, people are clustered densely together. In these developments kinship affiliations are ignored in assigning locations, which is conducive to arguments between families who have little or nothing in common.

All the incidents of abuse took place while the male was under the influence of alcohol (77 percent of the time) or drugs (23 percent of the time). Drugs at Pine Ridge usually mean marijuana, but in some cases young people sniff glue or paint solvent or gasoline, locally known as "huffing." Rarely is there any use of opiates or their derivatives, since they are too expensive whereas marijuana grows wild on the reservation.

At the time this survey was taken, 48 percent of the women abused had been seen at least once by the medical staff at the Public Health hospital.[9]

It is not uncommon to find that those acting to combat domestic violence on the reservation are women. In August 1979 an organization called the Sacred Shawl Society (Tašina Wakan) was formed to establish a shelter and resource center for battered women and their children who are forced to seek refuge. Members of the Sacred Shawl maintain:

> Traditionally, if a man beat his wife, he could expect severe retribution from her family and he

would be made to feel ashamed by the community.
If he continued, his wife could leave him and not
feel like she was a failure as a wife and home-
maker. Today we have fallen away from a lot of
traditional values and beliefs; a man can beat his
wife near death and not receive punishment.
Almost everyday women are brought to the PHS
hospital in Pine Ridge whose husbands or boyf-
riends have beaten them up. These men are rarely
prosecuted in a court of law.[10]

The Sacred Shawl attempts to provide temporary emergency
shelters for such women as well as helping them obtain legal aid,
medical assistance, and social services. Providing safe homes is
the hardest, simply because the small-town atmosphere and
kinship network make it almost impossible to place women in
shelters without everyone's knowing where they are—including
the aggressors. Furthermore, the "safe house" must belong
either to the woman's consanguineal kin or to no kin at all. In the
latter case, many are afraid of retribution if they offer their
homes as refuges.

Critics of the Sacred Shawl say that such an organization is not
relevant to most women, who are likely to stay with the men who
beat them. What is needed, they contend, is an organization that
can understand the frustrations on the reservation that lead men
to abuse their families and do something about them. According
to another woman:

In the old days they didn't have to worry about
women being abused, because men wouldn't just
go around hitting women. A woman had to do
something very serious before the tribe would take
action. And when they did it was usually some
kind of chastisement. But it wasn't something that
could be settled one to one. It was institutionalized, and it had to be for a very serious offense.
Nowadays, starting after World War II, men just
beat their wives. They learned it in the army when
they were able to go out drinking and socializing
with non-Indians. They saw a life different from
the one they lived on the reservation. When they
came home, they were so frustrated that there
were no opportunities available, they just lashed
out at their wives.

Another woman criticized the Sacred Shawl:

> If I was having problems I would want to go to
> someone who is well trained, professional, and
> who knows more than I do. The trouble is that
> some of those people are not trained and are not
> equipped to handle these types of problems.

Other women think that abused women get what is coming to them, not only from men but from other women. One woman told a story about a woman, abused by her man, who ganged up with her sister and beat up the woman currently living with the man who had beaten her. Both traditional and modern women agree with the Sacred Shawl's slogan, "Wife abuse is not traditional." But many of the younger activist women believe that the man reigns supreme today and that it always has been so.

The Pitiable

Some traditional women still believe in the pipe and the sacred rites. They do not believe in Public Health, and they do not believe in the new militancy. They are opposed to the Bureau of Indian Affairs and all the welfare programs that constitute the economic base for Pine Ridge. They spend their time picking herbs and curing people who suffer from the bureaucratic treatment at the Public Health clinics. They pray with and for those who are tired of standing in lines and waiting for the white man to decide their future. These women are concerned with what the Oglalas call *unšike* 'the pitiable,' the common people of the world. They help out with the sweat lodges, often taking part themselves. Today some of them go on vision quests, which a woman would not have done in the past. They participate in the Sun Dance and the memorial feasts, and some are married to medicine men and old chiefs.

These women, and not all of them are chronologically old, view the current scene—the teenage pregnancies, the abusive treatment of men, women, and children, the homicides and suicides, the general degradation of the Indian—as something that will end. They believe that the white man is nothing more than a visitor to their world and that one day he will pass into oblivion. Then the old Indian people and the buffalo will be born again, and life will be as it was before. These women and their men do not dance as was done in the Ghost Dance movement. They do not make loud predictions about the fate of white culture, and they do not join organizations that challenge the political status quo. They do not rebel, and they do not demonstrate or protest against the injustices of the past. They are silent. They sit and pray to Wakantanka. They smoke the pipe and wait. They are not particularly proud, and they are not defiant. They simply believe that everything—all the abuses and injustices created by the white man—will go away. They are not sullen, and they do not—as the Oglalas say—pout. They are quite capable of making jokes, particularly at their relatives' expense. They are a part of Oglala society that equates being Oglala and Lakota with being religious, with remembering the ways of their grandparents, and with telling their grandchildren stories about the old times. Such women are often old and wrinkled; their bodies are thick, and their eyes retreat behind fragile bones. They stand hunched over, sometimes supported by a cane itself as gnarled as their timeless legs. Their knuckles bulge over slender fingers and wrists, and sometimes they seem collapsed inside their worn and tattered clothing. They look longingly out at the prairies, and behind their ancient veneer they seem more insightful than others. But their fragility should be taken with caution, because the Oglalas consider them the powerful ones.

They are powerful because the Lakotas believe that as a person approaches death he or she has visions and premonitions. Frequently old people will rise in the morning and tell their families that they were visited during the night by a deceased relative—a husband or wife who preceded them—and that they talked about old times.

An old man whose wife had died when she was ninety-six told how she entered his room even during the daytime and talked with him about how good it would be to be together again. She sat on her favorite wobbly old chair, the man said, and said she had recently seen some cousins who had preceded her by two decades. They spoke about the buffalo-hunting days. He died shortly after these encounters.

These people are believed to be powerful because they are close to the spirit world. Their imminent death is heralded by recurring contacts with their deceased relatives. When this time comes, the younger people often become anxious that the old one will die before passing on some of the history of the Lakotas, particularly the sacred lore. They fear that the old women will fail to teach their now-aging daughters all there is to know about the old times and about the sacred medicines that women are entrusted to pick after menopause. The same ninety-six-year-old woman was sometimes chastised by her female relatives for not having taught her own daughter about the medicines she had once collected for her family. And it was with great relief that she called in her only daughter early each morning to tell her about the plants.

These "elderlies," as the old people are commonly called in English, often live private and public lives that are quite different. One small, frail-looking old woman with a kindly smile stood on the corner of the major intersection at Pine Ridge selling miniature tomahawks. The tomahawks cost two dollars apiece, and tourists were eager to buy them as they stopped at the crossing on their way to the Black Hills. She stood there with one tomahawk in her hand, holding a paper bag containing two or three more. When she sold out she began her walk back to the Sun Dance grounds, where she and her husband lived year round in a canvas wall tent. Her husband made the tomahawks from stones he had collected in the Badlands, and she decorated the handles with beads. As soon as another batch was ready, she put them in the paper bag and headed back to Pine Ridge. Few people realized that her husband was a medicine man and that the two lived a very religious life. A sweat lodge was built next to their tent, and once when I visited them they were busy curing a young man.

Still another woman, perhaps in her fifties, whom I met early in my travels to Pine Ridge spoke no English—somewhat of a rarity in the 1960s. She patiently followed her husband to the farmlands of Nebraska, where they and their children worked in the fields for white farmers and ranchers. They lived in barns, tents, or abandoned houses wherever they worked and had no real home of their own, on or off the reservation. Finally they moved back to Pine Ridge and occupied an abandoned cook-house east of town. Later I discovered that both were high-ranking officials of the Native American Church, and that the husband was called on to conduct "peyote" meetings far and wide. His wife also played an important part in the ceremonies.

Because the population at Pine Ridge is increasing and relatively few people who were born there leave except for temporary employment or to go to college, there seems no end to funerals one attends. Many of the old people travel great distances from one wake to the next, bringing gifts of food and staying up all night with the bereaved family at what the Lakotas call *hancokan wohanpi* 'midnight feast.' As we shall see in the next chapter, traditional religion and Christianity frequently meld in fulfilling the needs of the Lakotas, and the old people are quite capable of straddling religious persuasions during a lifetime.

11 All My Relations

Christianity and Traditionalism

Perhaps the most definitive way of distinguishing between traditional and modern Indian culture is to examine the religious institutions at Pine Ridge. The relationship between Christianity and traditionalism is complex. Although it is common to hear Oglalas describe people as Catholic, Episcopal, or belonging to one of the dozen or so other Christian denominations present at Pine Ridge, some are described as traditional—as those who follow the Indian way and "walk with the pipe." Indian women as well as Indian men move in both religious spheres.

Conceptually, the religious avenues open to Oglalas (and non-Indians who live on or near the reservation) fall into the following categories.

Christianity

The major Christian denominations have been represented at Pine Ridge since its establishment, and all of them are, not surprisingly, missionizing churches. The denominations that claim the highest memberhsip are Roman Catholic and Episcopalian. The former, for historical reasons, is frequently associated with modernism. Episcopalianism is strong where there are large numbers of traditional Oglalas, the main diagnostic feature being fluency in the native language.

The correlation between Lakota culture and Episcopalianism stems from the fact that the early progressives, who in the main were Catholics, insisted that their children be taught English so that the younger generation could speak the white man's language, whereas the Episcopalians observed a tradition of preaching to the Oglalas in Lakota. Somewhat ironically, the Catholics (read Jesuits) were always intellectual about their linguistic approach. They compiled grammars and dictionaries and

translated Bible stories, psalms, and missals into Lakota. Therefore they produced the greatest amount of literature in the
language. The Episcopalians, however, ordained native ministers who were fluent in both Lakota and English.

Christianity has fostered the idea of male superiority much
more than native religion has, particularly among the Catholics.
Although young women have been invited to join various con-
vents and today there are numerous Oglala nuns, Lakota men
have never been ordained as priests. Thus there is a replication of
the relationship between priests and nuns; the church does not
refrain from bringing women into religious orders, because it is
recognized that their vocations are subservient to men's. But it is
reluctant to bring men into the priesthood, where they may be
regarded as equal to white males.

Women do play an important role in Christianity, expectedy,
in the ancillary organizations that serve various supportive functions. Catholic or Protestant, it is generally the women who
organize the rummage sales and other fund-raising projects.
They run the day-care centers, summer camps, and other hu-
manitarian programs, such as feeding the poor and elderly,
helping people to get jobs and generally pursue a worthwhile
existence.

The Catholics have provided most of the educational facilities
for Oglala children on the reservation. Other denominations
have sent Indian children away to schools in other parts of the
country. There is some attempt today to change this pattern. For
example, some fundamentalist churches are beginning to operate schools. But still the Jesuits' influence is greatest. They have
an excellent reputation for educational programs that are superior to public schooling, and consequently they attract a number
of non-Catholic students whose parents want them to get the best
education. This emphasis on educating local children creates
more opportunities for women in the Catholic church, where
they can also be employed to perform various domestic duties.

Historically, the Catholics also have been noted for their
willingness to delegate some priestly tasks to lay catechists. In
the past, the Saint Joseph society for men and the Saint Mary's
society for women have provided a religious ministry to parts of
the reservation where priests could not travel owing to distances
or inclement weather. Holy Rosary Mission at one time main-

tained as many as thirty chapels in various communities where there were large populations of Catholics. The two lay societies were in charge of maintaining the chapels—cleaning them, cutting wood for the fireplaces in winter, and making repairs. Some of the men also served as prayer leaders when the priest was unable to say mass on Sundays and holy days. However, women did not preach: they simply helped the men in minor capacities such as arranging flowers on the altar, and if so inclined they frequently led the psalms that had been translated, albeit poorly, into Lakota.

The Episcopalians were and still are more democratic toward the duties of the reverend males and sisterly females, though still somewhat asymmetrical. They and other Protestant groups, of course, differed from their Catholic counterparts in that their clergy could marry. Almost invariably, Protestant ministers at Pine Ridge were accompanied by their wives. That some Christians could marry while others could not must have confused the Oglalas, who also could not understand why denominations fought among each other while all professing to believe in Jesus Christ (Powers 1976).

Although the combined membership of the Catholic and Episcopal churches accounts for approximately 90 percent of Christians, other denominations continue to minister to the Oglalas. In the early 1960s the Church of Latter-day Saints (Mormons) bought land near Pine Ridge Village and built a combination church and recreation facility. Young Mormon men, mostly from Utah, who are required to missionize for two years of their lives, take up residence at Pine Ridge and provide a number of services, mainly recreational. They also transport Indians around the reservation and perform charitable works. They have the reputation of flirting with young Indian girls, and Indians frequently joke about the Mormons' propensity for plural marriage. The Mormons have a tenuous following: their main objective is to recruit Indian students for Brigham Young University, and a handful of Oglala youths do attend at least for a short time. The Mormons of course teach that women are inferior to men, and needless to say they have few sympathizers among Oglala women. That they are being exploited by Indians who constantly ask them for favors that are always granted apparently escapes them in their youthful religious zeal. Thus they are useful to the Oglala people, particularly those living near their church.

Recently a number of fundamentalist churches have opened at Pine Ridge, and one at Wolf Creek is very popular because it also provides educational programs for young children. Known by their Oglala detractors as "Bible thumpers," the leaders of these churches conduct faith healing sessions, and their members, some of whom are non-Indian, occasionally speak in tongues and bear witness to their own salvation. Many of the Oglalas find their services fascinating, and since the churches serve free food, the evening camp meetings are often a source of entertainment. There are probably more women than men who participate in the prayer meetings, both Indian and white.

Christianity also provides a vehicle for acting out certain life crisis rituals. The Christian church or meetinghouse is the locus for christenings and to a lesser degree marriages when the latter are not "traditional." In many ways the federal, private, and parochial schools accommodate the ritual needs of young people, as they do in off-reservation schools. A young woman today is more likely to learn about household chores and cooking in a home economics class than at home from her mother. Instead of puberty ceremonies, young girls begin to attend high-school dances, outings, and picnics. Few girls of grade-school or even high school-age act out much of their life in a traditional way, except when they go home after school, on the weekends, and during vacation.

Babies are christened by priests and ministers in the same way they are off the reservation. Friends and relatives give showers for the expectant mother. Special clothes are bought or made for the baby. Grandmothers often insist on making the child a pair of fully beaded moccasins, a beaded bonnet, and a small star quilt for the crib. The parents and godparents take the baby to the church and watch it sprinkled with water. Later they retire to the church basement or to a relative's house for a celebration breakfast of bacon, eggs, sweet rolls, and coffee, not unlike their white contemporaries off the reservation.

Similarly, young people who wish to be married in church or "have the benefit of clergy," as the Catholics say, announce their engagement, and wedding showers are held. The weddings are sometimes formal, complete with a processional, white dress for the bride, and suit and tie for the groom. People pray and sing in the manner prescribed by each denomination, and the couple take their vows very much as is done in any American community. The ceremony is crowned by a wedding reception, again held in the church basement, or perhaps one of the district administration buildings, or in a private home. There is dancing, drinking, and eating. Young children scamper about, and before the couple slips away the bride throws her bouquet to the group of unmarried women waiting sheepishly to catch it. Except for a few of the old and middle-aged women who can be seen filling their *wateca* buckets with food left over from the wedding buffet, the marriage ceremony at Pine Ridge is identical to those held elsewhere in America.

Whether active in a Christian denomination or not, all Oglalas are conceptually linked to a church, either through their kin or through their attendance at parochial schools. Therefore when a person dies it is likely that he or she will be buried in a church cemetery and that Christian burial rites will be conducted. There are some exceptions. First, the Native American Church maintains its own cemetery, and its funeral rites are quite different from standard Christian burial practices. Second, many people are opting to bury their relatives on their own land, and today one can see small grave plots, frequently adorned with colored cloth offerings marking what is regarded as a traditional Lakota burial, though everyone recognizes that in the old times the dead were buried differently.

What is perhaps true of all the life-cycle rituals today, particularly those associated with birth and death, is that though Christian churches and meetinghouses are used, a persisting Lakota culture still impinges upon the rituals. Sometimes one sees a synthesis of traditional Lakota and white American cultures, sometimes the two religions are kept distinct. For example, the formality of the Christian burial is often interrupted by the spontaneity of Lakota ritual, as in one burial I attended.

A young man had accidentally killed himself. Since he had been baptized a Catholic, his two-day wake was held in the Catholic church in Pine Ridge Village. Mourners filed in each evening and sat silently in front of the casket. The young man was dressed in new clothing, and a feather fan was placed in his crossed hands. His wife and young child, still stunned, sat midway back from the casket, consoled by the wife's mother. Old female relatives greeted each other with the traditional laments, cooing softly on each other's shoulders. Alternately, old men and women stood up near the casket and talked about the young man's life. Some spoke in English, others in Lakota. A medicine man also arose to speak, to the obvious disapproval of the parish priest, who sat off to one side of the congregation.

At the end of the wake, people filed back to the church kitchen, where there were stacks of cardboard boxes filled with balogna sandwiches that had been quickly made up. Coffee and sweet rolls were also served, and many people wrapped uneaten morsels in makeshift *wateca* buckets made of tinfoil.

The next day and night the wake continued in much the same way. After the wake, however, various traditional foods such as soup and fried bread were served, because the young man's relatives had by then had time to prepare them.

On the following morning the burial took place at the Holy Rosary Mission cemetery. A large congregation had arrived at the mission church, but owing to the confusion created by the suddenness of the death, no one was quite sure where the body was. As it turned out, the casket had been left in town, and some of the pallbearers had to drive back in their pickup truck and retrieve it. Much later they arrived with the casket in the back of the truck and carried it into the church in the rather formal and somber procession typical of Christian funerals.

A funeral mass was said, and at its conclusion the coffin was carried to the door of the church and opened again. The members of the congregation filed by and paid their last respects, sometimes emotionally, and went immediately to their cars for the procession to the cemetery. The last viewer, the young man's older brother, became upset, crying out in Lakota, "Little brother, little brother, it should be me lying there instead of you!" Other relatives consoled him while the pallbearers closed the casket and carried it back to the waiting pickup. It was pushed unceremoniously into the truck, and the pallbearers jumped in beside it for the trip to the cemetery.

At the gravesite, a larger congregation gathered, including uniformed members of the local American Legion post, since the dead man had been in the military. A grave had been crudely dug, and as the pallbearers began lowering the coffin by hand with ropes, a number of people spoke. The priest prayed as it settled into place. A member of the American Legion gave a short eulogy and presented a flag to the young man's brother. An elderly man gave a short prayer in Lakota. The brother, keeping his eyes on the coffin, began singing a traditional song, and soon others joined in. Then, as women sobbed out loud, the pallbearers took up shovels and quickly began to scoop the dirt into the open grave.

The people dispersed, all retiring to a relative's house for another traditional feast that would continue throughout the day and night. And with this the funeral rites were concluded.

The degree to which Christianity and traditional religion combine is largely determined by each family itself. Traditional people who speak the native language at home and take part in native religious ceremonies nevertheless bury their dead in the Christian cemeteries, but the wake and funeral are likely to be more Lakota than Christian. When an old chief died recently, the family had a two-day wake, as in the funeral just described, but the feasts included buffalo, deer, and elk meat along with the other traditional foods, and giveaways were held afterward. The wake was held at home, and the room where the body lay in state was decorated with Indian artifacts and photographs of old-time Indians. Before the body was taken to the cemetery, the casket was taken outside and opened in the sunlight as the people filed by. After the burial, everyone returned for another great feast and giveaway.

It would be incorrect to say that the Christian and traditional religions are syncretic. Often the two are conceived as quite separate yet compatible. The Oglalas organize much of their life-cycle activity around the various Christian denominations, but for the traditional people spiritual life may often be fulfilled through Lakota religion. Even many Christian Oglalas believe that spirits of the deceased still roam freely around the countryside, and still others believe that when one dies there are two afterworlds, one for Indians and one for whites. The latter is somewhere around Europe.

Upon being asked what she expected to find when she died, one woman replied:

> My relatives—because I was raised with the belief
> that there is life after death and in that concept I

believe that we are just here on a visit. I was
raised in that belief. The great creator sent us here
on a journey. We are here on a visit and according
to his record one year is one day. According to his
record I've been here only forty-eight days and if I
reach one-hundred I will be very happy. I envy
people like my mother-in-law. She is over seventy
and I envy her. Someday she is going to make her
trip home naturally. Some kids today shorten their
lives by being here only twenty days. Accidents,
drugs, alcohol, committing suicide shortens their
trips. So in reality we are all going back, and I will
see them there.

Christianity, then, serves not only as an important substitute
for traditional religion, but as a viable adjunct to it. Most Oglalas
do not readily make a strong distinction between the two.

Native American Church

The number of Oglalas participating in the Native American
Church, also known in anthropological literature by the unfortunate term "peyote cult," has remained fairly constant since the
turn of the century. However, with dramatic population in-
creases, particularly over the past twenty years, a smaller per-
centage now participate in this church. Earlier estimates of fewer
than 10 percent membership should probably be reduced to
fewer than 5 percent.[1]

The Oglala version of the Native American Church emphasizes use of the Lakota language during the weekend services. As
in other tribes, these services are held in a tipi. Oglalas also use
many meaningful texts as opposed to vocabalic texts in the
peyote songs. These texts are often extracted from earlier religious songs such as those sung for the Sun Dance. The philosophy of peyotism that corresponds to living a good Christian life
(since Jesus Christ is regarded as the son of God) is not different
from other non-Oglala beliefs, but the rituals and their emphasis
on Lakota values as opposed to a larger Indian culture makes the
Pine Ridge variant analogous to a Christian denomination.

As in other parts of the country where peyotism vies with
either tribal religion or Christianity, the members are frequently
accused of being sluggish, lazy, and untrustworthy because they

use peyote buttons (*Lophophora williamsii LeMaire*), which though nonaddictive are hallucinogenic. Most members ingest peyote buttons raw during the meetings held from Saturday night to dawn Sunday, and others pulverize peyote and make it into tea or broth for minor ailments such as headache.

Although women play an important ritual role, this is usually limited to the wife of the male ceremonial leader, called the "Road Chief." The Native American Church as such is a negligible influence on Lakota culture, and it is perhaps better analyzed as a Christian denomination rather than a native religion, though Catholic and Protestant clergy alike obviously would disagree with this classification.

It is worth noting, however, that though peyote is as foreign to Lakota culture as Christianity is, in the origin stories told by its earliest American practitioners—the Kiowas, Comanches, and Apaches of the Southern Plains and the Menominis of Wisconsin—the ritual, songs, prayers, and directions for using the peyote cactus were taught to people suffering hardship by a mysterious woman, the "Peyote Woman," who directed them that the plant would enable them to live a long and fruitful life.[2]

Traditional Lakota Religion

Contemporary Lakota religion still emphasizes the White Buffalo Calf Woman, the Sacred Pipe, and the Seven Sacred Rites. Of the seven original ceremonies, the Sun Dance, Vision Quest, Sweat Lodge, Hunka, and Ghost-Keeping Ceremony are still performed. Today the Ghost-Keeping Ceremony is called "Memorial Feast" or colloquially *wohanpi*, a term applied to any feast. The Sacred Ball Game, and the female puberty ceremony have become obsolete, but this is not to say they will not be revived. The Hunka, which had fallen into disuse for almost fifty years, was revived in the early 1970s and is still an important ritual even though it has been somewhat modified. Judging by the significance the Lakotas still assign to the White Buffalo Calf Woman, it would be surprising if all seven rites were not performed in the near future. What is perhaps more interesting, particularly because anthropologists and historians, with little exception, have always considered the conversion of American Indians to Christianity a fait accompli, is that more and more young people, men and women, are becoming interested in native religion even though they may have at one time been active in a Christian church. Asked if he found conflict between Catholicism and the way of the pipe, one man responded:

> No. When I came back to Tunkašila I talked with
> my grandfather, Fools Crow.[3] And then I met
> several different medicine men like Crow Dog,
> Flying By, Catches, New Horse, Eagle Elk—I met
> them all. I've been to their ceremonies, I've
> prayed with them, I've sun danced under them,
> and the only conflict I had was that, in the Indian
> religion, there are colors that mean different things
> or different directions represented by different
> animals, winged or four-legged and each of these
> medicine people—maybe they had a different
> color. Maybe they don't use black, for example.
> And I couldn't understand this. For instance, the
> north is the Buffalo Nation, the east the Elk Na-
> tion, south the Owl Nation, west is the Thunder
> Being Nation. Some used different animals.
> This was the conflict I experienced, so I went
> back to grandfather and explained it. We had a
> sweat, and during that sweat he explained that not
> all medicine men are alike, and never put one
> down or above the other. Hold them at the same
> level and respect them. Even if the colors change
> or the four-legged or the winged change or the
> direction, it doesn't matter, it all means the same
> thing. It is just that their vision is different from
> the other, no two are alike.
> As for my Catholic upbringing, it wasn't hard.
> It doesn't matter whether you're Indian religion,
> or Baptist or Episcopal. There is only one supreme
> being that we pray to. We call him Tunkašila or
> Wakantanka and other people call him God or
> whatever. So the only conflict I had was the rein-
> troduction back into my religion. I had to get that
> straightened out.

With respect to the increasing number of young people joining in the Sun Dance, he added:

> To quote some of the medicine people, they say
> that the young people are coming back. They are

comming back and they are looking. The Sun
Dance is a sacred thing, a very sacred thing, and if
you dance and you are pierced, or they pierce you
and you are hurting, that's when you realize why
you are there. It's an individual thing. There is nobody helping you; your are on your own, all by
yourself. You are the only one out there who
knows what it feels like to be thirsty and hungry,
hot, tired, and hurting. I've heard a lot of people
say that some of the people who are dancing are
doing it for show. They want the scars. They want
to mutilate their bodies, and they do it to show
off. To me that hurts me, because I do it for my
own personal reasons, and also I do it for the old
people. Once we lose the old people, then we've
lost our legends, we've lost our way of life, we've
lost our traditions. I saw a young man who wanted
to dance with us. He wanted to do it. He promised
it two years ago and he promised it to his grandmother that he would do this and I prayed with
him last night and we talked and finally he is going
to do it. He is one of our students and I asked him
why he didn't do it before, and he said the agencies moved him around too much and he couldn't
do it before.

Now his grandmother is gone, but he is still
going to do it. That makes me feel sad and happy.
Finally he is going to be able to make it. But to
get back to your question. There are a lot of Sun
Dances. They are having them at Greengrass, at
Crow Dog, at Porcupine and other Indian communities, which is good. The young want to do it.

There are a number of reasons Oglala people can move from
one religion to the next, even go to mass on a Sunday and a
traditional ritual a few days later. First, from a historical point of
view, Indians at Pine Ridge had to belong to a church to receive
ration books. One declared membership in a church or risked
starvation for the whole family. Whole *tiyošpaye* tended to join
the same church, whatever denomination had established itself
in their community. Second, there was never any good reason
why Indians could not join a Christian church and still pray to
Wakantanka. Often such membership simply meant they would

receive rations and have access to clothing and sometimes shelter, since missionaries were always generous to their converts. Some of the lay catechists were even paid ten dollars a month to preach in the priest's absence. Interestingly, the catechists often moved from one denomination to the next, because they were bored or perhaps because they were offered better pay, a new place to live, and transportation. Not only did the common Oglala people become important Christian functionaries, so did even the medicine men. Well-known ones like Black Elk served for brief periods as catechists and lay readers for both Catholic and Episcopal churches. For some, being a Christian had nothing to do with one's spiritual life—it was an economic, political, and social means to an end.[4]

The presence of different denominations provided a framework to keep the old *tiyošpaye* organization alive even though it was now politically and economically defunct. Although an Oglala might belong to a Catholic community church, when he or she married the spouse was usually selected from another denomination, thus ensuring that the principles of exogamy of the *tiyošpaye* also held for one's religious affiliation (Powers 1976).

Of course Oglalas continued to be baptized and buried from local churches, even the medicine men and women, and certainly countless numbers sincerely converted to Christianity. On the other hand, some of the events that led non-Indian Americans away from formal religion in the 1960s also influenced young and old people at Pine Ridge. The difference was that on the reservation there was a viable alternative to Christianity. At least some—and one can perhaps argue the majority—still believed traditional religion had never died out.

Much of the recent resurgence of interest in traditional religion, however, can be traced to political activities on the reservation beginning in the late 1960s and coming to a head in 1972 when the members of the American Indian Movement participated in a large Sun Dance at Pine Ridge, at the traditional Sun Dance grounds one mile east of the village. Approximately thirty members of AIM took the opportunity of the large gathering to voice their opinion about the continuing oppression of Indians by the United States government. These ideas had been expressed before, but this year the members joined in the Sun Dance and were pierced. Furthermore, 1972 was the first year Sun Dances began to be well attended, numbering as many as three-hundred dancers by the end of the decade. It also marked the beginning of the proliferation of the Sun Dance itself. Soon there would be scores conducted by medicine men on all the reservations, whereas before 1972 only one or two were held by all the Lakota people.

In 1973 the AIM members occupied Wounded Knee, and since that time there has been an increased tendency to express one's Indianness through religious rather than secular means. The powwow, with its secular war dances and round dances, is no longer the focus of tribal solidarity. Today more and more young men and women join in the Sun Dance with all its forms of self-mortification, traveling the entire summer to take part in several Sun Dances on different Lakota reservations each week.

Women are participating more not only in the Sun Dance but in other rituals. At one time it was only males who went on the Vision Quest, fasting alone on a hill for one to four days and nights, waiting to receive a vision that would confirm their faith. Women prayed that their menfolk on the hill would pull through safely, but they did so from the security of the camp. Today women, old and young, even those attending college, make special trips back to the reservation to go out on the hill, placed there by a medicine man, to commune with their god in a traditional way now open to females as well as males.

The same obtains for the Sweat Lodge, which at one time was restricted to males. In the center of a small domed lodge made from willow saplings and buffalo hides, heated rocks were placed in a hole and water was poured over them to create steam. The men prayed and sang and communed with spirits in the darkened lodge, reviving themselves both spiritually and physically. Occasionally, when the men had finished and left the lodge a woman and her children could enter while the last traces of heat emerged from the cooling stones and crawl clockwise around the lodge, exiting after one circuit. But today Indian women join the men in the Sweat Lodge whenever they want to purify themselves. The only restriction is that they cannot participate when they are menstruating.[5]

Today the *Hunka* is performed no so much to create an adoptive bond between people as to serve as a puberty ceremony for both boys and girls. Those wishing to sponsor a *Hunka* for their child or children must smoke a pipe with a medicine man, and if he agrees to conduct the ceremony the sponsors will provide a feast for all their relatives. Frequently the *Hunka* is held as a part of another function such as a powwow, where a large gathering is already assured. The medicine man, accompanied by his wife, in front of the entire audience ties to the hair of the child a white plume from the breast of an eagle called *wacihin*. A wooden bowl of chokecherry juices is then communally drunk by all the participants, but especially the children, their parents, and the medicine man and woman. The purpose of the ritual is to formally announce that the children are ready to become responsible members of the tribe and to uphold Lakota cultural values. Any adult who has gone through the ceremony may conduct the ritual, but in practice it is usually led by a medicine man and his wife. After the plume tying has been concluded, the parents distribute large quantities of beef, *wojapi, taniga*, and fried bread as well as store-bought foods to the assembled group. After the feast the parents and close kin employ an announcer to call out the names of perons to whom the parents want to present gifts. At larger giveaways, when the parents can afford it, the ceremony is enhanced by the amount given away. Even a small feast and giveaway accommodating under a hundred people—a small gathering compared with large community feasts of over three-hundred—may cost several thousand dollars. And though both mothers and fathers participate equally in the ritual, the giveaway is under the supervision of the female, who determines all the gifts and supervises the manufacture of homemade items such as star quilts and shawls and the purchase of store-bought items. It is also the woman, usually the child's mother, who determines just who will receive gifts.[6]

Of all the contemporary ceremonies that underscore the importance of the woman, however, the most important is the Memorial Feast, the functional equivalent of the Ghost-Keeping Ceremony, which like its predecessor is conducted approximately one year after the death of a loved one. Memorial Feasts are not conducted for every person who dies; most are either for the young—perhaps babies, favorite children, important adults—or for those who die unexpectedly. What is important is the continuing belief that the spirit of the deceased lingers near the place of death for about one year. If a person elects to *wašigla* 'mourn,' then certain precautions must be taken to ensure that proper respect is paid to the spirit so it will not harm those who are near the place of death, particularly the relatives.

Men may grieve, but women are the only ones who formally engage in the mourning. The period is difficult, for one cannot leave the house, go shopping, go to powwows, or generally carry on one's normal life. To help out the mourner, a woman's female relatives buy her groceries and deliver them to her home. They also help her by making star quilts, shawls, embroidered towels, pillowcases, and sheets as well as other fancy needlework. All of these items, will be accumulated over the year until it is time to have the Memorial Feast.

Although one may sponsor a Memorial Feast without the more formal aspects of the mourning period, traditional women are bound by a strict regimen. Today they must wear black for the entire year. But most important, they must be sure not to make quick moves with their hands or turn around suddenly, because any motion that disturbs the air is likely to irritate the nearby spirit. The woman must, if she pledges to do so, ritually feed the spirit at every meal. A place is set for the spirit with its own plate and cup or glass. A morsel of food, perhaps a piece of meat or fried bread, is placed on the plate, and water or coffee is poured. After the family eats the meal, the place set for the loved one is cleared. Usually the food is burned or buried and the beverage is poured on the ground.

The feeding is very important, because if one elects to keep the spirit one must be sure not to anger it in any way, by words or by deeds. Only the dead person's friends will come to visit, lest the spirit enact some retribution on the living in payment for past offenses.

The time of the Memorial Feast is announced over what is known as the "moccasin telegraph" an informal network usually made up mainly of kin. When people hear there is to be a Memorial Feast or "dinner," they pack up the articles made for the giveaway, and perhaps some food. The mourning family will provide the staples: relatives will either buy or persuade someone to donate a side of beef, and the immediate family will prepare the other traditional foods such as soup, jerky, *taniga*, and *wojapi*—perhaps several varieties made from chokecherries,

buffalo berries, or wild plums. There will also be coffee, and
sometimes iced or hot tea. Alcoholic beverages are never served
at traditional feasts. Augmenting these traditional foods will be a
variety of store-bought foods such as bread, salted crackers,
sweet rolls, and canned fruits. Some families may provide a wide
range of meats, including venison, buffalo, and elk and also some
poultry, usually chicken.[7]

At Memorial Feasts, men help the women with the cooking.
The men normally build pit fires outside, over which iron grills
are placed. Large pots of meat and soup are placed on the wood
fire and cooked all morning. The women usually cook indoors,
perhaps using a church community house kitchen, where groups
of them prepare the fruit dishes, pies, cakes, fried bread, and
coffee.

Customarily, as is true for all traditional feasts, more food is
cooked than can possibly be eaten at the feast. Individuals may
be served up to ten pounds of food, and to take it home each
person brings a bucket, usually an empty lard bucket with a
handle, or cardboard boxes or other containers. People also
bring their own silverware and dishes. One learns to carry these
whenever there is a feast, and the man or woman who forgets his
eating utensils and *wateca* bucket is ridiculed.

Most Memorial Feasts begin at noon nowadays, and frequently even people who are working attend during their lunch
hour. In the center of a cleared area outdoors (though the feast
may be held indoors in inclement weather), folding chairs are
arranged in a large circle perhaps twenty-five to fifty yards in
diameter. In the center of the circle are several tables bearing
pots of soup and other foods. Because as many as three hundred
people attend these feasts, the cooked foods are likely to be
placed in fifty-five-gallon plastic or galvanized garbage cans, and
members of the family carry these cans of food around the circle
serving each visitor. As many as two dozen men, women, and
youths may help in the distribution, ladling out soup and pouring
coffee for the seated guests. People begin to eat as soon as they
are served the food, which is done in no particular order. After
the servers have distributed food to each guest they begin
another round, dishing out the food as people eat. Food that will
not fit into the plates and bowls is placed in the *wateca* buckets

and containers. The servers continue making their way around the circle until all the food is gone, serving each guest several times before they finish.

If the spirit is to be fed, a special ritual is usually conducted by a medicine man. *Wasna*, better known as pemmican, must be served at the Memorial Feast, and it must be made by an old woman. A young puppy may also be cooked, and both traditional foods will be served first to the old people and then, if any remains, to anyone else who wants them. *Wasna* is particularly powerful because it is symbolic of the old times when it was the special food of hunters and warriors out on the trail. It is regarded as so potent that it can never be *wateca'd*,[8] and it can be served only during the daytime for fear that at night it will attract the spirits, who might harm people by bumping into them and causing "stroke." If the sponsors of the feast are traditional, the mother of the deceased will give *wasna* and perhaps some fried bread and coffee to the medicine man, who will stand up and pray that the spirit may go on its way to the spirit land. He then offers the food to the four directions, the sky, the earth, and the spotted eagle before burying the food at his feet and spilling the cup of liquid on the ground before him. This ritual is the final act before the spirit is deemed "freed."

When everyone has finished eating and packing up the *wateca* buckets, the woman and her family clear the center tables of cooking utensils and replace them with the articles they and their relatives have accumulated over the year for the giveaway. The family employs an *eyapaha* or announcer to call out the names of the guests who are to receive gifts. Occasionally a Christian minister or priest may say a few words about the merits of the deceased, as will some old men such as chiefs or medicine men. As the speeches are made and the names of the recipients called out, some members of the family "present" the picture of the deceased, usually in an elaborate frame, to each of the seated guests. As each person is called, he or she walks to the center of the area, receives the gift, and shakes hands with the members of the family, who stand near the tables laden with gifts. When all the gifts have been distributed, the guests rise and begin to file past the family, who stand in front of the empty tables. This is a particularly dramatic moment for the woman, who has been mourning for the entire year. As if on cue, sometime before all the guests have had time to file by and shake hands with her, she begins to sob hysterically, gasping for air and flailing her hands, and cries out the name of the departed. Her family expresses great concern for her condition, and immediately she is picked up and carried off to her home or to a place where she can lie down. There she is given some water, and her family talks to her to calm her. After several minutes she regains her composure and returns to normal behavior, almost as if nothing unusual had happened. With that the Memorial Feast ends and the people go home.

Yuwipi

A modern-day curing ritual called *Yuwipi*[9]—a term that refers to a segment of the darkened room ceremony in which the medicine man is wrapped up and tied in a star quilt, then freed by spirit helpers—is the focus of much of the religious life of contemporary Oglalas. These ceremonies, and variants of them that can be traced back to the old dream "cults," occur ad hoc, usually initiated by a person who is ill with Indian sickness. The patient, or one of his relatives, consults a medicine man, or *Yuwipi* man as they prefer to be called, and if he diagnoses the case as Indian sickness, he will smoke the pipe with the patient and agree to perform the ceremony.

In several days, unless it is an emergency, in which case an abbreviated ritual can be held as soon as the sun sets, a time and place are arranged. Usually a sweat lodge takes place first, followed by the ritual itself, which is held in a house or room from which all the furniture has been removed. After dark the ceremony begins, and most of it takes the form of an invitation to spirit helpers to enter the meeting place, which is in total darkness, and advise the *Yuwipi* man how to cure his patient. During the ritual twenty-five to thirty adepts sit around a specially prepared altar and sing and pray communally. The cure usually comes in the form of a request from the spirits, communicated through the *Yuwipi* man, to offer tobacco or in some other appropriate traditional manner appease the spirits who have provided the cure.

During the course of the meeting, the *Yuwipi* man is tied up in a star quilt by his assistant and some of the singers and placed face down on a bed of sage. The lights are turned out, and the adepts sing and pray until the spirits arrive, marked by the sound of rattles and the emission of bluish "sparks." The spirits are perceived to be about three feet tall, dressed in breechclouts and moccasins, their bodies painted with clay. They carry miniature bows and arrows. The human spirits are often accompanied by the spirits of animals and birds that are believed to dwell somewhere between the sky and the earth.

The spirits commune with the *Yuwipi* man, who is also known as *iyeska*—in this context meaning "medium"—and the patient is usually advised that he or she will become well after praying to Wakantanka and being mindful of his or her responsibility as a Lakota. The meeting ends with the departure of the spirits. The patient feels better, and when the lights are turned back on the *Yuwipi* man has been miraculously untied and is sitting in the middle of the altar with the quilt neatly folded beside him. The ropes that bound him and the tobacco offerings are rolled into a ball. The meeting ends with the communal drinking of water, the smoking of the sacred pipe by all, and the repetition of the prayer formula *mitak oyas'in* 'all my relations,' meaning that part of the reason for these ceremonies is so that all may sing and pray that they may live a long time with their relations. The *Yuwipi*, like all traditional ceremonies, concludes with a feast, usually featuring traditional foods, particularly dog stew, which is considered sacred.

Although *Yuwipi* ritual specialists are always males, women play an important part in the entire ceremony. Nearly all *Yuwipi* men are married, and though it is the man who goes on a vision quest in order to receive power to cure, once the power has been vested in him and he decides to "walk with the pipe," his wife and all his female relatives are expected to live up to the standards he sets for himself. These include being particularly attentive about menstrual restrictions and never entering the *Yuwipi* meeting or going near any of the *Yuwipi* man's paraphernalia while menstruating, including his pipe, tobacco, rattles, and the special altar he sets up at each meeting. It is still believed that menstruating women diminish the power of sacred things, and if they should accidentally come in contact with them, the objects must be taken into a sweat lodge and be prayed and sung over by the medicine man to restore their power.[10]

The female relatives of the *Yuwipi* man are also expected to exhibit behavior exemplary for an Oglala woman and should by all means avoid situations that may lead to gossip. Any incrimination of the woman is likely to reflect on the *Yuwipi* man, diminishing his power, and may even cause sickness or death in the family. All these restrictions are considered difficult to live with, and this philosophy is enunciated in every vision quest when the *Yuwipi* men receive their power. They are told that it will be "hard to walk with the pipe" and that eventually one will "stumble." Although not consciously articulated, it is perhaps one of the ironies of the Indian way that the *Yuwipi* men, upon whom the people depend, all eventually lose their power and often are shunned in old age.

The wives of *Yuwipi* men or medicine men are generally active in all traditional religious ceremonies such as the memorial Feast and the Sun Dance. They not only supervise the feasts but instruct the families of patients how to get ready for the *Yuwipi*. There are normally several days of preparation for the one- to two-hour ritual, and this includes purchasing and preparing the *wannunyanpi*, the cloth offerings that adorn the altar, and making hundreds of *canli wapaȟte*, the minute tobacco offerings that delineate the sacred space in the darkened room.

The wife of one *Yuwipi* man I knew for several years served as his translator in the meetings, since he was partly deaf and responded only to the particular pitch of her voice. When she died the *Yuwipi* man announced that his power had been broken and that he could no longer practice as a ritual specialist.

The wife of a *Yuwipi* man may also be a medicine woman in her own right and either practice spiritual curing or, more frequently, serve as an herbalist. The woman who practices herbal medicine is usually past menopause, because she must continually select and prepare various medicines and would diminish their efficacy if she were menstruating.

Finally, though the woman who participates in the Sun Dance does not pierce her breast because of modesty, she may offer one or several pieces of flesh from her arms during the course of the dance. She may also dance beside her husband or brother who has pierced himself until he breaks through. During the Sun

Dance in 1980, over 250 women offered flesh each day at the four-day ceremony.

The rationale for a woman's sacredness is still the White Buffalo Calf Woman. The story is told again and again and continues to be the major inspiration of Oglala religion and Oglala femininity.

12 Sex Roles and Social Structure

Myth and Reality

I began this study with an investigation of the cosmological matrix out of which the Lakota woman emerges and followed with what I perceive as the ideological basis for being a contemporary Oglala woman. I chose to describe this ideological background from the perspective of life cycle:

> The description of a life cycle is a classical methodological exercise for anthropology. It can also become a heuristic tool, indispensable for the investigation of the processes of change that marked the life of this woman who was able to move out of the private social arena and into the public arena, thus obtaining access to the power structure. (Bunster 1976, 302–3)

If one compares the myth of the female past with the reality of the female present, it seems that the cosmological relation between males and females in the prereservation period has reversed itself in the contemporary period. In myth it is the woman who brings the sacred pipe and the seven sacred rites and thereby guarantees that the people will live long with relations. She and the buffalo are one—that is, there is an equation between nourishment nad reproduction, symbolized in the manifestation of the buffalo that is at the same time female. The men in the myth defer to the woman's wishes, and the penalty for disobeying is death—the extinction of the people—so dramatically expressed in the episode when the hunter who lusts for the White Buffalo Calf Woman, the source of life and hope, is enveloped by the fog of ignorance and reduced to a pile of bones.

The empirical reality for this historical period, however, was that males and females participated equally in ensuring their very survival. Each had a contribution to make, and in the tough

Plains existence one did not have the luxury of arguing over the division of labor or possible dominant and inferior status.

Today both the male and female ideology and the real gender roles have been disrupted, partly because of the establishment of the reservation and partly because the white man promotes, conciously or unconciously, a division of labor that stresses the dominant/subordinate relationship between males and females.

According to this American ideology, which many Oglala males undeniably subscribe to, the male is superior, the female inferior both in myth and in everyday life. And what is projected ideologically by the Oglala female today is that the men are in charge. They were and continue to be the chiefs, the warriors, the leaders, the workers, even though it is commonly recognized and verbalized that men have a harder time adjusting to modern life than women because they have been stripped of their historical role as provider. The myth, then, is that today women defer to men and that the Oglalas will survive through the men, particularly the men's ability to negotiate and maintain harmonious relations with the federal government.

But empirically it is the women who are more stable as workers, educators, students, and professionals, and there is a current increase in the participation of women not only in the work force, where they have always felt comfortable, but in the ranks of leadership: as superintendents of reservations, district and community leaders, judges, and contenders for the presidency of the Oglala Sioux Tribe. The reality is that men increasingly defer to women. But this is clouded owing to the influence of the Euramerican, or at least non-Indian, ideology forced on Oglala children in the schools and by the necessity of living in a white man's world. The mythic superiority of womanhood and the real deference of men in the early cosmology are replaced today by the real superiority of females and their mythic deference to men.

In the past, the United States government was accustomed to treat and otherwise interact with male leaders. Thus, to project a picture of a strong Oglala male was an important survival strategy; it was tantamount to presenting an image of a strong Sioux nation. Today, whether or not the women are in authority, they continue to bolster their men, presenting them as leaders, bosses, persons in charge, whether of a store, a community, a district, or a tribe. Oglala women support their men consciously as part of an ongoing strategy for survival in the white man's world. Ironically, this strategy may in the long run diminish the ability of the Lakota people to truly take charge of their own destiny. This false sense of security, supported by the continuing myth that the men are in charge, makes it impossible for male leaders to really compete in a society free from the control of the United States government through agencies such as the Bureau of Indian Affairs.

For example, though at Pine Ridge local government is strangled by petty bureaucracy to the extent that even minor decisions are difficult to make, tribal leaders travel to Washington, D.C., or write letters and resolutions to congressmen or even to the president of the United States making outrageous demands. The tribal leaders who cannot control even the limited economy of the reservation—such basic necessities as gas stations and grocery stores—appeal to the federal government to give them control of the Black Hills with all their resources so that the Sioux can underwrite their own tribal programs. And the chasm between myth and reality is unusually wide. The real, pressing needs are counted in relatively small loans to businessmen, the opening of light industry, and the establishment of an economy that will offset high unemployment; but rather than looking at the possibilities for local development at Pine Ridge and its relation to interstate trade, the tribal leaders are planning, if given the Black Hills, how they will contribute to the gross national product. The goals of the tribe are global and therefore unrealistic, and all are destined to fail.

While Oglala men set impossible goals at the national and regional levels, the women take charge at the local level, in the community and in the family. The man who cannot manage to earn profits in a small business set up by the federal government will neglect the realities of product manufacture and invest his energies in organizing a regional sales force. And the women who stand behind him permit him to fantasize about his role in American business—until the few products are given up to pay the bills, the business is closed, and the man is busy developing another scheme with which to approach the Small Business Administration or a similar funding agency for another loan.

Against this grim reality we see that the most successful

businesses on the reservation have frequently been started by enterprising Oglala businessmen but usually end up being leased to white entrepreneurs or chains.

Sometimes, even when circumstances are embarrassing to individuals or the tribe, they are overlooked because "that's the Indian way." Thus failure has been incorporated into the value system so that it is acceptable because Indians are expected in the long run to fail at the white man's jobs. In summer 1981 when members of the Oglala Sioux Tribe, with the support of part of the tribal council, decided to "invade" the Black Hills to protest the failure to settle the Black Hills claim, the "invaders" were required to purchase a camping permit from the National Park Service, an act that most Oglalas on the sidelines considered ridiculous. Nevertheless the invaders bought the permit, set up camp in an isolated area where no one could see them, and finally were ejected because they were littering the landscape. A white backlash group was quick to question whether Mother Earth really deserved such treatment from those who at least in rhetoric regarded the Black Hills as sacred. In the meantime other factions of the tribal council were distressed because the "invasion" took place at the very time when their lawyer was trying to argue the case reasonably in the courts.

Of course symbolic statements about oppression do not take the place of action. There is some indication that most Oglalas at Pine Ridge are aware that militants who want to invade the Black Hills or take over Wounded Knee, as happened in 1973, are essentially playing into the federal government's hands. For as long as the Indians continue to make *symbolic* last stands, they will continue to lose their land to large corporate interests.

And if the people want the image of the Oglala warrior as one who goes out to take over a remote section of the land, the government is willing to tacitly support it. One woman told me a story that illustrates just how far the federal government believes the Indian status quo should be preserved:

> There is a story about an anthropologist who was sent out to Pine Ridge by the government to see what could be done for the Indian people. After being out here for some time the agent in charge asked for his recommendations. Well, the anthropologist said, "The Indian men either stir up trou-

ble or they go hunting. And when they go hunting they bring the game home and the Indian women butcher it, clean it, and cook it. They make food out of it, they make clothes out of it, and they make shelter out of it. When they get ready to move, the Indian women roll up the tipi, pack up the kids, pack up the horse, and pull the travois. When they get to their new location, she sets up the tipi, cooks the food and takes care of the kids while the men go out hunting again."

And the agent said, "Who could improve on that?"

But women are very much aware of the myth and reality of the stereotypical Indian woman, and frequently they favor perpetuating the myth, particularly in front of their own men. It is not only in positions of leadership and control that men are made to feel they are the bosses—this myth begins at home. According to one woman:

Maybe I could learn to cook better, and maybe I should be a little more tolerant with my kids, but that's about all I'd want to change. My husband is domineering, and I think that's good because a strong father image is good for the kids. Maybe I put my husband on a pedestal, but a man should be a strong figure in his own home.

The same woman believes:

As for being aggressive, I don't think I am aggressive in the household. I think it's more at work where my job is concerned, that's when I am more aggressive. At home I am more docile, I cuss less. I noticed that in my friends' homes who don't let the man be in charge, who insist on ruling the homes, that's where I see the family problems. I think my husband is a better person to handle the money, so even though I work he handles all the money, and I think he does it well. He built this house and keeps us in fine shape financially.

Many of the contemporary women believe that even though women work the men should control the money. According to another:

I have a friend, and she and her husband have a
lot of problems because she controls the money
and he thinks that she is the smartest person in the
home. Maybe she is, but she should let him be because I think that men definitely have to be put in
a position where they are the major head of the
household and make the major decisions because
even in the background you [women] always play a
major role in what happens anyway.

Nevertheless, it is still recognized that women are beginning
to gain acceptance in leadership roles. As another woman said:

Now I see that women are not only leading the
households but that they are leading a lot, they are
on the tribal council, they are leading the community, and maybe they do it by using the best of
both worlds, by being aggressive when you have
to. My own experience is that the women out here
have a hell of a lot to say about what's going on
here.
   And they always have. I remember my mother
used to tell me about an old chief's wife, Sharp
Tongue. They called her that because she ruled
the roost.

Many Oglala women I interviewed were of the opinion that
without Indian women there would be no Indian culture:

So many of our so-called leaders, and I use that
advisedly, mostly are people that white culture has
picked out as our leaders, are people who are married to or living with white women who are willing
to wag their feet and are willing to do whatever it
takes to be an Indian. There is such a groundswell,
a return to the earth, a return to the ancient culture that we have a whole bunch of people outside
of the Indian culture who want so badly to identify
with Indians they are willing to do anything, whatever it takes. If it means doing all the shit work,
work that Indian women won't do or which we do
only in a partnership situation, then they have to
find someone who is willing to do it, someone who
is not an Indian but wants to be one. I think that

we are incredibly strong. I think that Indian
women are much stronger than Indian men.

Without exception, all the women I interviewd who are active
in politics, law, religion, and professional roles in general were
all expected to be able to perform so-called male activities when
they were growing up. And they were expected to excel in female
activities as well. In other words, their parents had high expecta-
tions for them, and today these women expect more of their
daughters and granddaughters than they do of their sons and
grandsons in their education and professions. Even some men
have higher aspirations for their daughters and granddaughters.
One man said:

> I never got acquainted with my wife until I retired.
> I never got to know her, but now we're really get-
> ting acquainted, and she seems to have had a lot
> of influence on me. And she seems to be very ac-
> tive in church even though she stays home most of
> the time. She was really active in the community,
> even though she never did work. And she's still
> active and so is her sister—she works—so it seems
> to run in the family. So probably my granddaugh-
> ter will be a lawyer one of these days.

Some women see their role as similar to those in other cultures, not as associated exclusively with being Oglala or Indian:

> I think most minority cultures end up with the
> same thing. I think with minority cultures women
> usually end up being the hub of the family. Being
> the head of the family, I feel the reason for that is
> that the white power structure has set up a form-
> ula for existing and living and subsisting, and I
> think one way of existing in certain cultures is that
> you conform to certain rules and that is, if there is
> not a male in the house to take care of you, you
> care for yourself and your family. So women have
> ended up this way, the head of households.
>   One of the things that happened in our culture
> here and I'm sure maybe happened in Indian
> tribes everywhere is that we [women] fit in a lot
> easier into the mainstream, the mainstream of the
> marketplace. We fit in a lot quicker because we

were domestics sooner and evolved into secretaries
a lot sooner, but men were hunters and warriors
and when we got fences, restricting people physically, they couldn't hunt and be warriors.

And some believe that the white man's culture has tended to
diminish complementarity between the sexes:

Women were the ones who were trained, so they
got the upper hand, and this emasculated a lot of
our population. There wasn't a ready role for the
men as there was for the women. So I think that it
really pitted Indian women and men against each
other in the sense that they had never really vied
with each other in the same way that white men
and women had. They had always sort of meshed,
and they didn't anymore.
I don't know if women would have made a dis-
tinctly different decision from the men. The men
that made the decisions essentially made the right
decisions for the time they were making them.

But still others are of the opinion that

Indian men appreciate what they have a lot more
than a white man would. What I am saying is,
once white influence was interjected into our own
cultural picture it's a little bit hard to weed it out
and to pretend it was never there, for me. But I
am an Indian, and I just think that Indian men
appreciate their counterparts a little more than
white men.

This sentiment has been carried even further in the past:

These people [whites] endured great hardships,
and all the while they were thinking that our
women were slaves we felt that theirs were. It may
not flatter the white man, but the Lakota did not
think him considerate toward his women. (Standing Bear 1933, 172)

Something Old, Something New

It is perhaps not unusual that colonized peoples not only construct a past that is more satisfying than their real history but also construct a more satisfying present. The current myth holds on to the superiority of the male even though since the Indian Reorganization Act Indian women have been as well educated as Indian men. Though missionaries came to be the greatest purveyors of education, implicitly if not explicitly teaching Indian girls to be submissive to men, it was women who, because of their ability to manage the household, were able to employ these skills in managing important programs and thus to acquire better jobs.

The women who have become professionals tend to exhibit the same aggressive capabilities as men. They can do most things as well as a man, from riding horses to driving tractors—they are carpenters, construction workers, and policewomen. As one woman's father said: "If you can't ride a horse right, just get the hell off the horse." But they are also the ones who express the greatest fear of losing their traditional culture and langauge, even though the occupations they profess are for the most part identifiably Euramerican in nature—nurses, judges, businesswomen, arts and crafts experts, lawyers, and community leaders. While the men are still sent off to fight the great battles in Washington and even the United Nations, it is the women who establish stability at home, making it possible for the modern-day warriors to succeed—or to fail gracefully.

What makes the Oglala woman particularly adept at what she does in running the family and running the tribe and at the same time making the man believe he is the real chief is that she exhibits a number of dimensions to her personality. She is not simply Indian or white, she is not simply traditional or modern, and she is not simply female—often filling a male role. What makes her most capable in her roles as wife and mother on the one hand and as effective community leader on the other is her ability to move along a number of continua with ideological Indianness at one end and the white world at the other. The successful Oglala woman can while away her day seeking Indian medicines or sit in the shade and sing old Indian songs to herself. But she can also pick up a guitar and accompany herself singing "Rock of Ages." She is neither one nor the other and can easily make the transition to either, situationally.

The successful Oglala woman is also aware of another continuum. She can be a traditional Indian, a grandmother if you will, giving advice to young girls and women and transmitting the code of the Lakotas through the stories and legends of fantastic cosmological beings as well as the brave heroes of the historical past. But at another time she moves to the other end of the scale where she is the modern Indian woman participating in treaty demonstrations or other activities such as the Sacred Shawl Society or WARN. Today the traditional woman may even pray alone on the vision quest and take part in the sweat lodge, while her modern counterpart dons a shawl and takes part in a contemporary powwow dance that her great-grandmother would not have recognized as even being Indian.

Finally, the successful Oglala woman glides along a most precarious continuum, back and forth from behaving as the ideal wife and mother whose role it is, as in the old days, to carry out the dictates of the White Buffalo Calf Woman—to reproduce and to nurture future generations of Oglala people, males and females. But she will also have the capacity to occupy the same position as a male with respect to community, district, and tribal activities and programs, recognizing that the men will not compete with her for female roles and responsibilities.

Oglala women are adept at working within the white man's system. If they cannot work in the factory, the white man allows them to take their work home, where they can participate in his system while living in their "natural environment," the household—near the kitchen, near the children, and near the bed. On the other hand, the male who cannot regularly punch a time clock, who gets drunk or gives up what jobs he does get out of the frustration of being an Oglala in a white man's world, has no alternative except to go home to his wife or mother.

Some Oglala men are of course successful. Many are leaders, and many in fact exhibit admirable characteristics of resoluteness and sensitivity to the demands of being an Indian leader in the twentieth century. But the goals a male Indian leader sets for himself are quite different from the ones a woman sets for herself. While men are organizing the Black Hills Treaty Council and the Black Hills Alliance, dealing with issues that involve the United States government—issues like uranium mining and control over natural gas and other resources—women tend to limit themselves realistically to immediate problems—what to do about abandoned children, teenage pregnancies, battered women, and hungry senior citizens. In this they are never challenged by their peers, their men, or especially the white man; these are issues that in retrospect would have been championed by the White Buffalo Calf Woman, who after all represents not simply Lakota culture, but the entire range of humanity. From an anthropological perspective, Oglala women, like women elsewhere, respond to an evolutionary imperative to reproduce and nurture. They continue to follow the dictates of the white Buffalo Calf Woman, who is not so much an exemplary Lakota woman as she is Everywoman endowed with the perspicacity to know that what is good for the individual is good for the species— metaphorically known as "the People" among the Lakotas.

Oglala women, it seems, like women in all parts of the world, are making the right choices. Certainly some have fallen prey to alcohol. Some have left the reservation and despite their blood quantum have become white women. Some have stayed at home, the mistresses of their menfolk, succumbing to their husbands' and fathers' wishes like automatons. Some have married well, some have married poorly, some have not married at all. Some have children, and the children may be raised well or not, and some are abandoned. In many ways Oglala women are no different from their non-Oglala or non-Indian contemporaries except in the particular way they choose to identify their femaleness, which distinguishes them from other communities, other tribes, and other nations.

Yet in many ways Oglala women are very different from their white peers. Given the same region of the United States, the Great Plains, Oglala women are probably tougher than most white women. They drink, and they fight in ways that are decidedly unladylike by white standards. But they are also genteel in ways that white women are not. Oglala women are extremely generous—those raised in a traditional household will give away everything. It is second nature to them. They dress more modestly, and sometimes they point with their chins rather than their fingers, and age-old Oglala custom. They are just as distressed as white women are when their daughters become pregnant by a casual boyfriend. But they will not seek abortions and they will not give away their babies if they deem themselves traditional. A fatherless child—if that term has meaning cross-culturally—will be brought into the mother's family as a full member, cuddled and tossed around from grandmother to grandfather, from aunt to uncle, from niece to nephew, and from sister to brother without concern that its biological father is not present. And it will grow into an adult without stigma, because that is the Indian way.

Oglala women, in myth, ritual, and reality, have adapted to their ever changing environment as a product of their heritage. Their particular culture, historically rooted in the culture of the Plains Indians, emphasizes living according to standards that fall between the teachings of another woman, the White Buffalo Calf Woman, and all of Western Euramerican society that has subjugated them, at least politically and economically.

The Oglala female (and male) assigns the highest priority to welfare of the tribe. As such, traditional culture—myth and reality—obliges her to participate fully as leader, worker, and sometimes follower. But she is primarily *Oglala* and secondarily *Indian*. Unlike many of her non-Indian counterparts, who view womanhood exclusively in terms of gender differences, being a wife, sister, and mother only partially defines her role as an Oglala woman.

Notes

Introduction

1. Ortner's explanation for women's universal subordination also attributes it to female physiology, specifically the maternal role, from both a biological and a cultural perspective. Ortner maintains that because of the natural procreative functions specific to women, females are more closely associated with "nature" while males are associated with "culture." She asserts that since culture is regarded as superior to nature, males are seen as superior to females.

2. No berdache arrangement existed for Plains Indian women; there were no institutionalized means by which a female might change her role and status to "male" (Forgey 1975, 1–2).

3. Lily Shangreaux, "A Look at Domestic Violence," *Lakota Times*, 20 August 1981, 4.

Chapter One

1. Sandoz 1961, 103.

2. DeMallie 1971, Feraca 1966, Feraca and Howard 1963, Hyde 1937, 1956, 1961, Olson 1965, Robinson 1904, and Utley 1963 provide the essential historical treatments.

3. In Lakota, women's speech is distinguished from men's, particularly in the use of interjections and by various enclitics marking declarative, imperative, and interrogative sentences. For example, the expression "come here" is rendered *hiyu wo!* by a man and *hiyu we!* by a woman.

4. For a discussion of these political distinctions, see DeMallie 1971, Densmore 1918, and Howard 1966. For problems in the nomenclature see Powers 1977, 3–14.

5. For a discussion of eastern sedentary life see Meyer 1967. See also Murdock 1949 and Powers 1977 for relevant information on social structure.

6. The penchant for organizing political units by sevens is discussed by Powers 1977, 30–31.

Chapter Two

1. Brown 1971, 133.

2. The major criticism has been by Deloria 1937. However, the works of Melody 1977, Powers 1977, *Ehanni ohunkakan*, n.d., and Walker 1980 clarify many of the issues once challenged.

3. This analysis follows Powers 1977, 167.

4. I have shown that this relationship is prevalent in a number of ritual performances, particularly those related to menstruation and reproduction. See M. Powers 1980.

5. Maȟpiyato 'blue sky' is also known as Takuškanškan 'that which moves' or by its abbreviated form Skan; it connotes energy or the force that moves things (Walker 1917).

6. The quotation is from Beckwith 1930, 408. See also Powers 1977 and Walker 1917 for characteristics of the four winds.

7. The expurgated story appears in Buechel 1978. Other stories about the pipe appear in Brown 1971, Densmore 1918, Dorsey 1906, Powers 1977, Walker 1980, and Wissler 1907, among others.

8. Densmore 1918, 67–68. I have revised the translation somewhat.

9. The American Horse count in Mallery 1886, 130.

10. The White Bull count in Howard 1968, 8.

11. Lone Man's account in Densmore 1918, 66.

12. These references may be found for the year 1798 in the Colhoff account in Powers 1963 and the Battiste Good count for 1797–98 in Mallery 1886.

13. In Powers 1963, 29.

14. The Battiste Good count in Mallery 1886, 103.

15. The winter count of the Oglalas, Ben Kindle, is probably the same as the Colhoff account, but it appears with greater elaboration in Beckwith 1930, 355.

16. Cited in Beckwith 1930, 356; but see also Brown 1971, Densmore 1918, Powers 1977, and Walker 1980.

17. Parallels in other religions are obvious.

18. The idea of revitalization movement is appropriate here in that the White Buffalo Calf Woman is in fact a prophet (Wallace 1956).

Chapter Three

1. Bean et al. 1976, level 2.

2. The Lakota term for pregnant is *igluš'ake*, the reflexive form of *yuš'ake*, meaning to be burdened or overloaded, to have as much as one can carry (Buechel 1970, 653). Another term is *hokšiipignaka*, meaning to gird oneself with child. To be in labor is *hokšikiksuye*, literally 'to remember the child' (but the meaning is not clear). To beget is *hokšikaga*, literally 'to make a baby.' The term for abortion is *hokšihiyukiya* 'to cause the child to come forth.'

3. Most writers refer to this as a turtle without giving the Lakota term. However, *t'elanunwe* is clearly 'lizard.'

4. In Lakota *hantkan* (?).

5. *Hupestola* 'sharp-pointed stem.'

6. *Waȟpewaštemna* 'sweet-smelling leaves.

7. *Pejuta skuya* 'sweet medicine.'

8. *Maka canšihu* 'gumwood stem.'

9. *Pejizizila* 'yellow medicine.'

10. *Waȟpe ceyaka* 'leaf mint.'

11. *Heȟaka tapejuta* 'elk's medicine.'

12. *Hokšicekpa* 'baby's navel.'

13. *Icaȟpehu* 'strike-down stem.'

14. *Sinkpe tawoyute* 'muskrat's food.'

15. *Pejuta janjans'ele* 'glassy medicine.'

16. Radin (1956) provides Winnebago and Assiniboine trickster myths whose themes are identical to those of Lakota myths. A number of Lakota "spider stories" were collected in Lakota and translated by Deloria (1932).

17. Densmore (1918, 68–77) provides an excellent description of the *Hunka* she witnessed. Also see Brown 1971, Powers 1977, and Walker 1917, 1980.

18. Literally the state of being a younger sister, for a female speaker.

Chapter Four

1. Brown 1971, 120–21.

2. For a description of this ritual see Brown 1971, Fletcher 1884, Powers 1977, M. Powers 1980, and Walker 1917, 1980.

3. See also Wissler (1907), who considers the cocoon a symbol of procreation.

4. Walker 1980, 107. See also M. Powers (1980) for an interpretation of menstrual rules.

5. The Lakota term closest to our idea of rape is *wiiyuȟ'aya*, derived from *kiyuȟ'a* 'the way animals copulate.'

6. For a description of the Sun dance see, among others, Brown 1971, Densmore 1918, Dorsey 1889, Powers 1977, and Walker 1917, 1980.

Chapter Five

1. Standing Bear 1928.

2. I plan a comprehensive study of Oglala kinship. Available works include Hassrick 1964, Lesser 1928, and Walker 1914, the last being the most important because it includes a Lakota text on kinship. But no definitive work yet exists.

3. A term also used to mean prostitute.

4. Hence "natal" here refers to the *tiyošpaye*—the environment, albeit nomadic, into which one is born.

5. The Lakota term that signifies the husband's presentation of horses to the wife's parents is *opetun*, today glossed 'to buy.' However, there is no evidence that this gift resembled bride-price, since nothing was returned should there be a divorce. The exchange was essentially reciprocal, the bride later presenting gifts to her husband's parents.

6. Since "marriage" is not marked by single ceremony but rather is a drawn-out process of gift exchanges and feasts, the term "bride" is at best arbitrary.

7. The idea of *wicawoȟ'a* suggests asymmetry in male/female relationshps only because of the negative values it connotes. It also suggests that the Oglalas, despite their ideological emphasis on egalitarianism between males and females, in fact displayed some form of hierarchy in relationships between families.

8. In fact, "co-wives" form another kinship domain called *teyakiciyapi* 'they call each other *teya*.'

9. Hence the extreme joking relationship tended to reduce the very real possibility of sexual relations between potential spouses before their actual spouses died. The Oglalas are still very much aware of this potential and joke about it in speech and in song.

10. See Faculty and Students of Crazy Horse School 1978 for some modern-day recipes. See also Nurge 1970 for an essay on Indian diet. A more comprehen-

sive analysis of food from the perspective of procurement, preparation, distribution, consumption, and redistribution may be found in Powers and Powers 1984.

11. Wissler 1940, 159–60, discusses various uses for the buffalo. See also Mails 1972, 190–91.

12. Standing Bear 1933, 91. For design elements and decorative techniques see Lyford 1940. For an excellent description of pictographic drawing see Blish 1967. Orchard 1916 and 1929 contain techniques of beadwork and quillwork, and Hanson 1975 provides a catalog of metal utensils acquired through trade.

13. For a description of a woman's dress see Lyford 1940.

14. In Lakota *ungnahela hotun* means to make the voice come forth suddenly.

Chapter Six

1. Bean et al. 1976, level 3.

2. This is the opposite of the Euramerican notion that if one forgets one's umbrella it will rain. Here the Lakota point of view is Frazerian but in a positive way. Lighting fires under the kettles causes the buffalo to be born—and eventually eaten.

3. There is no question that Indians responded to these diseases with horror. Recording them became a significant part of the winter counts.

4. Feraca 1963 provides some information on medicine women at Pine Ridge.

5. This figure is based on the botanical work of Buechel 1970 and on Rogers's useful manual (1980) compiled from Buechel's work.

6. In Lakota known variously as *poipiye* 'to cure swelling'; *canhlogan waštemna* 'sweet-smelling reed'; and *canhlogan unzipakinte* 'reed for wiping the anus' (because it was used for toilet paper).

7. In Lakota, *sinkpe tawoyute* 'muskrat's food.'

8. *Iniyan pejuta* 'breathing medicine.'

9. *Hehaka tapejuta* 'elk's medicine.'

10. *Wahpe ceyaka* 'leaf mint.'

11. *Pejizizila* 'yellow medicine.'

12. *Icahpehu* 'strike-down stem.'

13. *Pejuta skuya* 'sweet medicine.'

14. Called the *wanagi wapahte* 'ghost bundle or wrapping.'

15. Called *wanagi tipi* 'ghost lodge.'

16. It was considered bad manners to walk between a seated person and the fire. The proper way was to pass behind the person.

17. Called *wanagi glepi*.

18. Buechel 1978. There is no evidence for bachelorhood or spinsterhood in Oglala culture.

19. Traditional Oglalas continue to believe that the white man goes to a special hereafter when he dies.

Chapter Seven

1. McNickle 1973, 82–83. Under the Dawes Act of 1887, tribal lands were allotted according to a formula: 160 acres to the head of household, 80 acres to

single persons over eighteen and orphans under eighteen, and forty acres to other single persons under eighteen. All land remaining after allotment was deemed "surplus land" and was open to homesteaders or sold to the United States government or to others. For example, the Sissetons of South Dakota occupied 918,000 acres. The two-thousand members of the tribe received their allotment (300,000 acres according to the formula), and over 600,000 acres were in the surplus category.

2. *Vital Statistics*, South Dakota Department of Health 1970–78.

3. "Lakota Women's Council Initiated," *Lakota Eyapaha* (Pine Ridge, S.D.) 3, no. 6 (1979): 53.

4. Ibid.

5. "An Interview with Hildegarde Catches/Red [War] Bonnet Woman," *Lakota Eyapaha* 4, no. 2 (1980): 10.

6. Shirley Plume ran for tribal president but was defeated in primaries held in February 1982.

Chapter Eight

1. The districts are Wakpamni, White Clay, Wounded Knee, Porcupine, Medicine Root, Eagle Nest, Pass Creek, and La Creek. Recently, owing to its large population (three-thousand persons), Pine Ridge was given district status, bringing the total to nine.

2. It is recognized by Indian and white store owners even today that one cannot operate a business catering to Indians without providing some form of credit.

3. "Alcohol and the Pine Ridge Reservation," *Lakota Eyapaha* (Pine Ridge, S.D.) 5, no. 2 (1981): 29.

4. Ibid., 27.

5. Most "Indian" beadwork found in tourist shops is made in Japan or Hong Kong.

6. Holy Rosary Mission provides an outlet for arts and crafts, as does the Arts and Crafts Co-op, run by Zona Fills the Pipe on behalf of the Oglala Sioux Tribe.

7. Indian arts and crafts are today regularly auctioned off at such prestigious places as the Parke-Bernet Gallery in New York and command high prices.

Chapter Nine

1. Public law no. 383, 73d Congress, S. 3645. For a description of the IRA and its effects on tribal government, see Burnette and Koster 1974, Grinnell 1967, and McNickle 1973.

2. Oglala Sioux ordinance 79:47; Oglala Sioux Tribe 1965.

3. The *Lakota Times* was established in Pine Ridge in July 1981 and promises to be a source of records heretofore unobtainable. As a result of redistricting, Indians are now potential candidates for the South Dakota state senate. One of the five Indians running for this office is a woman.

4. "Plume to Run for President," *Lakota Times*, 17 December 1981, 1–2.

5. The suit is for damages and "back rent" on the Black Hills. For a statement on the position of the Oglala Sioux Tribe see the *Lakota Times*, July–August 1981.

6. "Women of All Red Nations," *Lakota Eyapaha* (Pine Ridge, S.D.) 4, no. 2 (1980): 31–34.

7. For a description of the Washington, D.C. episode see Deloria 1974.

8. For a commentary on the Wounded Knee occupation from AIM's point of view, see *Akwesasne Notes* 7, no. 3 (1975).

9. *Rapid City Journal*, 6 June 1980. This same woman traveled to Los Angeles with another woman to meet with David Wolper and protest his proposed television miniseries based on the novel *Hanta Yo*.

10. "An Interview with Hildegarde Catches/Red [War] Bonnet Woman," *Lakota Eyapaha* 4, no. 2 (1980): 10.

11. "Alcohol and the Pine Ridge Resevation," *Lakota Eyapaha* 5, no. 2 (1981): 27–29.

Chapter Ten

1. These figures represent the number of persons making up the hospital staff. Frequently the hospital operates with fewer.

2. White wives of Indian men have always been eligible for treatment at the Public Health hospital, but it was not until 1981 that white husbands of Indian women also became eligible.

3. My own opinion is that the Public Health Service doctors are no better or worse than one would expect to find off the reservation. I believe most of the frustrations exhibited by Indians and whites could be relieved through education programs, particularly for the physicians.

4. Racism is rampant at Pine Ridge, particularly since the Wounded Knee occupation. It is expressed rather openly by Oglalas in high tribal council positions.

5. In the old days expectant mothers were advised to eat proper foods and to limit their participation in household activites, which amounts to a kind of prenatal care.

6. Of course no one questions the abusive treatment of men by men, which is held to be normal behavior by both Indians and whites.

7. Ridicule is still the major form of chastisement in traditional homes.

8. Lily Shangreaux, "A Look at Domestic Violence," *Lakota Times*, 20 August 1981, 4.

9. These statistics are derived from a survey conducted by the Community Mental Health Program, United States Public Health Service, at Pine Ridge, June–December 1979.

10. Flier from Sacred Shawl Women's Society.

Chapter Eleven

1. Feraca (1963) provides a good description of peyotism at Pine Ridge.

2. On Southern Plains peyotism see LaBarre 1932. On Menomini peyotism, see Densmore 1932.

3. A well-known medicine man at Pine Ridge.

4. Powers (1976) regards even Christian ritual as one of these means, suggesting that medicine men believed the white man's god had power and attended church to discover how he could best be propitiated.

5. For a description of a modern vision quest and sweat lodge, see Powers 1977 and 1982.

6. My ethnography of the *Hunka* is forthcoming.

7. For a lengthy description and analysis of the Oglala food system see Powers and Powers 1984.

8. *Wateca'd* is the anglicized past participle of *wateca*.

9. For a complete description of Yuwipi see Kemnitzer 1976 and Powers 1982.

10. For Oglala values related to menstruation and a new analysis that sees menstrual restrictions as positively stressing female reproduction, see M. Powers 1980.

References

Ardener, Edwin. 1972. Belief and the problem of women. In *The interpretation of ritual*, ed. J. LaFontaine. London: Tavistock.

Basso, Keith, H., and H. Selby, eds. 1976. *Meaning in anthropology*. Albuquerque: University of New Mexico Press.

Beach, Frank A., ed. 1965. *Sex and behavior*. New York: John Wiley.

Bean, Sharon, Hildegarde Catches, Edwin Fills the Pipe, Elizabeth Makes Him First, Marla N. Powers, and William K. Powers. 1976. *Lak'ota wicozanni, ehank'ehan na lehanl* (Indian health, traditional and modern). Pine Ridge, S.D.: Oglala Sioux Community College Title IV Bilingual Health Program.

Beckwith, Martha W. 1930. Mythology of the Oglala Dakota. *Journal of American Folklore* 43 (October–December): 339–442.

Bermont, Gordon, and Julian M. Davidson. 1974. *Biological bases of sexual behavior*. New York: Harper and Row.

Blish, Helen H. 1967. *A pictographic history of the Oglala Sioux*. Drawings by Amos Bad Heart Bull. Lincoln: University of Nebraska Press.

Briggs, Jean L. 1974. Eskimo women: Makers of men. In *Many sisters*, ed. Carolyn Matthiasson. New York: Free Press.

Brown, Joseph Epes. 1971. *The sacred pipe*. Baltimore: Penguin Books. Originally published 1953.

Buechel, Eugene. 1939. *A grammar of Lakota*. Saint Francis, S.D.: Saint Francis Mission.

———. 1970. *Lakota–English dictionary*. Pine Ridge, S.D.: Holy Rosary Mission.

———. 1978. *Lakota tales and texts*. Pine Ridge, S.D.: Holy Rosary Mission.

Bunster B., Ximena. 1976. The emergence of a Mapuche leader: Chile. In *Sex and class in Latin America*, ed. June Nash and H. I. Safa. New York: Praeger.

Burnette, Robert, and John Koster. 1974. *The road to Wounded Knee*. New York: Bantam.

Bushnell, David I. 1927. *Burials of the Algonquian, Siouan, and Caddoan tribes west of the Mississippi*. Bulletin 83. Washington, D.C.: Bureau of American Ethnology.

Bushotter, George. 1887–88. Lakota texts. Manuscript in the National Anthropological Archives, Smithsonian Institution, Washington, D.C.

Cahn, Edgar S., ed. 1969. *Our brother's keeper: The Indian in white America*. New York: World.

Catlin, George. 1973. *Letters and notes on the manners, customs, and conditions of North American Indians*. Vols. 1 and 2. New York: Dover.

Cole, Michael, and S. Scribner. 1974. *Culture and thought*. New York: John Wiley.

Cooper, John M. 1932. The positivism of woman in primitive culture. *Primitive Man* 5:31–46.

Costo, Rupert. 1968. The American Indian today. *Indian Historian* 1 (Winter): 4–8.

The Crusader. 1948. Pine Ridge, S.D.: Holy Rosary Mission.

Daly, Martin, and Margo Wilson. 1978. *Sex, evolution and behavior*. North Scituate, Mass.: Duxbury Press.

Darwin, Charles. 1859. *The origin of species by means of natural selection*. New York: Modern Library.

———. 1871. *The descent of man*. New York: Modern Library.

DeBarthe, Joe. 1958. *Life and adventures of Frank Grouard*. Norman: University of Oklahoma Press.

Deloria, Ella C. 1929. The sun dance of the Oglala Sioux. *Journal of American Folklore* 42:354–413.

———. 1932. *Dakota texts*. Publications of the American Ethnological Society, vol. 14. New York: G. E. Steckert.

———. 1937. Dakota commentary on Walker's texts. Manuscript in the collection of the American Philosophical Society, Philadelphia.

———. 1979. *Speaking of Indians*. Vermillion, S.D.: Dakota Press. Originally published 1944.

Deloria, Ella C., and Jay Brandon, trans. 1961. The origin of the courting-flute, a legend in the Santee Dakota dialect. [*W. H. Over*] *Museum News* 22 (June):1–7.

Deloria, Vine, Jr. 1974. *Behind the trail of broken treaties*. New York: Dell.

DeMallie, Raymond J., Jr. 1971. Teton Dakota kinship and social organization. Ph.D. diss., University of Chicago.

Denig, Edwin Thompson. 1967. *Indian tribes of the upper Missouri*. Seattle: Horey Book Store.

Densmore, Frances. 1918. *Teton Sioux music*. Bulletin 61. Washington, D.C.: Bureau of American Ethnology.

———. 1932. *Menominee music*. Bulletin 102. Washington, D.C.: Bureau of American Ethnology.

——. 1948. *A collection of specimens from the Teton Sioux.* American Notes and Monographs, vol. 11, no. 3. New York: Museum of the American Indian, Heye Foundation.

Dorsey, J. Owen. 1889. A study of Siouan cults. In *Eleventh Annual Report of the Bureau of American Ethnology*, 351–544. Washington, D.C.: Government Printing Office.

——. 1891. Games of Teton Dakota children. *American Anthropologist* 4 (October): 329–45.

——. 1906. Legend of the Teton Sioux medicine pipe. *Journal of American Folk Lore* 19:326–92.

Douglas, Mary. 1966. *Purity and danger.* Harmondsworth, Middlesex: Routledge and Kegan Paul.

——, ed. 1984. *Food in the social order.* New York: Russell Sage.

Durkheim, Emile. 1915. *The elementary forms of the religious life.* London: Allen and Unwin.

Eastman, Elaine Goodale. 1978. *Sister to the Sioux.* Lincoln: University of Nebraska Press.

Ehanni ohunkakan. n.d. Pine Ridge, S.D.: Red Cloud Indian School.

Emery, M., and Ann Laquer. 1981. Perspectives on Native American women. *Indian Truth* (Philadelphia, Indian Rights Association) 239 (May–June): 5–7.

Erikson, Erik H. 1939. Observations on Sioux education. *Journal of Psychology* 7:101–56.

——. 1950. Hunters across the prairie. In *Childhood and society*, 114–65. New York: Norton.

——. 1965. Inner and outer space: Reflections on womanhood. In *The woman in America*, ed. Robert J. Lifton. Boston: Houghton Mifflin.

Ewers, John C. 1970. Contraceptive charms among the Plains Indians. *Plains Anthropologist* 15:216–18.

Faculty and students of Crazy Horse School. 1978. *Pute tiyošpaye* (Lip's camp). Wanblee, S.D.: Crazy Horse School.

Fay, George. 1967. The Sioux tribes of South Dakota, part 1. In *Charters, constitutions, and by-laws of the Indian tribes of North America.* Greeley: Colorado State College, Museum of Anthropology.

Feraca, Stephen E. 1963. *Wakinyan: Contemporary Teton Dakota religion.* Browning, Mont.: Museum of the Plains Indian.

——. 1966. The political status of the early bands and modern communities of the Oglala Dakota. [*W. H. Over*] *Museum News* 27:1–2.

Feraca, Stephen E., and J. H. Howard. 1963. The identity and demography of the Dakota Sioux tribe. *Plains Anthropologist* 8:20.

Finerty, John F. 1890. *War-path and bivouac.* Norman: University of Oklahoma Press.

Flannery, Regina. 1932. The position of woman among the Mescalero Apache. *Primitive Man* 5:26–32.

Fletcher, Alice C. 1883. The sun dance of the Ogallala Sioux. *Proceedings of the American Association for the Advancement of Science* 31:580–84.

———. 1884a. *The elk mystery or festival of the Ogallala.* Peabody Museum Reports, vols. 3–4. Cambridge: Peabody Museum.

———. 1884b. The white buffalo festival of the Uncpapas. In *Sixteenth and seventeenth annual reports of the Peabody Museum, Harvard*, 3, nos. 3 and 4, 260–75. Cambridge: Peabody Museum.

———. 1904. *The hako: A Pawnee ceremony.* Twenty-second Annual Report, pt. 2. Washington, D.C.: Bureau of American Ethnology.

Ford, C. S. 1970. Some primitive societies. In *Sex roles in changing society*, ed. Georgene H. Seward and Robert C. Williamson, 25–43. New York: Random House.

Ford, C. S., and F. A. Beach. 1952. *Patterns of sexual behavior.* New York: Harper.

Forgey, Donald G. 1975. The institution of berdache among the North American Plains Indians. *Journal of Sex Research* 11 (February): 1–15.

Fox, Robin. 1975. *Encounter with anthropology.* New York: Dell.

Frazer, James G. 1963. *The golden bough*, vol. 1. Abridged ed. New York: Macmillan. Originally published 1922.

Friedl, Ernestine. 1975. *Women and men: An anthropologist's view.* New York: Holt, Rinehart and Winston.

Geertz, Clifford. 1973. *The interpretation of cultures.* New York: Basic Books.

Goldfrank, Esther S. 1943. Historic change and social character: A study of the Teton Dakota. *American Anthropologist*, n.s., 45:67–83.

Goll, Louis J. 1940. *Jesuit missions among the Sioux.* Saint Francis, S.D.: Saint Francis Mission.

Graham, W. A. 1926. *The story of the Little Big Horn.* New York: Bonanza Books.

———. 1953. *The Custer myth.* Harrisburg, Pa.: Stackpole.

Green, Rayna. 1980. Native American women. *Signs* 6 (Winter): 248–76.

Grinnell, Ira H. 1967. *The tribal government of the Oglala Sioux.* Special Project 22. Vermillion: Governmental Research Bureau, University of South Dakota.

Grobsmith, Elizabeth S. 1981. *Lakota of the Rosebud.* New York: Holt, Rinehart and Winston.

Hagan, William T. 1966. *Indian police and judges.* New Haven: Yale University Press.

Hanson, James A. 1975. *Metal weapons, tools, and ornaments of the Teton Dakota Indians*. Lincoln: University of Nebraska Press.

Hassrick, Royal B. 1964. *The Sioux: Life and customs of a warrior society*. Norman: University of Oklahoma Press.

Hewitt, J. N. B. 1910. Woman. In *The handbook of North American Indians*, ed. F. W. Hodge, 2:968–73. Bulletin 30. Washington, D.C.: Bureau of American Ethnology.

Honigman, John J. 1973. *Handbook of social and cultural anthropology*. Chicago: Rand McNally

Howard, James H. 1966. The Teton or western Dakota. [*W. H. Over*] *Museum News* 27:1–6.

———. 1968. *The warrior who killed Custer*. Lincoln: University of Nebraska Press.

———. 1976. Yanktonai ethnohistory and the John K. Bear winter count. *Plains Anthropologist* 21, no. 73, pt. 2, memoir 11.

Hubert, Henri, and Marcel Mauss. 1964. *Sacrifice: Its nature and function*. Chicago: University of Chicago Press. Originally published 1898.

Hutt, Corinne. 1972. *Males and females*. Harmondsworth, Middlesex: Penguin Books.

Hyde, George E. 1937. *Red Cloud's folk*. Norman: University of Oklahoma Press.

———. 1956. *A Sioux chronicle*. Norman: University of Oklahoma Press.

———. 1961. *Spotted Tail's folk*. Norman: University of Oklahoma Press.

Kelley, Jane H. 1978. *Yaqui women*. Lincoln: University of Nebraska Press.

Kemnitzer, Luis. 1976. Structure, content and cultural meaning of Yuwipi: A modern Lakota healing ritual. *American Ethnologist* 3:261–80.

Kluckhohn, Clyde, L. Gottschalk, and R. Angell. 1945. *The use of the personal document in history, anthropology and sociology*. Bulletin no. 53. New York: Social Science Research Council.

Koch, Ronald P. 1977. *Dress clothing of the Plains Indians*. Norman: University of Oklahoma Press.

LaBarre, Weston. 1932. *The peyote cult*. New Haven: Yale University Press.

LaFontaine, J., ed. 1972. *The interpretation of ritual*. London: Tavistock.

Landes, Ruth. 1971. *The Ojibwa woman*. New York: Norton. Originally published 1938.

Langness, L. L. 1965. *The life history in anthropological science*. New York: Holt, Rinehart and Winston.

Leach, Edmund. 1958. Magical hair. *Journal of the Royal Anthropological Institute* 88, no. 2:147–64.

———. 1964. Animal categories and verbal abuse. In *New directions in the study of language*, ed. Eric H. Lenneberg. Cambridge: MIT Press.

———. 1969. Virgin birth. In *Genesis as myth and other essays*, 85–112. London: Cape Editions.

———. 1976. *Culture and communication*. London: Cambridge University Press.

Leacock, Eleanor. 1978. Women's status in egalitarian society. *Current Anthropology* 19:247–76.

———. 1981. *Myths of male dominance*. New York: Monthly Review Press.

Lessa, William, and Evon Z. Vogt. 1972. *Reader in comparative religion*. 3d ed. New York: Harper and Row.

Lesser, Alexander. 1928. Some aspects of Siouan kinship. Paper presented at Twenty-third International Congress of Americanists, New York.

Levine, Seymore. 1971. Sexual differentiation: The development of maleness and femaleness. *California Medicine* 114 (January): 12–17.

Lewis, Emily H. 1980. *Wo'wakita*. Sioux Falls, S.D.: Center for Western Studies, Augustana College

Lewis, Oscar. 1941. Manly-hearted women among the North Piegan. *American Anthropologist* 43:173–87.

Linderman, Frank B. 1972. *Pretty Shield*. Lincoln: University of Nebraska Press. Originally published 1932 as *Red mother*.

Lowie, Robert H. 1913. Plains Indian age-societies: Historical and comparative summary. *Anthropological Papers of the American Museum of Natural History* 11:877–984.

Lurie, Nancy Oestreich. 1972. Indian women: A legacy of freedom. In *Look to the mountaintop*, 29–36. San Jose, Calif.: Gousha.

———. 1974. *Mountain Wolf Woman*. Ann Arbor: University of Michigan. Originally published 1961.

Lyford, Carrie. 1940. *Quill and beadwork of the western Sioux*. Washington, D.C.: U.S. Office of Indian Affairs, Education Division.

Macgregor, Gordon. 1946. *Warriors without weapons: A study of the society and personality of the Pine Ridge Sioux*. Chicago: University of Chicago Press.

McNickle, D'Arcy. 1973. *Native American tribalism*. London: Oxford University Press.

Mails, Thomas E. 1972. *Mystic warriors of the Plains*. New York: Doubleday.

Mallery, Garrick. 1886. The Dakota winter counts and the Corbusier winter counts. In *Fourth Annual Report, Bureau of American Ethnology*, 89–146. Washington, D.C.: Government Printing Office.

Matthiasson, Carolyn, ed. 1974. *Many sisters*. New York: Free Press.

Mauss, Marcel. 1954. *The gift*. New York: Free Press. Originally published 1924.

Maynard, Eileen. 1968. Pine Ridge reservation population by districts, communities, and village-rural distribution. *Pine Ridge Research Bulletin* (U.S. Public Health Service) 6 (December): 1–10.

————. 1969a. Felt needs, dependency and community development. *Pine Ridge Research Bulletin* 7 (February): 1–10.

————. 1969b. Some notes on denominational preferences among the Oglalas. *Pine Ridge Research Bulletin* 10 (July):1–6.

Maynard, Eileen, and Gayla Twiss. 1970. *That these people may live*. Pine Ridge, S.D.: U.S. Public Health Service.

Mead, Margaret. 1967. The life cycle and its variations: The division of roles. *Daedalus* 96, no. 3:871–75.

Medicine, Bea. 1977. The role and function of Indian women. *Conference on American Indian Language Clearinghouse Newsletter* 5 (March): 7.

————. 1978. *The Native American woman: A perspective*. Austin, Tex.: National Educatonal Laboratory.

Mekeel, Scudder. 1936. *The economy of a modern Teton Dakota community*. Yale University Publications in Anthropology 6. New Haven: Yale University Press.

Melody, Michael E. 1977. Maka's story: A study of a Lakota cosmogony. *Journal of American Folklore* 90, no. 356: 149–67.

Meyer, Roy W. 1967. *History of the Santee Sioux*. Lincoln: University of Nebraska Press.

Michelson, Truman. 1933. Narrative of an Arapaho woman. *American Anthropologist* 33:595–610.

Mindell, Carl. 1967. Notes on identity diffusion and focal symbiosis in an American Indian tribe. Paper presented at meeting of the American Psychiatric Association.

Mirsky, Jeannette. 1937. The Dakota. In *Cooperation and competition among primitive peoples*, ed. Margaret Mead. Boston: Beacon Press.

Montagu, Ashley M. F. 1940. Physiology and the origins of the menstrual prohibitions. *Quarterly Review of Biology* 15 (June): 211–20.

Murdock, George P. 1949. *Social structure*. New York: Free Press.

————. 1960. *Ethnographic bibliography of North America*. 3d ed. New Haven: Yale University Press.

Nadeau, Remi. 1967. *Fort Laramie and the Sioux Indians*. Englewood Cliffs, N.J.: Prentice-Hall.

Neihardt, John G. 1961. *Black Elk speaks*. Lincoln: University of Nebraska Press.

Niethhammer, Carolyn. 1977. *Daughters of the earth*. New York: Collier Books.

Nurge, Ethel. 1970. Dakota diet: Traditional and contemporary. In *The modern Sioux*, ed. Ethel Nurge. Lincoln: University of Nebraska Press.

Oglala Sioux Tribe. 1935. *Constitution and by-laws of the Oglala Sioux Tribe of the Pine Ridge reservation of South Dakota*. Approved 15 January 1936. Pine Ridge, S.D.

———. 1965. *Revised code of the Oglala Sioux Tribe of the Pine Ridge reservation of South Dakota*. Pine Ridge, S.D.

O'Kelly, Charlotte G. 1980. *Women and men in society*. New York: Van Nostrand.

Olson, James C. 1965. *Red Cloud and the Sioux problem*. Lincoln: University of Nebraska Press.

Orchard, William C. 1916. *The technique of porcupine quill decoration among the Indians of North America*. New York: Museum of the American Indian, Heye Foundation.

———. 1929. *Beads and beadwork of the American Indians*. New York: Museum of the American Indian, Heye Foundation.

Ortner, Sherry. 1974. Is female to male as nature is to culture? In *Women, culture and society*, ed. M. Rosaldo and L. Lamphere. Stanford: Stanford University Press.

Parkman, Francis. 1950. *The Oregon Trail*. New York: Mentor Books. Originally published 1846.

Petrullo, Vincenzo. 1932. *The diabolic root*. Philadelphia: University of Pennsylvania Press.

Pommersheim, Frank, and Anita Remerowiski. 1979. *Reservation street law*, Rosebud, S.D.: Sinte Gleska College Press.

Powers, Marla N. 1980. Menstruation and reproduction: An Oglala case. *Signs* 6 (Fall): 54–65.

Powers, William K. 1963. A winter count of the Oglala. *American Indian Tradition* 52:27–37.

———. 1969. *Indians of the Northern Plains*. New York: G. P. Putnam's Sons.

———. 1976. Dual religious participation at Pine Ridge. Manuscript. Available from author.

———. 1977. *Oglala religion*. Lincoln: University of Nebraska Press.

———. 1980a. The art of courtship among the Oglala. *American Indian Art* 5, no. 2:40–47.

————. 1980b. Plains Indian music and dance. In *Anthropology on the Great Plains*, ed. W. Raymond Wood and Margot Liberty. Lincoln: University of Nebraska Press.

————. 1982. *Yuwipi: Vision and experience in Oglala ritual.* Lincoln: University of Nebraska Press.

————. 1983. The North American berdache. Reply to Callender and Kochems. *Current Anthropology* 24, no. 4:461–62.

Powers, William K., and Marla N. Powers. 1984. Metaphysical aspects of an Oglala food system. In *Food in the social order*, ed. Mary Douglas. New York: Russell Sage.

Radin, Paul. 1956. *The trickster.* New York: Schocken Books.

Red Cloud Indian School. 1963. *Red Cloud's dream.* Pine Ridge, S.D.: Holy Rosary Mission.

Riegert, Wilbur A. 1975. *Quest for the pipe of the Sioux.* Rapid City, S.D.: Printing, Inc.

Robinson, Doane. 1940. *A history of the Dakota or Sioux Indians.* Minneapolis: Ross and Haines.

Rogers, Dilwyn J. 1980. *Lakota names and traditional uses of native plants by Sicangu (Brule) people in the Rosebud area, South Dakota.* Saint Francis, S.D.: Rosebud Educational Society.

Rogers, Susan Carol. 1975. Female forms of power and the myth of male dominance. *American Ethnologist* 2:727–56.

————. 1978. Woman's place: A critical review of anthropological theory. *Comparative Studies in Society and History* 20 (January): 123–73.

Rosaldo, Michele, and Louise Lamphere, eds. 1974. *Women, culture and society.* Stanford: Stanford University Press.

Ruby, Robert H. 1955. *The Oglala Sioux: Warriors in transition.* New York: Vantage Press.

Sanday, Peggy. 1981. *Female power and male dominance.* Cambridge: Cambridge University Press.

Sandoz, Mari. 1961. *These were the Sioux.* New York: Dell.

Schlegel, Alice. 1977. Male and female in Hopi thought and action. In *Sexual stratification*, ed. Alice Schlegel, 245–69. New York: Columbia University Press.

Schwatka, Frederick. 1890. The sun-dance of the Sioux. *Century Magazine* 34:753–59.

Shapiro, Judith. 1982. Women's studies: A note on their perils of markedness. *Signs* 7 (Spring): 717–21.

South Dakota Department of Health. 1970–78. *South Dakota vital statistics, annual reports.* Pierre, S.D.: Health Statistics Program.

Spencer, Robert F., Jessie D. Jennings, et al. 1977. *The Native Americans.* 2d ed. New York: Harper and Row.

Spier, Leslie. 1921. *The sun dance of the Plains Indian: Its development and diffusion.* Anthropological Papers, vol. 16, pt. 7. New York: American Museum of Natural History.

Standing Bear, Luther. 1928. *My people the Sioux.* Boston: Houghton Mifflin.

———. 1933. *Land of the spotted eagle.* Boston: Houghton Mifflin.

Stephens, William N. 1967. A cross-cultural study of menstrual taboos. In *Cross-cultural approaches: Readings in comparative research,* ed. Clelland Ford. New Haven: Yale University Press.

Sword, George. n.d. Story of the woman from the sky. Manuscript edited by Ella C. Deloria, deposited at American Philosophical Society, Philadelphia.

Teitelbaum, Michael S., ed. 1976. *Sex differences: Social and biological perspectives.* New York: Anchor Books.

Thomas, Robert K. 1966–67. Powerless politics. *New University Thought* 4 (Winter): 1–3.

Tibbles, Thomas H. 1905. *Buckskin and blanket days.* Lincoln: University of Nebraska Press.

Tiffany, Sharon, ed. 1979. *Women and society.* Montreal: Eden Press Women's Publications.

Tiger, Lionel. 1970. *Men in groups.* New York: Vintage Books.

Tiger, Lionel, and Robin Fox. 1971. *The imperial animal.* New York: Dell.

Tiger, Lionel, and Joseph Shepher. 1976. *Women in the kibbutz.* New York: Harvest Books.

Turner, Victor. 1961. *The forest of symbols.* Ithaca: Cornell University Press.

———. 1969. *The ritual process.* Chicago: Aldine.

———. 1975. Symbolic studies. In *Annual review of anthropology,* vol. 4. Palo Alto, Calif.: Annual Reviews.

Tyler, Lyman S. 1973. *A history of Indian policy.* Washington, D.C.: U.S. Department of the Interior, Bureau of Indian Affairs.

Underhill, Ruth M. 1965. *Red man's religion: Beliefs and practices of the Indians north of Mexico.* Chicago: University of Chicago Press.

Utley, Robert M. 1963. *The last days of the Sioux nation.* New Haven: Yale University Press.

Van Gennep, Arnold. 1960. *The rites of passage.* Chicago: University of Chicago Press.

Vestal, Stanley. 1956. *Sitting Bull, champion of the Sioux.* Norman: University of Oklahoma Press.

Vogel, Virgil J. 1970. *American Indian medicine.* Norman: University of Oklahoma Press.

Walker, J. R. 1914. Oglala kinship terms. *American Anthropologist* 16:96–109.

————. 1917. *The sun dance and other ceremonies of the Oglala division of the Teton-Dakota*. Anthropological Papers, vol. 16, pt. 2. New York: American Museum of Natural History.

————. 1980. *Lakota belief and ritual*. Edited by R. DeMallie and E. Jahner. Lincoln: University of Nebraska Press.

Wallace, Anthony F. C. 1956. Revitalization movements. *American Anthropologist* 58:264–81.

————. 1966. *Religion: An anthropological view*. New York: Random House.

Wauneka, Annie. 1976. The dilemma for Indian women. *Wassaja* (American Indian Historical Society) 4, no. 9:8.

Wax, Murray L., Rosalie H. Wax, and Robert V. Dumont. 1964. Formal education in an American Indian community. *Social Problems* 11, suppl., 4.

Weist, Katherine M. 1980. Plains Indian women: An assessment. In *Anthropology on the Great Plains*, ed. W. Raymond Wood and Margot Liberty. Lincoln: University of Nebraska Press.

Wissler, Clark. 1907. Some Oglala Dakota myths. *Journal of American Folklore* 20:195–206.

————. 1912. *Societies and ceremonial associations in the Oglala division of the Teton-Dakota*. Anthropological Papers, vol. 11, pt. 1. New York: American Museum of Natural History.

————. 1938. *Red man reservations*. New York: Collier Books.

————. 1940. *Indians of the United States*. Garden City, N.Y.: Doubleday, Doran.

Wood, W. Raymond, and Margot Liberty, eds. 1980. *Anthropology on the Great Plains*. Lincoln: University of Nebraska Press.

Young, Frank W., and A. A. Bacdayan. 1967. Menstrual taboos and social rigidity. In *Cross-cultural approaches: Readings in comparative research*, ed. Clelland Ford. New Haven: Yale University Press.

Index